1500
75P

FOUNDATIONS OF EDUCATIONAL RESEARCH

Second Edition

Alfred L. Papillon
DePaul University

University Press
of America™

Dedication

To my wife Eleanora

and my son Leo

TABLE OF CONTENTS

iv

Acknowledgments

The author wishes to express his appreciation to the many people who were involved in the production of this book. Numerous graduate students who took the course presented challenges which elicited many of the viewpoints developed in the book. Publishers have kindly granted permissions to reproduce pertinent materials, and acknowledgements are made in customary formats at appropriate places. Thanks are also due to Ms. Nina Piekarz for her assistance in preparing the field-test materials and the final draft of the manuscript.

PREFACE

Today research is a major human endeavor, especially in education.
Research is in the vanguard of educational activity because it is only
through educational research that the quality of education can be improved. New knowledge and new uses of knowledge are the means to progress,
and research is the best process known to humans for acquiring them; the
quality of human education rises or falls with the quality of educational
research.

Therefore, the requirement of an introductory course in educational
research has become well nigh universal for programs on the master's
level and the doctoral level, a requirement which usually comes early in
the graduate student's program. This course and these students are the
target of the present book. It is intended as the first graduate course
in educational research design, and requires no previous statistics.
Furthermore, it does not necessarily anticipate any subsequent course in
educational research. In line with this comprehensive concept, the
text has fo r broad objectives to prepare the beginning graduate student
as a consumer and as a producer of educational research. Admittedly,
within the limitations of a single introductory graduate course, it will
not be possible to develop him into an accomplished producer of educational
research, but a sound basis will be laid for satisfying immediate research
needs in the present and conducting more long-range research in the future.

For the student as a consumer of research, the text seeks to build competencies with bibliographic tools and resources for becoming informed about
completed research, and skills in reading research reports meaningfully
and synthesizing them.

The orientation of this text is toward decision-making. By this is
meant that its concern is primarily with the "how" and process of educational research rather than the "why" and theory. This is not to say
that there is not an adequate theoretical foundation for research in the
text, but that, as the title selected for the book implies, theoretical
issues remain foundational. The safeguard sought in the text is for students to understand thoroughly what they are doing in educational
research, so that they do not engage in mechanical practices devoid of
conceptualizations. However, in terms of student understanding of
research principles and statistical procedures, the safeguard must be
achieved through the teaching approaches of the instructors as much as
through content selection for the textbook. If the teacher cannot
ensure that the students understand what they learn, the textbook cannot
do it for him; it can only facilitate the achievement of this objective.
Hence, the approach in this text is to present fundamental concepts and
to follow up such presentation with procedures for implementation. The
framework for which such implementation is envisioned is the school setting. Throughout the book, the pervading assumption is that the purpose
of educational research is to provide an empirical base for educational
theory and educational practice. This is what is meant by the opening
statement of this paragraph, that the orientation is toward decision-
making.

The orientation toward decision-making raises some issues about
content selection for the foundational course in educational research.

Admittedly, there can be no strict prescription of a single body of content which is foundations of educational research. On the other hand, there is the distinct possibility of attempting to teach more than can be meaningfully learned in the time period of one quarter or one semester in graduate school. The resolution of this dilemma depends upon one's perception of the course in educational research. If one considers it in terms of subject matter, content selection will be governed by consideration of what is known about educational research design and statistics. If the course attempts to include all that is known, it becomes encyclopedic. If the course attempts to include what is commonly known, it becomes various things in various places. If the course attempts to include essential knowledge only, it becomes minimal. The alternative to these diversities is to perceive the course in terms of the student as well as of subject matter. From this viewpoint, the course is controlled by what needs to be known about research by practicing educators, and a unifying principle organizes the content. This rationale supports the approach of the text, described in the preceding paragraph as a decision-making orientation.

This text is unique, content-wise, in its greater recognition of non-experimental types of research. The author is convinced that the needs of schools today are more comprehensive that they were in the past; they are also of a different nature. Today's schools are faced with basic questions related to human nature, human learning, and human society. Answers to them call for research designs involving factorial analytic, predictive, and even historical techniques. This is not to demean the experimental design. It simply recognizes that many generalizations needed today involve demographic and sociological data from representative samples rather than measurements on comparative groups.

The author sees evidence for these needs in the research topics for which graduate students express preferences, and in the purposes which they state as felt needs. There is an urgent demand to develop competencies among practicing educators for these types of educational research, and this book is committed to placing an emphasis upon them. The emphasis constitutes what might be termed the new educational research.

As instructional strategy, this text utilizes cases and analytic models in addition to expository writing, Just as content selection is functionally oriented by considering practicing educators in the school setting as guide, so likewise instructional mode is functionally oriented by use of research samples as teaching materials. A systematic presentation of principles of research design and statistics is made in the first part of the book. This is followed by representative research reports of different types, with a brief of each, and three sample research proposals in the second part. The briefs and the proposals are called analytic models because they point out the elements of research designs in the completed reports and proposals. Thus, the book achieves a functional approach to educational research by combining practice with theory.

A final trait in the uniqueness of this text is the computer-assisted approach to educational statistics. In the controversy over whether to teach or not to teach computations in statistics, the book lines up squarely on the side of "to teach." However, it does so with the difference of providing computer programs that eliminate the drudgery of low level arithmetic computations. The computer is utilized as a problem-solving mechanism. Program writing is not taught, and no special skills are required, rather only a normally favorable attitude toward electronic technology. The author has written "teaching programs" which print out the step by step operations which the researcher would perform long hand with pencil and paper if he did not have the assistance of the computer. Students learn how to call up these programs, enter their own data, and read printouts with understanding. The programs are inclusive enough to do real research. The programs are innovative mainly in their application of the computer to classroom teaching. A notable exception to this is the process for ranking scores by the computer. This is an original invention of the author and is utilized in several statistics involving ordinal data. The principal limitation to the computer assisted statistics is that Hewlett-Packard equipment is needed to utilize the pre-punched program tapes.

The book can be utilized without computer assistance because statistical computations are included and illustrated along with all the statistical concepts. However, the computer programs listed in the book are copyrighted and may be purchased by arrangements with the author.

There is a thriving market for educational research in all of its phases, and a number of good textbooks teaching how to do it are on the market. However, there are still needs to be met in the field and this book is planned to satisfy some of them. Herein lies the justification for bringing out a new book in educational research.

I am grateful to the Literary Executor of the Late Sir Ronald A. Fisher, F.R.S., to Dr. Frank Yates, F.R.S. and to Longman Group Ltd., London, for permission to reprint Tables III and IV from their book STATISTICAL TABLES FOR BIOLOGICAL, AGRICULTURAL AND MEDICAL RESEARCH. (6th edition, 1974).

Alfred L. Papillon

CHAPTER I.   THE NATURE AND DEVELOPMENT OF EDUCATIONAL RESEARCH

Educational research is truth-finding about any phase of education. Its function is to produce empirical evidence that is adequate to validate educational theory and to evaluate educational practice.   Its goal is to generate and extend educational concepts rather than to solve educational problems.   To this end it assembles educational data which is accurate, objective, and sufficient to be the basis for sound principles setting forth the structure and the processes of education.   To achieve these purposes empirically, educational research utilizes the inductive thinking process.   From within the array of specific educational measurements and observations which it assembles, research discovers uniformities, causes-and-effects, and inter-relationships which it synthesizes into principles that can be utilized in school practice to improve the quality of education.

Historically, several sources of truth have been available to the human mind.   The earliest was authority and tradition, which usually prevailed in primitive settings where the individual was completely absorbed in a struggle to secure food, clothing, and shelter, and to survive from the attacks of enemies--wild beasts, the elements, and other humans.   As groups of individuals organized some elemental form of group living which assured the individual of the essentials in life, personal experience emerged as a source of truth.   The modicum of leisure and self-direction which individuals enjoyed permitted them to formulate their own answers to human problems.

Personal experience is very fallible as a source of truth. Its hazards are that it is limited, its basic facts are often inaccurate, and conclusions which the human mind draws from them are subject to bias and prejudice. In all thinking based on personal experience, it is important to keep an open mind. Subsequently in the human experience, the mind evolved the deductive, so-called "philosophical," method of thought. It is a method because it is governed by rules and it has a vehicle, the syllogism. The handicap of the deductive method throughout the centuries of its existence was the scarcity of proven universal propositions on which to anchor the chain of syllogisms, but today the explosion of knowledge has largely remedied this weakness and the method is now more viable rather than less. The fourth source of truth for the human mind is the inductive method. It originated as the "scientific" method because the first truths developed by it were in the natural sciences-- the heliocentric theory, circulation of the blood, refraction light, etc.--which were discovered during the century from 1550-1650. The "scientific" method of thinking is basically more applicable to the field of the natural sciences because its demand for accurate and objective data can be met more precisely in studying the physical universe, but the method has been adapted to investigations involving behavioral and social data although it operates with less precision in these fields of knowledge. As a result of generalizing the method, to all fields of human truth, it is now less commonly called the scientific method, and more commonly called the inductive method of thinking.

A few basic assumptions about data must be satisfied to make inductive thinking feasible per se. The first such assumption is that phenomena be classified into categories.

This prerequisite is necessary to facilitate the operation of the mind alternately by analysis and by synthesis. Fortunately this prerequisite is met both in nature and in human nature. For instance, it is possible to measure and observe children in terms of physical development, of mental development, and/or of affective development. A second assumption is that phenomena be reliable, by which is meant that phenomena repeat themselves with predictable regularity. This prerequisite is demanded by the permanence of truth; it can be formulated only on the basis of sustained uniformities and cause-effect relationships. Phenomena occurring by chance are incapable of supporting laws or theories. Unfortunately, the prerequisite of reliability of phenomena is not as fully met in behavioral phenomena as in natural phenomena. For instance, the scores of children on standardized tests will normally vary from five to ten points on successive administrations of the same tests. Nevertheless, there is enough regularity in the recurrence of the behavior of children to make it possible for research to improve practice in education, although the variations in the recurrence of the same acts in learning behavior are a serious handicap to educational research. The third assumption without which there could be no inductive thinking is that causes and effects must be operative in phenomena, a prerequisite inherent in the nature of a principle or law. Causal relations exist in all phenomena, both natural and behavioral, but they are difficult to discover, and herein precisely lies the challenge in all research. Thus the prerequisite characteristics of phenomena for inductive processes are satisfied in educational research data albeit not as well as in scientific data.

The inductive process also assumes that the researcher possess three capabilities: 1) the capability to measure and observe,

2) the capability to record and remember, and 3) the capability to interpret data and apply findings. The human researcher possesses these capabilities by human nature. Through the five sensory powers, he is capable of measuring and observing. Sensory powers are, however, very fallible and human ingenuity resorts to technology of various sorts to refine and multiply the effectiveness of measurement and observation. Also, the human researcher has a memory, which is very prone to error. Here, technology improves on human nature, and the recent introduction of computers as support systems for recording and remembering data has been a boone to educational research. Finally, the human researcher is capable of thinking with educational data. There is no specific technology to extend and perfect this aspect of human nature, but the human mind has developed statistical science, with its strict force of logic to make interpretative and evaluative thinking more rigorous. In addition to satisfying assumptions essential to the feasibility of inductive processes, educational research also has the same purposes as inductive thinking. These include: 1) To understand and explain phenomena and processes, 2) To achieve control of forces and events, and 3) To achieve prediction of outcomes and results. The consistency of these goals with educational research is obvious.

The beginning educational researcher may ask about its historical development. As competent research, it does not extend to more than fifty years ago. Some initial attempts at educational research were made during the last quarter of the nineteenth century, but research methodology even up to 1930 was over-inclusive and inaccurate. Beginning with World War II and since, research methodology has been refined sharply. Instruments and procedures for securing criterion data have been perfected , especially scales for affective factors.

Sampling theory and statistics have expanded into a specialization. Inferential statistics have been extended by creation of new concepts and procedures. There is movement toward a radically different system, Bayesian Statistics, for interpreting behavioral and social data.

The past is definitely prologue and a long future laden with promise stretches ahead. Educational research is undoubtedly part of the way of life even on the level of the local district and school.

CHAPTER II. SELECTING A TOPIC AND SURVEYING THE LITERATURE

A multiplicity of topics demand investigation in all aspects of education: curriculum, instruction, administration, guidance and counseling, measurement and evaluation, etc. Even research itself is researchable. Yet, despite the availability of topics the uninitiated to research fail to recognize the researchability of educational materials, activities, and procedures. Such insensitivity to research topics may be called "topic blindness," and its opposite may be termed "topic sense." Development of a topic sense is one of the primary purposes of the introductory course in educational research.

By way of definition, "topic sense" is an unerring insight into the feasibility of empirical data collection and the applicability of inductive thinking to educational topics. For instance, it is readily discernable that utilization of materials and procedures whereby children can be taught in smaller groups or individually will yield outcomes that are measurable objectively. These measurements can be used to test the hypothesis that individualizing instruction yields better learning outcomes. The topic sense is not the prerogative of a few rare individuals, it is teachable and learnable by the careful student who is guided through appropriate learning experiences. A topic sense consists partially of attitudes and habits as well as partially of specific knowledges and skills. To some extent it consists of re-directing knowledges and processes which most good students already possess toward the specific purpose of recognizing and delimiting

educational topics which need to be researched. To this extent, a
research topic sense is a state of mind: it consists of being alert
and constructively critical of all that goes on in the field of education.
It includes what is happening immediately around oneself, in one's
school, and in one's classroom. The continuous concern for the improvement of education will lead one to recognize aspects of education in
which there are felt needs, lack of means to ends, and unexpected
results. These are the hallmarks of researchability--the indicators
of research topics.

Some activities of a specific nature may also be taken to develop
a topic sense. The first such exercise is to read reported research.
It is advisable for this purpose to begin by reading research reports of
a capsulated type. Thus, the future researcher gets more exposure to
a variety of research topics. The primary sources in which may be found
capsulated research reports are the Encyclopedia of Educational Research,
The Handbook of Research in Teaching, Dissertation Abstracts, and books,
periodicals, or sections of periodicals aimed at surveying or synthesizing
the research literature in an area of education. It is profitable to
peruse even the bare listings of research authors and titles in such
listings as doctoral dissertations accepted by American Universities,
found in issue No. 13 of each volume of Dissertation Abstracts, or
listings of Master's Theses found in Master's Theses in Education,
edited annually by H. M. Silvey.   Occasional publications of
bibliographies of research on given topics belong to the same category
as listing dissertations and theses, and their attentive reading also
contributes to development of a topic sense.

The cultivation of an inquiring mind toward researchable topics
and the use of bibliographical tools to familiarize oneself with

research topics of record are basic training preparatory to selecting a
topic but they are not an inherent part of the selection process itself.
The selection process per se includes three phases, each becoming
progressively more specific. The first phase consists of determining
that broad field in education within which the researcher wishes to
select a topic for investigation. Topic selection at this level is concerned with choosing from among curriculum, instruction, administration,
guidance, personnel, educational psychology, etc. Having elected the
field from which to choose a topic, the investigator next singles out
an area within the field from which to elect a topic. For instance,
within the field of school curriculum, the researcher may choose to do
research in curriculum theory building, or curriculum innovation, or
curriculum evaluation. Having specified a research area within a
research field, the investigator now turns to the selection of a specific
topic within the chosen area. Thus, within the area of curriculum
innovation the researcher may decide to investigate the effectiveness
of curriculum innovation utilizing multi-media learning aids, or
discovery learning, or inquiry learning, or individualized learning.
Through the topic selection approach described above, the researcher
successively narrows the limits of his concern for a topic so that the
process may be symbolized by a large letter V, with the research topic
ultimately emerging at the point of the V. In some cases a research
topic is thrust upon the researcher by the pressures of social change,
needs of the school, or by the stark outcomes of ineffeciency. In such
cases the researcher should proceed through the topic selection procedure
inversely for the sake of clarifying the context within which his topic
lies for the sake of placing the topic in its context.

Not only should the researcher have knowledge of the setting external to the topic he selects but he must also have knowledge internal to the topic. On one hand he must be cognizant of the forces which influence the topic from the outside but he must also have insight into the factors which are inherent in the topic itself. For instance, in relation to the use of multi-media materials in teaching science, the researcher needs to be aware of various types of technology and the strategies that are being taken to utilize types of technology in teaching science. The researcher must also be knowledgeable about the problems challenging the learner in science and the conditions under which they can be met. Only if the researcher possesses knowledge fundamental to the topic does he have the capacity for setting up an adequate research design. In other terms this means that the researcher should have both some formal educational preparation and some educational experience in the area. He is not required to be an expert on the topic, but neither is he permitted to be uninformed about it. Only with knowledge of the topic can the researcher formulate meaningful purposes and hypotheses, discriminate pertinent data, and interpret significance of criterion data to create a research design for an investigation.

If the researcher has identified several possible topics, he may take several steps to arrive at a final decision. Select a topic only after having determined upon the context in education which is preferable for doing research, as described above. Selection of one topic from among several should be influenced by both the experience and the formal study of the researcher. Background is needed for topic selection, purposing, hypothesizing, collecting criterion data. Beyond this, work out answers to the following specific questions, which are criteria for selecting a topic.

Is the data that will be required for the research amenable to observation
and measurement? One ought not attempt as topic to determine the effect
of voluntary library reading on reading achievement because it is well
nigh impossible to isolate the influence of voluntary library reading
from the influence of formal lessons and life experiences on reading
achievement. How technical is the topic? What level of expertise is
demanded by the topic to do meaningful research about it? Does the
researcher have sufficient preparation and experience in the topic?
Some topics in learning theories require advanced competencies in
psychology which the Master's level graduate student may not possess.
Are tools available for collecting information needed, or can they be
reasonably adapted or constructed? Researchers usually can construct
questionnaires, check-lists, score cards, and are now developing rating
scales. But to develop a standardized test is too complex and technical
for a beginning graduate student. Will permission be available for
access to data? For example, will a Board of Education permit access to
minutes of board meetings for the past ten years? The special projects
committees of school boards refuse permission to do certain investigations
on a variety of grounds. Is extensive administrative authority needed
to conduct the research on this topic? Researchers should not request
to set up homogeneous or heterogeneous groups in schools, or to assign
teachers to administer a certain test or compile certain information.
The research should be possible within the administrative framework
existent. This criterion is pertinent to aspects of research design as
well as to the topic per se. Because of administrative realities, we
may have to limit the purposes and hypotheses of the research, and the
population to which findings are generalizable, but the topic may still
be worth investigating.

What are the requirements of the investigation in terms of time, money and geography? The cost of incidentals such as postage, materials, typing, is a reality which must be faced. The time, expense, and inconvenience of travel for collecting data must not be overlooked. For instance, these factors might become considerable if very much interviewing were necessary for collecting data and the sample were located geographically over one or more states. For the purposes of master's degree theses, the sampling and data collecting can usually be planned at reasonable cost without sacrificing adequacy of the research design. How crucial and worthwhile is the topic? The sources of the topic are the professional conditions in education, and the individual conditions of the researcher. Maybe the topic is recent and very acute, such as the education of gifted and disadvantaged. Maybe it is a persistent problem that is still not satisfactorily answered, such as the role of phonics in teaching reading. Perhaps it is a "new" topic that is evolving at a reasonable rate, such as educating the disadvantaged. Even if it is not a newly arrived topic, it can still qualify as a "new" topic because it will gather information that never before has been gathered and interpreted. Previous research on a topic does not disban it, especially if there are differences in the design planned, because the topic is not exhausted.

When a researcher first becomes aware of a topic, it is tentative in his mind. The very meaning of the topic and the variables involved in it frequently need clarification in his thinking. Even for the fewer topics that are more obvious and more easily justified, the researcher will not take any steps toward creating a research design or begin action toward data collection without first reviewing the status of the topic. This step among educational research procedures is known as the Survey of the Literature on the topic.

There are several reasons for surveying the literature. The most obvious one is to canvas current knowledge, opinion, and thinking on the topic. The state of the topic review will show to what extent the idea has been explored, what problems included in it have already been solved, what issues are still unresolved, what questions are up for investigation at present and in the foreseeable future. Although, as has been stated earlier, a research topic does not have to be unexplored to be new, the researcher might think of abandoning the topic either because the survey of the literature shows that much has already been done about it, or vice versa, very little has been done about it. A second purpose which the survey may serve is to guide the researcher in limiting the topic. From the literature he may discover aspects of the topic which are more in need of research, or which are more meaningful to him and his organization. A third reason for surveying the literature is to evaluate his experimental treatment. From the literature he may gather what approaches to the independent variable seem to hold promise for results and which ones seem to lead to dead ends. Fourthly, the researcher usually will pick up clues for creating or remodeling his own research design from the reports of previous research. As a specific example, he may learn of new measuring instruments or new techniques for collecting accurate and objective measurements and observations as his data. Fifthly and finally, the researcher may arrive at a more comprehensive grasp of related aspects of education in which the topic falls. Thus, it may become evident to him that some supporting research needs to be done in an area which relates to his topic.

To do the survey of related literature for the topic, the researcher needs bibliographic tools.

The Bibliographic Index is especially versatile as the first tool to utilize in compiling a bibliography on a topic because each item in it is in itself a bibliography, not just one title. The _Mental Measurements Yearbooks_ and their spin offs _Reading Tests and Reviews, Personality Tests and Reviews, Intelligence Tests and Reviews,_ and _Vocational Aptitude Tests and Reviews,_ are essential in deciding on instruments for collecting criterion data. The Handbook by Orval G.Johnson and James W. Bommarito entitled _Tests and Measurements in Child Development_ is also useful in choosing measuring instruments. The beginning researcher must especially become adept at using _The Encyclopedia of Educational Research, The Handbook of Research on Teaching, Dissertation Abstracts_ and periodicals such as the _Review of Educational Research,_ the _American Educational Research Journal,_ the the _Journal of Experimental Education,_ and the _Journal of Experimental Psychology._ These sources contain the research literature on topics, and research literature is of course valuable from the viewpoint of data collection, statistical treatment, and interpretation of data. Other tools,dictionaries, bibliographical sources, and directories have occasional uses which can economize much in time and effort.

In terms of procedure in using bibliographical tools, a workable plan is to proceed through three operational stages. The first is to search exhaustively for sources on the topic. To avoid discontinuity, it is suggested in this phase to accept any source by title and or author which may be thought to deal with the topic. Such activity will yield what this author terms an Exhaustive Bibliography on the topic. The second cycle is to eliminate from this bibliography those sources which prove to be removed from the topic in purposes or subjects in the study. This reduction of the bibliography is achieved by "skimming" the sources that were located in the first round.

The retrenched bibliography may well be referred to as a Working Bibliography. Quoted Sources are the researcher's Definitive Bibliography.

It is assumed that the graduate student is by now familiar with some
format of note-taking from bibliographical sources, and this book, therefore,
ignores the matter. As to footnote references, format is neither right
nor wrong, but a convention, and the main issue is to be expedient and
consistent. The sources which are specifically referred to in the
finished research report are the only ones which merit to be included
in the final bibliography of the investigation. The researcher may
give himself credit for all the sources he has found pertinent to his
investigation by attaching as many footnote references as he needs to
any work, phrase, sentence, paragraph, table, etc. in his research report.

As a concluding thought for survey of the literature of a research
topic, it is useful to indicate that data which the researcher collects
from related sources is his Secondary Data. By contrast, the measurements
which he obtains on his sample are his Primary Data. He will organize
and interpret this latter data which he has collected. Secondary data
performs research functions in a number of aspects of research design.
It serves in making the analysis of the topic and it may serve in
interpretation of the data by relating findings of other researches as
comparison norms. Although survey of the literature plays a secondary
role in original research activity, it is nevertheless very important,
and only too often it does not receive the time and attention it deserves.

Selection of a topic and survey of the literature give a research
project its orientation. They deserve the researcher's best efforts.

CHAPTER III.   ANALYSIS OF THE RESEARCH TOPIC

Each research topic is a more or less broad educational concept which includes one or more sub-concepts within itself. The concern of analysis of the topic is to identify these sub-conceptual elements in the topic. Identification of these variables in the topic is an important step in educational research because they are the basis to constructing a research design. The research topic for different types of research varies in the nature and complexity of its sub-concepts and a considerable portion of this chapter will be concerned with the explanation and interpretation of these differences in terms of analysis of the topic.

Because of the prominence of experimental investigations in the field of educational research, the treatment of analysis of the topic in this chapter begins with the topic for experimental research. An experimental research topic focuses on some variable in education which is hypothesized to be able to produce different or greater educational outcomes of some sort. This experimental factor is referred to as the "Independent Variable". There is an almost limitless number of such independent variables, and they exist in every aspect of education. A few examples are: team teaching, homogeneous grouping, programmed instruction, discovery learning, individualized instruction, social and personal values, group counseling, administrative teams, pre-school education, flexible scheduling, unit school district, and compensatory education.

All of these concepts, materials, procedures, organizational patterns, whatever they may be, can be hypothesized to improve education in some way. They are devised by the imaginative insight of educators, based upon experience complemented by knowledge, especially knowledge discovered by previous research.

The hypothesis that the independent variable will improve education specifies some factors in education which will be created, or changed, or increased as a result of the influence of the independent variable. These specified effects anticipated from the independent variable are referred to as the "Dependent Variables" in the topic. Achievement is the dependent variable for many independent variables. It may be specified as mastery of organized knowledge or the acquisition of mental skills, or the establishment of motor-sensory coordinations. Dependent variables may be drawn from the affective domain as well as the cognitive domain. Thus, it may be hypothesized that teaching by discovery learning will increase pupils' motivation for learning, or that the study of sub-cultures in American society will develop the attitude of tolerance in children. Also, both the independent and the dependent variables may be derived from the area of school administration. Thus flexible scheduling may be the independent variable which facilitates more effective utilization of faculty as its dependent variable or con-solidation of rural school districts may be an independent variable with cost of education as its dependent variable.

The definition of the outcomes of the experimentation as dependent variables is based upon their relationship as effects to the independent variable, which is their cause. This cause and effect relationship be-tween the independent and the dependent variables in the topic distingui-shes the experimental investigation as a research type and it is the reason why the experiment is the most powerful type of educational research. This power of experimental research to discover cause-effect relationships will appear in a number of ways throughout this book.

Identification of the independent and the dependent variables, does not exhaust the analysis of the research topic. Although individualized instruction will normally produce greater achievement, the size of the class may be such that individualization can not be implemented effectively, and so the expected increase in learning does not materialize. In a similar manner, the poverty of a school district may be such that materials are lacking to effectively individualize instruction, and again the anticipated increase in learning may not materialize. These variables may handicap or facilitate the independent variable to influence the dependent variable. Such factors which may intervene between an independent variable and its dependent variables, are referred to in this book as "mediating variables." They are otherwise widely known as "Control Variables" in experiments since they must be prevented from interfering between the independent variable and the dependent variables. The term mediating variable is used preferably to control variables in this book because it presents a more logical sequence of nomenclature in conjuction with the terms independent variable and dependent variables, and because it is applicable for other types of research as well as experimental. A mediating variable, such as complete interest in the study of mathematics, may conpensate for the relative inefficiency of the experimental factor, in which case the results are attributed to the experimental variable whereas they were largely caused by the students' motivation. If mediating variables are not controlled, sources of the outcomes are clouded and the cause-effect relation of the independent variable and the dependent variable cannot be reliably inferred from the data.

The practical implications for controlling the mediating variables
associated with an experimental research topic are to achieve assurance
that the groups of individuals involved in the treatments are equivalent
to each other on those factors which are capable of intervening between
the independent and the dependent variables. For many topics, the
mediating variables which occur most frequently are: The intelligence
and/or other aptitude level of the treatment groups, their reading
ability level, their mathematical ability level, their socio-economic
backgrounds, their backgrounds of formal schooling, the identical
curriculums content involved in the experimentation, the equivalence
in experience, formal preparation, and effectiveness of the teachers
involved in the research, and the duration of the treatments. For some
of these mediating variables, such as I.Q., reading ability, or mathematical
ability, scores of the individuals can be secured and then statistical
tests can be made to determine whether there are significant differences
between the means of the groups. If there are no significant differences,
there is assurance that these mediating variables are controlled. For
other mediating variables, such as socio-economic background and equivalence of teachers involved, control of these mediating variables is
achieved by consulting the information one has on the individuals and
matching them on those traits which are of concern to the research topic.

The concept of the educational experiment is to investigate the
effectiveness of a variable to produce certain effects dependent upon
it. This concept yields the model of independent variable, dependent
variable, and mediating variable for analyzing the experimental research
topic. But the model of independent—dependent—mediating variables may
not apply for analysis of the topic in all other types of research. The
researcher must differentiate his model for analysis of the topic by type

of educational research. Most books now in print treating the theory
and practice of research design, unfortunately fail to make this
distinction clear. If analysis of the topic is dealt with at all, it is
limited to the independent-dependent-control variables of the experimental
type. The beginning researcher attempting to do other types of educational research often seeks to analyze his topic along this model and
it does not work. The inexperienced researcher is thus frustrated and
confused as to what factors are involved in his topic and how they are
related. It is obvious that a bungled research design is likely to be
produced if the researcher is in such confusion about his topic. Hence
this chapter deals with the analysis of variables inherent in research
topics for each of the types of educational research.

Descriptive research is possibly the second most frequent type of
research after the experimental. The two types differ in that descriptive studies can show only concomitance among variables whereas experiments show causes and effects. In the topic of a descriptive study there
is an independent variable, such as Advanced Placement Programs, Team
Teaching, Core-Curriculum, etc., concerning which the purpose is to
establish the present record. The researcher limits himself to establishing the record in terms of several aspects of the topic. For instance
in a survey of Advanced Placement Programs in high schools, the
researcher would need to establish the record about (1) administrative
arrangements for Advanced Placement Programs, (2) the Curriculum of
Advanced Placement Programs, (3) Personnel in Advancement Placement
Programs, both teachers and students and (4) Methods of Instruction in
Advanced Placement Programs. These four aspects of advanced placement
programs are the dimensions on which the advancement placement is described in the study and they may therefore be termed the "Descriptive

Variables" of the topic. The descriptive variables are to descriptive
research topics what dependent variables are to experimental research
topics. In addition to the independent variable and the descriptive
variables in a descriptive research topic, there are also mediating
variables. As in the experimental and other types of research topics,
mediating variables are factors which have an impact on the topic.
For advance placement programs, the size of the district, the per capita
assessed valuation, and the ability level of the students are definitely
factors which help determine whether a district will have advanced
placement and how much of it. Mediating variables in descriptive research,
however, are not controlled. Their role in research design is to provide
different environments for the investigation. An important use for them
may be as the strata in a stratified sample for the survey. The mediating
variables are also used as structures to organize the data for its
presentation and interpretation. For example, detailed data on advanced
placement programs grouped by size of districts may constitute one
or more tables, a section of a chapter, or even an entire chapter in
a written report of a survey.

Historical Research is concerned with establishing the past record
for an educational topic. Thus, so far as the topic is concerned,
descriptive and historical research have the same goals, but for different
points in time. The model for analysis of the topic for historical
research is therefore the same as for descriptive research, i.e. Independent-
Descriptive-Mediating variables.

In Factorial Analysis Research, the concern is for the nature
and relationships of factors and correlates in the topic. Thus, the
independent variable may be the type and/or extent of adjustment, or
achievement, or retardation, or behavior of racial groups of individuals.

The general factor being investigated is the Independent Variable, and the factors to which it is related are the Correlate Variables. These latter are the counterparts of Dependent Variables in experimental research. There are also mediating variables in the topics of factorial analytic studies. As usual, they are variables which have an influence on the topic. Thus, this type of research may reveal that reading is largely involved in Intelligence Scores, and that they both vary as found in disadvantaged children as compared to advantaged children. In this setting, intelligence is an independent variable, reading is a correlate to it and socio-economic status is a mediating variable which influences the relationship of the two variables.

Predictive Research is concerned with projecting the future status of a variable based on some known characteristic or performance of an individual. Obviously, the predictor variable must correlate at least substantially with the predicted variable. In this context, the topic of a predictive study includes the Independent Variable, which is being used as the predictor and the Predicted Variable, which is the dependent variable. An independent variable which has been used in many predictive studies is I.Q. There are mediating variables in a topic for a predictive study. Again, such traits as the socio-economic background may inhibit the effectiveness of I.Q. to predict success in reading because intelligence cannot develop fully in a setting of severe poverty. The mediating variables have to be controlled in predictive as in experimental research.

The final type of educational research, Developmental Research, is concerned with engineering innovative educational practice, especially by developing educational technology. For instance, a researcher may develop a set of slides from a selection of still pictures, plates,

and/or photographs which he has collected because of their relevance to
a concept or skill in mathematics, language arts, social studies or
science. He then records a script for each slide in the series
using a two-track cassette. The result is a set of sound-motion slides.
Their creation constitutes the developmental phase of the research and
it usually includes some "formative" survey, such as a survey of use
of such devices while the technology is being worked out. This may
even involve research activity, or the survey type or of the action
research type. Then once the technology has been refined, it is
necessary to conduct "summative" research of it utilizing an experimental
design. In the first phase, an experimental variable is created and
in the second phase, it is evaluated. The topic in developmental
research therefore includes an independent variable and dependent
variables, but these latter may be broader than the dependent variables
in an experimental topic, including for instance such criteria as
the cost of electronic equipment, or the need for in-service re-training
of teachers to use it, as well as the criterion "Do children learn with
this new material?" Mediating (control) variables are also present in a
developmental research topic, and they are of the usual varieties: intelligence score, reading ability score, etc., and must be controlled.
Because of numerous innovations and a rapidly expanding technology in
teaching, developmental research is very necessary today. It is a relatively newer research type, but is growing and becoming sophisticated
rapidly.

The parallels in analysis of the topic for various types of research
set forth above are summarized in the chart below to bring them into
contrast with each other.

ANALYSIS OF THE TOPIC BY RESEARCH TYPE

I. DESCRIPTIVE RESEARCH:

Independent Variable: The factors whose present record is being established. They are any factors of some importance in education.

Descriptive Variables: Dimensions of the description. They are inherent in the independent variable(s).

Mediating Variables: Factors closely related to the independent variable(s). They are different environments for the descriptive study.

II. HISTORICAL RESEARCH:

Independent Variable(s): Subject(s) whose past record is (are) being established. A topic is historical when living witnesses no longer exist.

Descriptive Variables: Dimensions of the record described. They are inherent in the Independent Variable(s).

Mediating Variables: Factors closely related to the independent variable(s). They are conditions of time, place, and culture which were the setting for the independent variable.

III. FACTORIAL-ANALYSIS RESEARCH:

Independent Variable(s); The factor(s) defined in the research. They include numerous cognitive, affective, and social factors.

Correlate Variables: The related variables analyzed in the research. They are correlated with the independent variable.

Mediating Variables: Factors closely related to the independent variable. They are different environments in which the independent variable operates.

IV. EXPERIMENTAL RESEARCH:

Independent Variable(s): The factor(s) whose effectiveness is (are) tested in the research. They may be drawn from any aspect of education.

Dependent Variable(s): Factors which are criteria for measuring effectiveness of the independent variable. They are outcomes of the independent variable.

Mediating (control) Variables: Factors closely related to the independent variable. In experimental research they must be
controlled.

V. PREDICTIVE RESEARCH:

Independent Variable(s): The factor(s) which is (are) used to
predict outcomes for another variable. Good predictors are
limited in number.

Dependent Variable(s): Factor(s) whose outcome is predicted. They
are correlated to the independent variable.

Mediating Variables: Factors closely related to the independent
variable(s). They are different environments for the independent
variables. In predictive studies they must also be controlled.

VI. DEVELOPMENTAL RESEARCH:

Independent Variable(s): They are innovations. The educational
concept(s) for which research is (are) engineering educational
practice, especially technology. Regression is computed.

Dependent Variables: As in experimental research. Criteria for
measuring the effectiveness of the independent variable. They
may be outcomes of the independent variables or factors which
make it feasible.

Mediating Variables: Factors closely related to the independent
variables. They are external to the independent variables.
They must be controlled.

As was mentioned in passing at the beginning of this chapter the conceptual elements in the topic are fundamental to the research design.
As a result of the elaborations on the analysis of the topic in the
above pages, it is possible to point out succinctly the role of elements
in the topic for establishing research design. The independent variable
is the source of the experimental treatments in the design. The dependent
variable(s) is (are) the criterion data by which the effectiveness of
the independent variable(s) will be measurable. For this reason, the
dependent variables dictate to the researcher the choice of his instruments for data collection. The mediating variables are the factors which
must be controlled in the research design. All of these roles of the
variables in the topic arise when they are considered singly

and independently of each other. When we consider them related to each other, the independent-dependent-mediating variables interaction produces the purposes and the hypotheses in the research design.

CHAPTER IV. DESIGN FOR COLLECTING DATA

In educational research design, there are three critical elements:
the purposes, the hypotheses, and the criterion data. The purposes are
the most basic issue, and hypotheses and criterion data derive from the
purposes. All three factors combined are the center complex of the
design for any given investigation. The only matters of research
design which take precedence over them are selection and analysis
of the topic. The next step is to set purposes. Once purposes have
been set, procedures are controlled by the purposes. As stated, topic
selection precedes purposing, but setting purposes affects even the
topic itself, for this is the way to limit the topic. Certain aspects
of a topic are more meaningful to education and the research limits
itself to dealing with them only. For each purpose and sub-purpose
set, there must be a corresponding hypothesis or sub-hypothesis.
Similarly, for each purpose-hypothesis it is imperative to identify
data that will serve to test the hypothesis and answer the purpose.
This is what is meant by saying that purposing controls hypothesizing
and collection of criterion data.

An illustration of the principles stated above is found in the case
of an experiment designed and controlled by Francis R. Hunkins, a copy of
which is included among the Analytical Models later in this book. The
research topic is the effect of different types of questions on
achievement, and the title is "The Influence of Analysis and Evaluation
Questions on Achievement in Sixth Grade Social Studies." The broad
purpose of the investigation is to answer the question:

31

"Will students who utilize study materials consisting of analysis and evaluation questions acquire more learning than students who utilize study materials consisting of recall questions?" Beyond this general purpose, researcher Hunkins sets three sub-purposes, included in the general purpose. The first sub-purpose is the question: "Will superior achievement due to utilization of higher cognitive questions rather than lower cognitive questions depend on the sex of the student?" In other words will the superiority of type of questions hold when only the boys or the girls in each group compete against each other? The second sub-purpose is the question: "Will superior achievement due to utilization of higher cognitive questions rather than lower cognitive questions depend on the reading ability of the student?" Otherwise stated, will superiority of type of questions hold according to the reading level of the student?" The third sub-purpose is the question: "Will superior achievement due to utilization of higher level cognitive questions rather than lower level cognitive questions depend upon interaction among type of questions, sex of student, and reading level of student?" This last question is answered by statistical procedures and not by any re-grouping of the subjects in the sample. The reader will notice that these purposes are clear, significant to the topic, and give depth to the research. These are characteristics of good purposing. It is obvious that if the researcher is to be able to set effective purposes he must have some measure of competence related to the topic. He must also be analytic-minded to clarify his thoughts as to what he is trying to accomplish through the investigation. Since purposes are in them-selves inquiring and interrogative, it follows that the best grammatical format in which to state them is the interrogative form—as a question.

The beginning researcher needs to be warned of the hazards to research design which exist in the area of purposing. Defective purposes can defeat a good research project.

Beginning researchers have a tendency to "go into action," collecting data too soon without carefully setting purposes. In written research reports, purposing is often slighted by not stating purposes clearly and thoroughly enough. The researcher is, therefore, cautioned that if purposes are not adequately formulated and the research design controlled by them, no amount of elaborate testing or sophisticated statistical treatments later on can save the project from producing findings which are of dubious validity.

Once the purposes have been determined for an investigation, the researcher sets up a hypothetical answer to each question in his purposes and sub-purposes. The use of hypotheses was introduced into inductive research designs about a century ago. The function of hypotheses in research design is to simplify and reduce the data collection in research. If the researcher approached his topic as an unanswered question, he would have to collect evidence for both a Yes-answer and a No-answer until one or the other answer seemed to command more evidence. By means of a hypothesis the researcher formulates the best answer he can justify for each of his purpose questions, then he collects a set of data and analyzes his data to see if it supports his hypothesized answer beyond mere chance occurrence. If it does, he concludes that his hypothesis is confirmed: if it does not he rejects his hypothesis and revises it or searches for another one. The use of hypotheses thus streamlines research procedures while also introducing elements of chance and proba-bility into them. There is no stigma attaching to non-confirming of the hypothesis for hypothesizing involves some guessing, albeit informed guessing. By this is meant that the hypothesis should be justified on the basis of one or more from among the following sources: educational philosophy and psychology, widespread school practice, widespread judgmental consensus, and any assumptions basic to the hypothesis, which must be clarified. The hypothesis combines the independent-dependent factors in a predication. For instance, Hunkins probably hypothesized that the analysis and evaluation questions would produce greater learning than the recall questions. In research terminology, this logical statement of the hypothesis may be referred to as the "Positive Hypothesis" as opposed to the statistics-oriented "Null Hypothesis." This latter is derived from the logic basic to all statistical formulas, which begin with the assumption that there will be no significant differ-ence between results from the comparative treatments. This logic gives rise to the term "Null" hypothesis. Research reports of projects which involve use of inferential statistics will usually state only null hypotheses whereas reports of other projects, such as surveys, which involve little if any inferential statistics will likely state "positive" hypotheses.

They hypotheses arise from purposes and lead into criterion data. The researcher establishes his purpose-hypothesis units, and for each one he must then assemble some empirical data by which he tests each hypothesis. This empirical data is referred as the "Criterion Data." Obviously, the data needed must be determined by the question to be answered. If greater achievement is hypothesized, achievement scores must be collected to verify whether achievement was greater. If a change or improvement of attitude is hypothesized, some score on an attitude or interest scale must be secured to verify whether an affective change occured. Criterion data in survey or historical investigations often consists of observations and their frequencies.

The preponderance of criterion data consists of test scores. One caution to be exercised in the selection of criterion data is to design criterion data which is as close to the independent variable and the experimental treatment as possible. Sometimes, graduate students utilize one or two units over a few weeks as the experimental treatment. As criterion data they use scores on a standardized examination on the field as the criterion data to measure outcomes from the experimental treatment. This is patently poor procedure because one or two units taught by some new approach will not make much difference on what the students know about the entire field. It would be more effective research design to construct a test on the dependent variable and limit it to what was taught in the experiment. In this case the researcher-made test is not standardized and is less sophisticated but it is more valid for the purpose of the research. In this connection, Hunkins did a very commendable job of constructing his own 42-item examination on the unit on "Western Africa, Australia, and New Zealand." In spite of the amount of work put into it and the expertise brought to bear on it, the test had a low reliability coefficient of only .68, but it yielded more valid criterion data for his investigation than would have been yielded by a standardized Social Studies Examination with a reliability coefficient of .90.

Criterion data in educational research exists in three categories. "Nominal Data" consists of categories, or items, and their frequencies. This type of data is commonly collected in descriptive and historical studies, especially normative surveys. There are relatively few inferential statistical procedures available for interpreting nominal data. The second type of data, "Ordinal Data" consists of the rank or position of individual subjects, compared to other individuals in the sample.

More statistical procedures exist for the interpretation of ranked data especially, several more recent ones. Finally, there is criterion data known as "Interval Data." These are scores, with which every one is familiar. Scores are expressed on a numerical series beginning with zero and going to infinity with an identical unit interval from one number to the next. Most of the statistical procedures known to educational research are intended for interpretation of interval data. The nature and extent of criterion data depends on the independent and the dependent variables involved in the research topic. The researcher must give careful attention to deciding what will be his criterion data. It must be the measurements or observations which most validly measure the dependent variables in the topic. Also, the criterion data must be chosen with a view to being as completely accurate and objective as possible. This point in the research design is important for assuring that the evidence collected in the investigation is truly empirical.

Now that purpose-hypothesis, and criterion data have been discussed, the following check-questions may be formulated for this area of research design. The first question is: "Is the design plausible?" By this is meant, are the purposes, hypothesis, and criterion data worthwhile and justifiable. Is there interest in them in the practice of education? The second question is: "Are consequences deducible from the purposes and hypothesis?" If possible, express these consequences, as behavioral objectives. Depending upon the resolution of these questions, it will then appear whether the criterion data will be nominal, ordinal, or interval. The third question is: "Are hypothesizing and criterion data exhaustive of the purposing?" The former two must cover the range of purposes but they must not go beyond them. The fourth question is : "Are sub-purposes and sub-hypotheses consistent with each other?"

They, as well as the criterion data must be logically related, they should not overlap in detail, and they should not contradict each other. A fifth question is: "Are they expressed in clear, simple, and direct language?" Above all, they should be clearly stated.

A final note to close this chapter is the distinction among fact, hypothesis, and theory. A hypothesis lies between facts and a theory. A body of facts will confirm or disconfirm a hypothesis, and several hypotheses will be synthesized into a theory (law). The ultimate goal of educational research is to build theories but this can be achieved only through the cumulation of related researches. The single individual investigation makes a contribution to some theory, but it is invariably limited only to some aspect of a theory. Investigations of individualizing instruction in certain subject fields or students of certain ability levels test hypotheses, but numerous such studies will be needed to build a comprehensive theory of individualized instruction.

CHAPTER V. SAMPLING DESIGN

Educational research is concerned with testing hypotheses on various aspects of education with a view to generalizing findings to large universes of students, or teachers, or schools, or programs, etc. For instance, educational research seeks to be able to say that sixth graders will achieve better in social studies if they utilize study materials involving analysis and evaluation questions rather than recall questions. The obvious way to achieve this far reaching goal would be to carry out research including all sixth graders as the subjects in the experiment, but this is not possible. The problem therefore arises: "Can research be done with a smaller group drawn from a universe, and still yield findings that are generalizable to the universe?" In terms of the topic mentioned above, could we conduct an experiment utilizing analysis and evaluation questions versus recall questions involving only 200 sixth graders, and still be able to consider the findings applicable to sixth graders generally? The reader will note the terms involved in this issue. Most importantly, there are the concepts universe and sample. In research terminology, a universe is a large number of subjects who are being investigated. The subjects may be human beings such as pupils, teachers, administrators, parents, etc. or they may be institutions such as elementary schools, secondary schools, colleges, etc.; or they may be programs, such as programs in remedial reading or individualized instruction. The term population may be used for the term universe. A sample is a much smaller number of subjects drawn from a given universe (population). The term sample is applied to the group of subjects drawn from the universe whether by some process or by no process at all. Also, both terms, universe and sample, are relative as to size. Thus, a sample of two may be drawn from ten, or sample of 200 may be drawn from a universe of 2,000 and so on. A sample is a group of subjects selected from a pool of such subjects, called the universe of the sample.

The basic question for sampling in research is, "Are findings from a sample generalizable to the universe?" The answer is yes, provided the sample be REPRESENTATIVE of the universe. A sample is representative of its universe if it includes all the relevant categories which exist in the universe and if it includes them in the same proportion as they are in the universe. For example, let us assume that the universe of public elementary schools in a given state consists of 2,000 schools of which 10% have enrollments over 1,500, 40% have enrollments between 500 and 1,000 and 35% have enrollments of less than 500. A sample of 100 schools drawn from the 2,000, in order to be representative of the universe by size of school, would have to include ten schools with enrollment above 1,500, fifteen with enrollment between 1,000 and 1,500, forty with enrollment between 500 to 1,000, and thirty-five with enrollment less than 500 pupils.

Pursuing the concept of representativeness, the question arises, "How does one secure a representative sample from a universe?" The traditional and laborious way is to identify all the categories in the universe and their proportionality, and to select individuals from all the categories of the universe in a smaller number, but in the same proportion to the universe. In the example of the hypothetical 2,000 elementary schools in a state, the individual schools in each enrollment category

may be identified from a state directory of schools. If schools of 1,500
enrollment are 10% of the schools, that means there are 200 schools with
1,500 enrollment. Of these 200, any 10 are selected to be the 10% of
schools of 1,500 enrollment in a sample of 100 schools in the state.
This procedure is repeated for each category of school by size of enrollment. Doing so, is often not feasible because the basic data of
categories and proportionality are not available and also because individuals in each category are not identifiable. School districts, for
instance do not have information on which students are very interested
in learning to read, which less interested in learning to read, and
which are not interested in learning to read; likewise, it is not known
what proportions of students fall into these categories. Because of
the lack of available information and because of the labor and time
involved in striving for such information, it became necessary to find
a more feasible and efficient way of drawing a representative sample
from a given universe. This need was met by random selection of individuals from a universe. The criteria of a randomly selected sample
are that the sample is so drawn that: (1) each individual in the
universe has the same probability of being included in the sample, and
(2) the selection of one individual from the universe does not in any
way affect the chances of any other individual to be included in the
sample. Different random sampling designs have been developed to meet
these criteria of random sampling.

The first random design which usually comes to mind is the lottery.
Names or numbers representing individuals are placed in a container and
"randomized" by mixing them thoroughly, and then units are drawn blind-
foldedly from the container. Weaknesses of this random design are the
difficulty of completely mixing the symbols in the container and the

defacto reduction in the odds of remaining individuals in the sample after
drawing of each member for the sample. In drawing the first member of
a sample from a universe of 2,000, the odds of each member being included
are 1 in 2,000. At the selection of the 200th member of the sample, the
odds of a universe member to be included have dropped to 1 in 1,800.
This problem could be solved if by means of some technology, all of the
members of the sample can be drawn simultaneously from the universe
rather than one after another. Other random selection designs are known
such as selection of every 20th or 50th member from a card file of
individuals. The problem here is to prevent the selection of any one
member of the universe from affecting the chances of other individuals to
be in the sample. To this end, no logical grouping of the cards in the
file may be permitted, such as chronological age or alphabetical order.
Before the interval selection begins, the cards must be shuffled into
a completely random order.

In a computerized age, random sampling designs which depend on a
"Manual" manipulation of gadgetry are anachronistic. Electronic equipment can produce sequences of Random Numbers, and the use of these tables
is the most efficient manner of randomly selecting a sample from a
universe. A table of random numbers consists of rows and columns of
numbers randomly dispersed, each number being repeated exactly as many
times as every other number. Thus, we may have a table of random numbers
composed of the digits 0,1,2,3,4,5,6,7,8,9, each repeated ten times and
the numbers randomly dispersed in rows and columns. Because all numbers
in the table occur the same number of times and because numbers are
randomly sequenced, the table of random numbers has a strict random design.

The first step in selecting a random sample by means of a Table of
Random numbers is to assign numbers to the individuals in the universe,

beginning with "one" and continuing until all individuals are numbered consecutively. To further randomness, the individuals should not be in any order or organization at the time of initial assignment of numbers. The next step is to enter the table of random numbers at any point. Beginning at that point, the researcher numbers one or more digits and the individuals they represent are included in the sample. Numbers are drawn until the sample is filled. Size of the numbers drawn in digits depends on the size of the universe. If it is in the thousands, four-digit numbers are drawn; if it is in the hundreds, three-digit numbers are drawn. Repeated numbers are ignored.

As an illustration, let us assume that we wish to draw a sample of ten from a universe of 99 children. First, we assign to each child a number from 1 to 99, in no special order. At this point, the reader is requested to refer to the sample table of random numbers reproduced among cases and models later in this book. Selecting any row-column intersection that comes to mind, let us enter the table say, at row 20, column 20. The number at this point happens to be zero. Now we mark off two-digits at a time. The first two digit number is00, which is ignored because no one in the universe was assigned 00. The following two-digit numbers are: 59,65,14,20,41,96,91,83,37, and 59. Since we want a sample of ten, we stop here, and the individuals in the universe who were assigned these numbers make up the sample. They constitute a random sample drawn from the universe of 99 children by means of the table of random numbers. As such, they are representative of their universe and they will be equivalent to any other sample of ten which may be drawn from the same universe of 99 by means of the table of random numbers.

There is no mathematical or logical proof that samples drawn by means of a table of random numbers will be representative of their universe and

willbe equivalent to each other. The proof is empirical: many such
samples have been drawn from universes and only by chance occurrence
did the samples fail to be representative of the universe or equivalent
to similar random samples. On the basis of this empirical proof, it is
accepted research procedure to consider samples drawn by means of the
table of random numbers to be representative and equivalent as stated
above. Equivalence is further enhanced after the total sample has
been drawn by assigning individuals to the treatment groups by a second
round of random selection, using the sample chosen as the universe for
the treatment groups.

Representativeness of the sample to the universe and equivalence of
treatment groups in the sample with each other are essential requirements for sampling in experimental research. Representativeness is
necessary for the findings based on the sample to ge generalized to
the universe; otherwise they are applicable only to the sample. Lacking
the proof of representativeness, the sample is its own universe; universe
and sample are coterminous. Random selection and/or assignment of the
control and experimental groups in the sample is proof in good standing
that the groups are controlled on the mediating variables which can
affect the dependent variables and must, therefore, be controlled to
satisfy the experimental research model. This model is that two situations
or phenomena are identical in all traits except one (the experimental
treatment), and hence, any differences in outcomes between the two situations or phenomena are attributable to the one trait on which they
differed (cause and effect relationship).

For research types other than the experimental, selection of a
sample from the universe by means of a table of random numbers guarantees
that the sample is representative of the universe and findings from the

sample may be generalized to the universe with assurance. Furthermore, in some descriptive studies, the researcher prefers to establish a stratified random sample. For this he needs information as to what categories exist in the universe and their proportion in it. The researcher may identify the individuals in each category and, using them as a universe, select by random numbers a sample for each category and in the same proportion to the sample as it is to the universe.

As a matter of practice in educational research, it is frequently not possible to define a particular universe and draw a random sample of specified size from it. Random selection is especially not feasible where research is done in the context of daily operations of the schools. Usually, the researcher accepts a number of individuals who are declared by school administrators to be "available" for the research. Such a "sample" of individuals is of course not representative of anyone but themselves and the value of research with such samples is sometimes questioned. The rebuttal to this challenge is that the criterion of representativeness can be waived in favor of replications of a project in numerous local investigations with non-representative samples. A so-called crucial investigation, one in which a final and definitive answer to a question is sought from a single exhaustive investigation, implies utilization of rather massive samples and the attempt to achieve perfect accuracy, objectivity, and control of variables. Cost, of course, is great. Crucial studies have been attempted, but were no more convincing than smaller scale projects. In their stead, the approach now is rather to conduct numerous replications of local limited investigations in various situations. Once a body of such replications has been accumulated, a synthesizer attempts to merge their findings into broader meanings toward comprehensive theory building. Hence, the local research based on non-representative samples has a valid purpose in the process of generalizing research findings. Often, the school or district in which a non-representative sample is used are primarily interested in the findings which emerge from "their children" so that local decisions and programs can be formulated.

Another issue of importance in sampling design is: "How large should the sample be?" The basic problem here is that of the sampling error. What the researcher means is what size should his sample be to make it free of error as a representative sample? Basically, the entire universe would be the most error-free sample of itself. Generally, the larger the sample, the greater is its chance to be free from error as representative of its universe. This does not necessarily follow, however, and a larger sample drawn by a looser random design is invariable less representative of its universe than a smaller sample drawn by a stricter random design. But given an equally strict random design, a larger sample will tend to be more representative of the universe than a smaller sample because the larger the sample the more it approximates the universe.

On the question of estimating the sampling error, statistics are available to determine the size of sample needed to meet a specified limit of sampling error. For instance, what size sample is needed to insure that the sample does not deviate more than two points in mean I.Q., from the universe mean I.Q., 100? The formula for computing such sample size is 1.96 x standard Error of Mean = 2. Standard error of a mean is the standard deviation of the series divided by the square root of the number in the series $(SE_m = SD/\sqrt{N})$. Replacing in the original formula, we get 1.96 x $(SD/\sqrt{N})=2$. The commonly accepted standard deviation of a series of I.Q.'s is 16. Again replacing, we get $1.96(16/\sqrt{N})=2$. Transforming algebraically this yields $(1.96 \times 16) /2 =\sqrt{N}$, since we are solving for the unknown N. Reducing, we get $15.68 = \sqrt{N}$. Squaring both sides gives N=246 approximately. In terms of sampling error this means that 95% of the time, a sample of 246 randomly selected individuals will not deviate more than two points from the universal I.Q. mean of 100; otherwise stated, the sample mean will fall between 98 I.Q. and 102 I.Q., ninety-five percent of the time. The size of sample needed for assurance 99% of the time that the sample mean will not deviate more than two points from the mean of the universe is computed by the formula $2.58 \times SE_m = 2$. Computing as with the previous formula N=426 is the sample size needed to meet the specified sampling error. All of the above discussion applies to randomly selected samples.

Errors in sampling may be spoken of as "random errors", and/or "constant errors". The errors which are inescapable in random sampling with its purely empirical basis, are random errors. An example, on the other hand, of constant errors, sometimes also called "systematic" errors, would be to include only children of business executives in a sample of school children. Since this sample would not contain children from all the categories of socio-economic backgrounds, this sample would be "biased". Sampling errors can be reduced by applying three remedies. The first remedy is to increase the size of the sample for, as stated earlier, a larger sample has greater probability of approximating the universe, other things being equal, than a smaller sample. The second remedy is to increase the homogeneity of the variable under study. This means simplifying or unifying the experimental treatments. A broader band of experimental variables increases the hazard of variance in the sample. In other words, this remedy is concerned with simplifying and unifying the purposes of the investigation. The third remedy is to re-examine the sampling design used and to searc h for means of making

it more rigorous. At times this may necessitate repeating the entire
process of selecting the sample,   to arrive at a new and improved
sample. The three remedies above are effective in reducing the margin of error in securing representativeness and equivalence of groups
in a randomly selected sample, but they do little for correcting a sample
in which the errors are constant. In such cases, usually, increasing
size of the sample only increases the error in it. For samples with
constant errors, the best remedy is to discard them and employ a design
which will involve randomness.

Sampling in educational research was refined during and since
World War II. There are now bodies of both sampling theory and sampling
statistics. Sampling has now become a field of specialization and there
are full-time specialists in sampling. The beginning researcher especially needs to understand the difference between sampling data and
sampling statistics as opposed to criterion data and criterion statistics. Sampling data and statistics involve measurements and computations
which are concerned with securing a sample that is representative of
the universe, and experimental treatment groups which are equivalent to
each other. The data involved in the sampling statistics are measurements and/or observations on the mediating variables. They may include
the pretest scores on the instrument for collecting criterion data
(post-test scores) which tests for differences on the independent variable. The statistical procedures used in sampling statistics are the
same as those used in interpreting criterion posttest data. The inferential
statistical procedures called the "t-test" of the significance of differences between group means and the "F-ratio" of the Analysis of Variance
are identical when used with sampling data and criterion data; only the
purposes are different.

Sampling is vital to inductive thinking and the design of all types of research. If the researcher is not certain of the sample on which his findings are based, neither can he be certain of the findings.

CHAPTER VI. TOOLS FOR COLLECTING DATA

As was pointed out in the Chapter on Design for collecting Data, the purposes of the investigation control the research design and procedures. This control relationship is obvious between purposes and the tool(s) for collecting the criterion data. If the purpose of the investigation is to test the effectiveness of an independent variable on cognitive achievement of children, the tool for collecting data must be an achievement test, possibly a standardized test, but preferably an achievement test constructed by the researcher and closely related to the learning involved in the investigation. If the purpose of the research is to test the effects of an independent variable on an affective dependent variable such as attitude toward learning, or the spirit of tolerance, then a rating scale of some type is needed for measuring these effects. The purposes-hypotheses of the research design determine the nature of the data which must be collected in the investigation, and the nature of the data determines the type of instrument which must be used to collect that data.

This principle implies that the researcher must have competencies for collecting a wide spectrum of data. The following discussion of ten different kinds of tools will be helpful to him. Ten types of tools may be grouped into five categories: 1) Collecting data through Seeing and Hearing, 2) Collecting Data through Soliciting, 3) Collecting Data through Measuring, 4) Collecting Data through Bibliographic Tools, and 5) Collecting data by means of Mechanical Devices.

The tool for collecting data through seeing and hearing is a
process really, observation. Unfortunately, much of the data collected
through observation during the early decades of the twentieth century
was inaccurate and subjective. Observations were faulty because a
single long observation period was used, and a multiplicity of objectives were targets simultaneously. Consequently, the observer did
not have a good sampling of behavior to observe and he could not keep
accurate records of his data. The upshot was that observation
fell into disrepute as a tool for educational research. However, the
increase in problems of delinquency during the 1950's created demands
for research in the affective domain, values, interests, motivation.
Attempts to secure measurements and observations of such data soon proved
that objective pencil and paper devices obtained responses which were
socially right and culturally inspired , but not true about the individual
respondent. It became evident that such data would best be collected
by means of observation if this latter could be made objective and
accurate. To this end, new procedures of observation were devised. They
include multiple observation periods scheduled at different times of
the day, different days of the week, and different weeks of the year.
This pattern yields a more representative sampling of behavior. Thus,
instead of twelve hours in two solid days of observation, the researcher
would carry out twelve visitations, of one hour each, spread over a term
of the school year. In addition to conducting multiple visitations, the
observation concentrates on a single criterion datum for each observation
session. This permits him to be more accurate in observing. Finally,
observation has been rehabilitated by developing forms and record formats
for recording data. All of these revisions make observation the best data
gathering device in the area of values and the affective domain generally.

Tools for collecting data through soliciting it include the Questionnaire, the Check List, and the Interview. In the questionnaire format
each item is presented followed by a space for providing an answer.
Such answers are termed unstructured. They are theoretically more valid
than structured answers because the respondent is free to answer exactly
as applies to his situation. In practice, however this theoretical
advantage is lost for the most part. Because the respondents must
formulate an answer, which involves time, effort, and some skills,
many individuals in the sample do not respond, and so returns are reduced.
Then, the researcher must read the unstructured answers he does receive, and in both directions of communication, self-expression by the
respondent and comprehension by the reader, a considerable amount of
exactness of the answers is lost. Finally, the researcher must
tabulate the unstructured answers and to do this he must compress
each one to its basic message so that similar responses may be tallied
with each other. By the time the researcher has reached this point in
collecting his data advantages of unstructured answers have greatly
dwindled away. However, the questionnaire format, a question followed
by a blank for indicating the response, remains the best format for a
specific, factual answer, such as: In what year was Research Director
first appointed in the school district? __1952.__

The second type of tool by which data is solicited is the Check-
List. The format for this device is an initial incomplete statement
(called the stub) followed by several verbal elements (called options)
which may meaningfully complete the statement. The respondent checks the
option(s) which most nearly describe(s) his situation. Such answers
are termed structured answers. All the items that are included in a
questionnaire could be formulated as a Check-List, and vice-versa.

The additional work of structuring responses is considerable. The options
for a given item must exhaust all the meaningful responses possible, but
they should not overlap. It will take considerably more time to formulate
a given set of items as a Check-List than as a Questionnaire. On the other
hand, the responses to a Check-List are much more quickly tabulated than
open-ended answers on a questionnaire. The accuracy of responses via the
structured options in each item of the Check-List is no doubt at least as
great ultimately as that of free answers in the Questionnaire. Check-List
validity can be increased by adding a blank option where-in the respondent
may enter an option formulated by himself if he wishes to describe his own
situation with greater accuracy. Experience shows, however, that few
respondents avail themselves of the opportunity to give a response "other"
than the options listed by the researcher. The responses tabulated from
a Check-List thus are usually as accurate as and certainly more objective
than responses tabulated from a questionnaire, and, to repeat, returns by
respondents are facilitated.

The third type of tool for soliciting information is the Interview.
Again, this type of instrument can include the same items as a Questionnaire
or a Check-List. The format for the Interview is an unstructured verbal
answer. Being verbal, the answer is invariably much longer than a similar written answer formulated in a questionnaire. The greatest advantage
of the interview over the questionnaire and the Check-List, however, is
its flexibility. Responses may be revised, follow-up questions to answers may be explored, and clarifications of answers may be secured. Thus,
the responses can be more valid, have more depth, and the data secured
is qualitative as well as quantitative. Unfortunately, much of these
theoretical advantages is not realized in practice.

To capitalize on the advantages of the interview, the interviewer must be able to motivate the interviewee and to establish rapport with him. These objectives are not extremely difficult to achieve, but they do require some planning and some mental alacrity to create effective communication.

There are a number of problems associated with collecting data by interviews. The interviewer and the interviewee must find a mutual time in their individual schedules to meet for the interview. An interview should be requested usually by a telephone call and then confirmed by letter. In the call and the correspondence, the researcher should introduce and describe himself and he should also brief the interviewee as to his topic, his purposes-hypotheses, and the data he needs. Geography and transportation are a hurdle for the interviewer who must travel from one interview to another. An interview may generate some pressure on both interviewer and interviewee. But the most difficult problem associated with interviewing is recording and tabulating the responses. The researcher should have forms developed for quick, unobtrusive recording of basic answers, for he must not interrupt the flow of communication by obtrusive note-taking. A tape recording of the interview is helpful, providing the respondent is agreeable. Even so there is still the need to transcribe the tape into written script, to abstract answers, and to cumulate them with other interviews. If an interview is not recorded, the researcher should draw up a summary statement of it as soon as possible after the interview, and especially before conducting any further interview, so as to prevent forgetting or overlap confusion among interviews. After a summary is arrived at for an interview, it should be submitted to the interviewee for his endorsement. At this time he has the opportunity to make any changes or revisions or to change it entirely

because an interview is admittedly an unrehearsed encounter and the
interviewee is entitled to a more deliberate consideration of his answers.
However, a researcher must have empirical records of his data, and
once the interviewee has had the opportunity to reconsider his statements,
he should be willing to certify his responses by signing of initialing
the summary of his deposition. The researcher should list these official
summaries in his bibliography and indicate the location where they are
preserved on file, and describe procedures by which the reader could
have access to them if he wished to examine them.

The student will readily note that the Questionnaire, the Check-List,
and the Interview are data collection tools utilized mainly in descriptive research of the Survey variety. The researcher invariably constructs
his own instrument except in cases where the researcher may find a
previously constructed instrument which merely needs revising. The researcher, therefore, must possess competencies to construct basic
descriptive instruments. The first step is to identify a set of items
which are to be included in the tool. The criterion for identifying
these items is the purposes of the research. A questionnaire should
include all the questions which are needed to achieve the purposes set.
Hence the issue of how long or how short a questionnaire should be is
a secondary question. A long questionnaire is not necessarily better than
a short questionnaire, nor vice versa. A questionnaire should be as long
or as short as the purposes dictate. Any decisions on the length of a
questionnaire should be guided by the purposes and hypotheses of the
research design. The researcher builds upon his own knowledge of the topic to begin his inventory of the items which should constitute a questionnaire, or Check-List, or Interview. He expands the list from his survey
of literature on the topic and, desirably, interviews with a few experts

in the field. He expresses these items in language as clearly as possible, then sequences them in some order, frequently by logical relationship. Having done these things to the best of his ability, he should submit his final draft of the instrument to a few experts on the topic for evaluation of the instrument as a questionnaire. This evaluation will include consideration of items that should be added or deleted to the instrument; the communication in the instrument, i.e., clarity of language; sequence and organization of the items; and format for recording responses. After making any revisions based on the evaluations of these experts, the researcher takes the final safeguard of mailing the instrument to a pilot group for trial run of it as an instrument. For this pilot run the researcher may well use 10% of his sample with the intent to retain their responses for inclusion in his criterion data. If any revisions of the questionnaire appear necessary from the trial run, they should be carefully made. The 10% who served as the pilot group are re-surveyed only if revisions are made in the instrument and only on the items affected by the revisions. The set of procedures described above exhaust the repertory of safe-guards which the researcher can take to assure validity and reliability of his questionnaire. The device is then ready for administration to the full sample. This is a critical point in a descriptive study, because the data is only as good as the instrument which collects it, and the findings will be only as good as the data on which they are based. Pro-bably, there is something left to be desired in the quality of the ques-tionnaires used in much of the descriptive research which is done.

The next category of research tools includes those which secure data by measuring. They are mainly tests, scales, and score cards.

Tests are of several varieties: aptitude tests, achievement tests, and performance tests.

The researcher in graduate school, single-handed, under the supervision of advisors, constructs tests on units in an experimental treatment, but it is beyond the scope of a Master's Thesis to attempt to develop standardized norms for an objective examination. Graduate researchers, however, can readily obtain coefficients of validity and reliability for their tests. It is also useful to note the growing use of performance testing in collecting educational data. New techniques for doing this kind of testing are evolving, especially to make them more objective. Whereas, performance measurements were not widely used for doing educational research in the past, they will apparently feature more prominently in educational research in the future.

Beyond the decision on what type of test is needed, there is the decision of finding the best test of the type needed, which may be in the market, from the viewpoint of empirical data, validity, reliability, and feasibility. Validity is the quality by which the test measures what it is intended to measure. Thus, a valid reading test measures reading achievement. The validity of tests is ascertained by computing their correlation with other tests of the same type which are commonly accepted as valid. In this sense, the coefficient of correlation is called the coefficient of Validity. Text publishers usually report the coefficient of validity of a given test, and it is frequently below .70. The researcher must not select a test solely because of its validity coefficient, he must also consider its validity for the purposes and hypotheses in his research design. To this end he may examine the items in the test individually. For instance, by examining if the items in a test are concerned with types of learning tasks which are related to his purposes. A given instrument may be more or less valid for certain research purposes.

In this connection, it is important in research design to note that standardized examinations in a subject field are often too general to serve for securing the criterion data needed in the investigation. The researcher may secure more valid criterion data by constructing a test of his own with the expertise at his command. His test will not be as sophisticated as a standardized instrument, but it will measure the dependent variables that are involve in his experimental treatment. A good example of the point here made is found in the research design of Hunkins as reported in his article included in Analytical Models in this book. He taught a unit on Africa, Australia, and New Zealand, utilizing analysis and evaluation questions as study materials for one group as opposed to utilizing knowledge questions as the study materials of another group. To test the effectiveness of the experimental variable (types of questions) he constructed a 42-item test on the unit Africa, Australia, and New Zealand, and used it as pretest and as posttest for his criterion data. His self-constructed examination was a more valid test, research-wise, than a standardized examination in social studies, because a standardized test on the field would have items beyond the unit Africa, Australia, and New Zealand. Students from both the experimental and the control groups would have missed items not becuase of the types of questions in their study materials, but because they had never been taught that particular content. Thus, Hunkins' self-constructed examination yielded more valid test scores than would have been yielded by a standardized examination on sixth grade social studies.

The next important characteristic of a test is its reliability, which is the quality by which the same test yields the same results when taken by the same testees. Data for computing the reliability coefficient are scores which may be obtained from a single group of students by means of

a test-retest with the same form of the test; or a test-retest with
equivalent forms of the test; or by split-halves of one testing, considering
odd-numbered items as one test, and even-numbered items as a second test.
In any case, the first step for computing reliability is to compute the
"r" correlation coefficient for the two series of scores. After that the
researcher may replace the correlation coefficient in the Spearman-Brown
formula:

$$r1 = \frac{r12}{1+r12}$$ where r_1 = reliability of a test and
$r12$ = correlation between two administrations of the test.

In the split-halves method the formula must be adjusted thus:

$$rtt = \frac{2\ rhh}{1+rhh}$$ where rtt = reliability of the total test, and
rhh = correlation between the two halves of the test.

The limit considered desirable in a reliability coefficient has
been variously set at .94, .90, or around .86. Test publishers publicize
the reliability of their test, but in a research design, other considerations need to be recognized; a test with a somewhat lower reliability
coefficient, may have greater validity, or suit the characteristics of the
sample better. The rationale for reliability of a test is that if some
items are not answered consistently by the same individuals, this is evidence that they should be revised in language, or modified in content, or
both; and if they still cause confusion, they should be eliminated as in-
appropriate.

Feasibility of a test includes its ease of administration, time, and
cost. Obviously, group tests are more feasible than individually administered tests, and a projective technique type test can be safely given only
by a trained psychologist or preferably a psychiatrist. In spite of their
advantages otherwise, projective tests are not feasible

for most graduate level educational research.

To assist the researcher to secure tools which have the characteristics discussed in the paragraphs above, there are several published sources. The most widely known is the Mental Measurement Yearbook, which does not appear anually, but at intervals, whenever enough new and revised instruments have appeared to justify publication of a new Yearbook. Instruments are listed by categories and the more prominent ones are reviewed. Cross references permit the interested reader to trace back to earlier instruments and forms included in previous yearbooks. Four new supplements to the Mental Measurements Yearbook are now published by its editors: Reading Tests and Reviews, Personality Tests and Reviews, Intelligence Tests and Reviews, and Vocational Aptitude Tests and Reviews. Also, certain listings and annotations of instruments are published elsewhere, such as in Johnson and Bommarito, Tests and Measurements in Child Development: A Handbook.

Scales and scale construction are prominent in data gathering today. The Likert-type scale and the Thurston-type scale are constructed and used quite frequently. A scale does not yield a score, it implies a description of individuals on certain traits and in terms of levels or degrees. For instance, it is almost impossible to arrive at a score for an individual on promptness, but it is possible to arrive at a description of him as invariable prompt or rarely prompt, or in-between these poles on promptness. The development of models and techniques for constructing scales is facilitating research greatly in the areas of personality and values.

The Likert Scale is popular and is least complicated to construct. The researcher assembles a set of statements relevant to his topic, and

significant to his purposes and hypotheses. The items are not cast
at any pitch or level or intensity of meaning, but they range from a
desirable outlook to an undesirable outlook on the topic. The respondent decides for himself the point at which he stands on the continuum from the positive pole to the negative pole for each statement.
The format for this continuum consists of columns bearing such headings
as agree-uncertain-disagree. The triple classification usually suffers
from the fact that people shun extremes and seek a middle position.
If three options are offered, many respondents will place themselves
in the middle, and the instrument will fail to discriminate among
individuals. For this reason, a five-category format is more effective. Given two options on each side of an issue, many people will
avoid the dead center and place themselves in the moderate position if
they do not favor an extreme position. It might seem that if this is
true, why not have a continuum of seven, nine, eleven, or more options.
To go beyond five options places a demand on the respondent to make
fine distinctions in his thinking so that many will either not respond
at all or give a random response. Items in the scale are either positive or negative according as agreement with the statement is desirable
or disagreement is desirable. To arrive at a score for an individual,
the researcher assigns values from 1 to 5 to the intervals on the
continuum. For positive statements the values are assigned as 5 to 1,
and for negative statements the values are assigned 1 to 5. The
individual's score on the scale is the sum of the values assigned the
positions which he checked on the continuum. For this reason the Likert
Scale is also referred to at times as the Summated Rating Scale. Because
of its feasibility both in terms of its construction and its administration, it is quite commonly used in educational research.

The Thurstone Equal Appearing Intervals Scale is the original type of scale pioneered for measuring affective characteristics. It created the concept of statements on a continuum of degrees or levels, proceeding from a positive pole through a neutral center, to a negative pole. In the Thurstone scale, however, the degrees of intensity are expressed in the wording of each item, and thought-difference between items should be equal. The task of the researcher is therefore to develop approximately two hundred items which range over a continuum of eleven positions of intensity from very favorable to very unfavorable. As said, the intensity gap from one position to the next must be as nearly equal as judgement can make it. Hence the term Equal-Appearing Interval Scale. Once the researcher has created the pool of such statements he submits them to be distributed over the continuum of equal appearing intervals by a panel of judges. Thurstone is reported to have used 2,000 to 3,000 freshman and sophomore judges, but presumably a group of fifty mature, graduate level people would suffice. After the researcher gets back the packets of statements he eliminates all of those that have been distributed over too wide a range of intervals by the judges. From the judges' experience with these latter items, it appears that they are not reliable. Up to fifty percent of the items may fall to this attrition. With the remaining items he arrives at a scale value for each item by graphing frequency of judges (y axis) who assigned it given positions from 1 to 11 on the continuum (x axis). He drops a perpendicular to the X axis from that point in the histogram where fifty percent of the judges are accounted for. The base of the perpendicular on the continuum is the scale value of the item. The researcher assigns approximately fifty items to Form A of the instrument and the remaining same number of items to Form B.

When the scale is administered, the testee is directed to check <u>only the items with which he is in agreement</u>. The scale values of these items are added up to give his score. Both of these types of scale are great assets to educational research in the affective domain.

The Score Card is a measuring device which is utilized in evaluating performance, being used to judge competition of various sorts. One problem in developing a score card is to know what are valid criteria of this type of performance, such as, what is good oratory, or piano-playing, or typewriting, or creative writing. The authorities in the field are the best sources to consult for these criteria. Once the criteria are selected, weighted values must be assigned to them. Weights are also assigned by the judgments of experts. The above steps yield a score card, but there is still the need for someone to utilize it. Once again, this demands an expert in the field who can recognize the presence of the criteria and judge the degree to which they are present. Unless the researcher has competence in his own name in the field, he may need to recruit judges to assign scores to the performers.

Another category of tools for collecting data is documentary sources. Schools maintain cumulative files on students and these files are sources of data for researchers. Often I.Q. scores and Reading scores for pre-testing purposes are available from cumulative records. Other school files such as in administration or guidance offices may also be sources of research data. As such, they may be considered tools for research. Data from files must not be accepted indiscriminately. Some data may be out-dated or records may be incomplete. Also, the researcher should criticize the sources of information he is considering for use. For instance, he may wish to know whether trained counselors administered the tests or whether all classroom teachers were used to administer the test. Cumulative files may be used more directly in the collection of

data, especially in longitudinal studies. However, they still remain
more a depository for data than a tool for measuring or observing.
Many researchers, however, look to cumulative files for greater depth
of information about their data.

Another documentary source of data is the index of publications
and other library resources. Several of the bibliographic tools have
been referred to or commented on at the appropriate places in this
text. For the most commonly used ones, the graduate student is expected
already to have familiarized himself with them and to have developed
competence in making bibliographies and taking notes. No further
mention is made of them in this book.

Finally, there is the category of mechanical devices for collecting
educational research data. Mechanical and electronic devices are
welcome as measuring and observing devices. Their objectivity, accuracy,
and efficiency greatly surpass that of unaided human sensory powers.
They are also more objective than printed tools. Unfortunately, there
still are not technological devices for measuring and observing most
variables with which educational research is involved. Eye cameras
are an excellent means of recording eye movements, but we do not have
equivalent electronic tools for recording non-sensory, non-motor human
behavior. Certain devices such as ordinary cameras and tape recorders
are second line tools which help indirectly in processing data. So are
computers and these have vastly extended the dimensions of educational
research.

The issue of tools for collecting data is crucial in educational
research. Inductive thinking is the best process for discovering new
truth, but it depends upon measurement and observation tools to provide
it with data which are objective, accurate, and sufficient in number

to justify making generalizations.

CHAPTER VII. ORGANIZING DATA FOR INTERPRETATION

The concern of this brief chapter is for the articulation of data collection with data interpretation. Basic to this concern is the assumption that there is a difference between these two processes. Since both are integral parts of the inductive thinking process, some research-ers may not see the need to differentiate between them. The argument in favor of thinking of collection and interpretation of data as separate is the truth that any interpretations can only be as good or as bad as the data on which they are based. If research data is not valid, accurate, and objective, not even the most sophisticated interpretation strategies will be able to draw from it generalizations that have the assurance of truth. Moreover, experience shows that educational researchers often feel a compulsion to assemble some data and get on with interpreting it. The best preventive against this syndrome is to implement a careful and thorough data collection design previous to interpreting. In this setting, organization of data is an appropriate culminating activity for data collection as well as an effective entry task to interpreting data, thereby, articulating the two phases.

The organization of educational data is controlled by the purposes set in the research design. Purposes may generally be either to determine significance of differences within the data, to determine significance of relationships within the data, or to determine uniformity within the data. Accordingly, the following paragraphs entertain considerations relative to organizing data when the research purposes focus on differences,

organizing the data when they focus on relationships, and organizing
data when they focus on uniformities.

If the concerns of the investigation are with differences, the
research design involves comparative groups, and the data includes
measurements on these groups on the dependent variables and probably
on some mediating (control) variables. Thus , in the case of experimental investigations, the data consists of pretest and posttest
measurements on all the dependent variables, and of at least one
measurement on one or more control variables. The format for organizing this data is a series of scores for each measurement, wherein
by series is meant a set of scores on a variable. The heading column
of the series is the name of the variable and each subject in the sample
is a row in the series. Since, in an experiment there are comparative
groups, a series of scores is organized on each measurement for each
variable in each group. For example, given an experimental design with
an experimental group and a control group, both of which are measured
for equivalence on I.Q. and Reading, and both of which are pretested
and posttested on achievement by a criterion - referenced test of
knowledge, by a standardized test of critical thinking, and by a
rating scale on attitude; there would result eight series of scores
for each group, or a total of sixteen groups of scores. The series of
scores on I.Q. and reading for the groups are sampling data (4 series)
and the pretest and posttests on the dependent variables are criterion
data (12 series).

Under research for differences, there would never be organization
of series from the competing treatments into a single continuous series
overarching the comparative groups. There is never any need to list
series of scores in any logical order, nor even in rank order.

Research purposes are concerned with relationships in the regression analysis and the predictive types of investigations. Data in these types of research are also organized into series. An important difference, however, between these research types and the experimental type is that although there are groups in regressions and predictions, the groups do not represent competing treatments. As a matter of fact, the purpose of the study may be to determine the correlation among variables for a total sample including all the sub-groups. In this case, the series for each variable will be a continuous series overarching all the groups, on each variable. It is entirely possible, however, that the investigation seeks to determine the correlation, limited to each group. Then the measurements are organized into one series for each variable for each group or environment for the data.

The remarks in the preceding paragraph pertaining to organizing data by groups and variables for correlation and regression analyses apply likewise for organizing data by groups and variables for predictive studies.

For research in which the purpose is to search for uniformities and concomitances, a different challenge exists. Whereas, data in the previous settings is invariably interval, or sometimes ordinal, the data in descriptive types of research is most often nominal.

The researcher must begin by grouping together large areas of nominal data which are held together by some unifying concept. If the questionnaire or other instrument for collecting data was logically organized, this task has already been done to some extent at least. The next step is for the researcher to break down each of these larger areas into smaller groupings of unified data. Thus, the process of analysis proceeds until small bodies of ten to twenty related items have been

distilled from the original mass of data. This is the appropriate
size of a body of nominal data for close scrutiny by means of deductive
and/or inductive thinking or for statistical treatments, say Chi-Square.

These segments of content can be further organized for interpretative
treatment by being presented in tables and figures. Tables convert the
nominal data into purely numerical expression at the intersections of
rows and columns. Figures convert the nominal data into a graphic-
pictorial representation. Both of these physical devices facilitate
discovering meanings in the data in the table. A table is more versatile than a figure for presenting data because each intersection of
a column and a row in the table is the equivalent of an intersection
of an X-Axis and a Y-Axis in a graph. Thus, a table can contain
the data of as many graphs as there are column-row intersections in
the table. Since the mechanics of organizing data into tables is
common knowledge, nothing is said about it here, for the chapter is
concerned only with the organization and meaning of tables and graphs.

The versatility of the table to present an extensive amount of data
must not be overtaxed for then the table loses its potential to present
data clearly and obscures its meanings. In constructing tables to present data, the researcher must strike a balance between overexpanding
the table on one hand and fragmentizing it on the other hand. The
unifying principle for each table may be more or less inclusive and the
table will accordingly include more or less data. The construction of
each table requires a decision to be made and all of these decisions
should only be made in the light of the purposes of the investigation.
The content of the tables is organized into columns and rows. The
label for columns are named Headings and the labels for the rows are
named Stubs. Hence the term "nominal" data. At the intersection of each

column and each row is a frequency, which indicates the number of times
the two are found in combination with each other in the responses
received. Every table should have a title which indicates the nature of
the data and accounts for the headings and the stubs.

Figures are pictorial in nature, being characterized by space and
direction. Thus, figures include graphs (histograms and frequency
polygons and all types of graphs involving symbols), charts, maps, etc.
This textbook assumes that the beginning researcher is already familiar
with the construction of figures and the concern here is with their
utilization for interpreting the data. Being pictorial, figures are
less abstract than tables, which are more numerical. Figures must have
a title which indicates the nature of the data and the categories included
in the figure. The decision should be made to present a set of data
either as a table or as a graph, but it should not be repeated as both
because such repetition does not contribute to the interpretation of the
data.

CHAPTER VIII.   DESCRIPTIVE STATISTICS

The role of statistics is to interpret the meaning of educational data. The full force of the logic of mathematical thought, which statistics entail, is brought to bear upon the data which has been assembled with a view to testing hypotheses and answering the purposes of the investigation.

As related to types of research and types of data, statistics fall into two broad classifications: Descriptive and Inferential. Descriptive statistics are basically associated with descriptive research, especially surveys, and these statistics usually deal with nominal data. Inferential statistics are basically associated with experiments and regression analyses and these investigations usually deal with ordinal and interval data (ranks and scores). Descriptive statistics describe numerically just as language describes verbally. Thus, a mean I.Q. of 100 tells us that the individuals it represents are average. Descriptive Statistics include the following statistical topics: Reporting Numerical Data, Measures of Central Tendency, and Measures of Dispersion. Measures of Relationship (Correlation) are largely descriptive, but since the coefficients are subject to inferring significance by referring to a probability table, they are included among Inferential Statistics in this text.

Reporting Numerical Data

The set of measurements or observations on a group of individuals is called a series. Such a series is termed ungrouped data whether

the numbers are all listed individually, including repetitions, or whether
only different scores are listed and the frequency of occurence of each
number is posted opposite it. Such numbers can be reported in a cumulative
frequency tabulation by listing the different numbers vertically from highest
to lowest and tallying the frequencies into a cumulative total from the
lowest score to the highest.

It has long been customary in statistics to group scores into frequency
tabulations. High speed computers have lessened the need for frequency
tabulations, but computers are equally effective with grouped scores as with
ungrouped. The original advantages of frequency tabulation of data are
therefore still meaningful. These advantages are: 1) to deal with fewer
numbers, 2) to deal with smaller numbers, and 3) to bring together a larger
body of data into physical juxtaposition for analysis and comparisions.
Frequency tabulation of scores consists basically of organizing them into
intervals of points and posting the frequency for each such interval, hence
the term grouped data. The first step in frequency tabulation of data is to
determine the range of the scores, i.e. difference between the highest score
and the lowest score. The second step is to approximate the interval size.
For this, the range is divided by 10 and by 20 because we do not wish to deal
with less than 10 nor more than 20 numbers. From the approximations of one-
tenth and one-twentieth of the range, one decides upon the most convenient
interval size for grouping the data, usually choosing from among 2,3,5, and
10 because these are familiar numbers. The third step is to mark off the
interval limits. The lower limit number and the higher limit number in each
interval are included in the interval size. The fourth step is to tally the
frequency, number of scores, for each interval. Finally, the fifth step
is to establish

the cumulative frequency column by adding the frequencies of the intervals from lowest to highest. Statistics computed from grouped data will be slightly less correct than the same statistics computed from ungrouped data, but the loss in accuracy is minimal when compared to the margin of error in the validity of the scores to begin with. Hence there is no significant devaluation of standards in research by utilizing frequency tabulations of data.

The steps for frequency tabulation of data can be illustrated with the following 50 hypothetical I.Q. scores.

Table I. Hypothetical I.Q. Scores

I.Q.	frequency	I.Q.	frequency
155	1	98	4
143	1	97	2
136	1	94	2
131	1	92	2
125	2	89	2
120	2	86	1
115	3	84	1
112	3	82	1
108	2	76	1
107	2	70	1
106	4	64	1
103	4	55	1
101	5		N = 50

Step 1. Range: 155 − 55 = 100

Step 2. $\dfrac{100}{10} = 10$; $\dfrac{100}{20} = 5$

Interval (I) = 10

Descriptive Statistics

		Interval		Cumulative
Step 3. Interval Limits	Step 4.	Frequencies	Step 5.	Frequency

Table IA. Frequency Tabulation of I.Q.'s

Interval Limits	Interval Frequencies	Cumulative Frequency
150–159	1	50
140–149	1	49
130–139	2	48
120–129	4	46
110–119	6	42
100–109	17	36
90–99	10	19
80–89	5	9
70–79	2	4
60–69	1	2
50–59	1	1

Total N = 50

At times the meaning of data can be made more obvious by resorting to graphic presentation of it. A common format is to represent achievement measures on the X-axis of a graph and the frequencies of these measures on the Y-axis. The coordinates can then be used to mark off rectangular columns based on an X-value and rising to a corresponding Y-value. In this case the graph is termed a histogram. Otherwise, the coordinated can be marked by a point at the intersection of the axes and the points may then be joined by lines. In this case the graph is called a frequency polygon. These types of figures show direction only; others utilize space and shape as well, but do not facilitate statistical interpretation in any way.

Measures of Central Tendency

The statistics known as Measures of Central Tendency are descriptive statistics. By a single numerical value they describe the series as to where is found the greatest concentration of scores (central

tendency). There are basically three Measures of Central Tendency:

the mode, the mean, and the median. The Mode is the most frequently

occurring score in the series. The mean is the arithmetic average,

and the median is the mid-point of rank-order of the scores.

The mode applies only to ungrouped score. It is too unstable

to be useful in educational research because there may be more than one

mode (ties) in series, or because it may be far removed from the

center of the series (toward the upper or lower end), and because there

may be several modes in the same series. In the series of scores

listed above in Table I, the mode is the I.Q. 101 because it occurs

five (5) times. Although the mode is not helpful to research, it is

helpful in school administration where, for instance, fixtures and

furnitures are planned with the most common height (mode) of students

in mind.

The mean, the arithmetic average of a series, figures prominently

in educational statistics. The concept of the mean is taught in

elementary school, but possibly the graduate student is not aware of

a symbolic formula for the mean. The formula is $\bar{X} = \frac{\sum X}{N}$, where $\bar{X}$

(bar X) is the symbol for the word mean, $\sum$ (capital Greek sigma) is

the symobl for the words "sum of", X is the symbol for each score in

the series, and N is the symbol for the number of scores in the series.

The sum of the 50 scores in Table I is 5150; when 5150 is divided by

the N, 50, the quotient we get is the mean, 103. When scores are

grouped, the formula for computing the mean is $\bar{X} = M' + \left(\frac{\sum fx'}{N}\right) i$. In

this formula, M' is the mid-point of any interval assumed to include

the mean. The symbol x' represents the deviation of other given intervals

above/below the interval where M' has been assumed, "i" is the interval
size, and N is the total number of scores. The mean of grouped data
in Table IA is computed as follows:

Interval	f	x'	fx'
150-159	1	10	10
140-149	1	9	9
130-139	2	8	16
120-129	4	7	28
110-119	6	6	36
100-109	17	5	85
90-99	10	4	40
80-89	5	3	15
70-79	2	2	4
60-69	1	1	1
50-59	1	0	0
	50		244

Place M' as the mid-point of the interval 50-59. Multiply each f by
its corresponding x' to get the fx' column. $\overline{X} = 54.4 + \dfrac{244}{50} \times 10 =$
$54.5 + 48.8 = 103.3$. In this case the mean for grouped scores is .3
different from the ungrouped scores. As stated previously, there is some
loss in accuracy in computing the mean from grouped scores rather than from
ungrouped scores, but the difference is almost never statistically significant.

In the computations for the mean, the column of x' (deviation of intervals from the mean), any interval may be selected as including the mean.
However, if any interval other than the lowest is selected, the computations
will involve positive and negative numbers. At this point in statistics,
computations of numbers with different signs remain

relatively simple. Later on, however, in computing Pearson Product Moment r coefficients of correlation, computations will also include assigning the assumed mean to some interval. For the Pearson r, computations become much more complex if there are positive and negative numbers in the x' column. It is therefore advisable for the student to customarily place the assumed mean in the lowest interval.

The mean is a statistic of a sample. The mean of the universe from which the sample is drawn is known as a parameter and is represented by the symbol μ (mu). Research utilizing descriptive statistics is sometimes interested in the closeness between the mean of the sample and mean of its universe. For this purpose, it is possible to compute the confidence limits above and below the sample mean within which the mean of the sample will probably fall 95 or some other percent of the time. For this computation the standard error of the mean is needed. The standard error of a mean is equal to the standard deviation divided by $\sqrt{N}$. For I.Q. scores as in Table I, a commonly accepted standard deviation is 20. The $\sqrt{50}$ is approximately 7, so if 20 is divided by 7, we get a standard error of approximately 3 for the scores in Table I. The confidence interval for a mean at the .05 level of probability is 1.96 times the standard error. In the case of Table I, this gives us 1.96 x 3= 5.98. Therefore, the mean of repeated samples of 50 scores selected from this universe would fall 95% of the time between 5.98 points above to 5.98 points below the sample mean of 103 (103 $\pm$ 5.98 = 97.02 to 108.98). For the .01 level of probability, the confidence interval is computed as 2.58 x 3 = 7.74. Therefore, the mean of repeated samples of 50 from the same universe would fall 99% of the time between 7.74 points above and 7.74 points below the sample of 103 (103 $\pm$ 7.74 = 95.26 to 110.74). In a study in which the mean of a sample of students has been found, it is sometimes of interest to know the limits within which the mean of repeated samples at different probability levels would fall. Confidence Limits provide this answer statistically.

The median is the central measure of the scores based on their rank order. The mean is the middle score if the series has an odd number of scores in it; it is the mid-point between the two mid-most scores if the series has an even number of scores. In the odd series of ungrouped scores, the median is determined by placing the scores in rank order and observing which score has an equal number of scores above it and below it. In the even series of ungrouped scores, the median is determined by adding the two middle-most scores and dividing their sum by two. For Table I, the median is mid-point between the 25th and 26th scores. Since both of these are 103, the median is 103.

For grouped scores, the formula for computing the median is:

$$\text{Median} = LL = \frac{(N/2 - lcf) \times i}{n}$$

In this formula, LL stands for lower limit of the interval which includes the median, N is the total number of scores, n is the frequency of the interval which includes the median, lcf (lower cumulative frequency) is the cumulative frequency of all the intervals below that which includes the median, and i is interval size. Computations of the median for the scores in Table I are shown on p. 78.

The interval which includes the median must be identified precisely. For the data in Table I, the median is the mid-point between the 25th and the 26th scores. By consulting the cumulative frequency column, we observe that these two scores fall among the 17 scores in the interval 100 - 109. In the formula, therefore, LL becomes 100. The other quantities which go into the formula follow according to LL.

Computations of the median for scores in Table IA are as follows:

Interval	f	Cumulative frequency
150–159	1	50
140–149	1	49
130–139	2	48
120–129	4	46
110–119	6	42
100–109	17	36
90–99	10	19
80–89	5	9
70–79	2	4
60–69	1	2
50–59	1	1

$$\text{Median} = 100 + \left(\frac{50/2 - 19}{17}\right)10 = 100 + \left(\frac{6}{17}\right)10 = 100 + \frac{60}{17}$$

Median = 100 + 3.57 = 103.57

When the mean and the median are considered as measures of central tendency, the mean is a more perfect measure than the median because the former is based upon the absolute values of the scores whereas the latter is based upon the rank order of the scores. The mean is, therefore, preferable to the median in research theory. On the other hand, many teachers prefer the median for purposes of classroom teaching because it is less abstract, since it has a pictorial element because of the position of ranks. The mean involves interval data, whereas the median involves ordinal data. For some immediate research purposes, the median may be preferable to the mean. With some topics, measurements of the dependent variable can only be obtained or best be obtained as ranks rather than as scores. For instance, this may be the case measuring performances, such as subject matter competitions, musical contests, shop skills, or physical education skills. The student will notice that a majority of statistical procedures utilize interval data (scores) and fewer statistics utilize ordinal data (ranks), and fewer yet utilize nominal data (frequencies). In learning each statistic, he must be aware of the type of data compatible with it.

Measures of Dispersion

The statistics known as Measures of Dispersion are another set of Descriptive Statistics. By a single numerical value they describe the series as to limits within which the scores in the series are deployed. Some of the statistics of dispersion are single values, and some of the statistics are intervals which determine the limits of dispersion of groups of scores.

The most obvious measure of dispersion, is the Range, which is the difference between the highest score and the lowest score. It is a weak statistical measure research-wise because about the only description it provides is whether the group represented by the scores is hetergeneous (wide range) or homogeneous (narrow range).

A more meaningful set of dispersion measures are the Quartiles. They are the First (Q_1), Second (Q_2), and Third (Q_3) Quartiles. Q_1 is that score which has one-fourth of the scores in the series below it, Q_2 is that score which has one-half of the scores below it, and Q_3 is the score which has three-fourths of the scores below it. For ungrouped scores, the quartiles are determined by ranking the scores and observing the values along the series which have the given proportions of scores below them, as for the median. For the scores in Table I, Q_1 is mid-point between the 12th and 13th scores. Both of these scores are 94 so Q_1 is 94. Q_2 is the mid-point between the 25th and 26th scores; these scores are among the four scores 103, so Q_2 is 103. Q_3 is the mid-point between

the 37th and 38th scores; both of these scores are among the three scores

112, so Q_3 is 112. Q_1 is identical with the 25th percentile, Q_2 is identi-

cal with the 50th percentile and also with the median, Q_3 is identical with

the 75th percentile.

Computation of quartiles with grouped scores is basically the same as

for the median. For Q_1 the formula became $Q_1 = LL + \left(\dfrac{N/4 - lcf}{n}\right)i$.

Replacing with values from the frequency tabulation, we get Q_1 = 90 +

$\dfrac{(12.5 - 9)}{10}$ x 10, and Q_1 = 90 + 3.5 = 93.5. For Q_3 the formula is $Q_3 = LL + \left(\dfrac{3N/4 - lcf}{n}\right)$ x i. Replacing, we get Q_3 = 110 + $\dfrac{37.5 - 36}{6}$ x 10 = 110 + 1.75

= 111.75. All deciles and percentiles are also measures of dispersion.

The basic formula is versatile. For instance for the 90th percentile,

$P_{90} = LL + \left(\dfrac{90N/100 - lcf}{n}\right)$ i. Replacing, we get P_{90} = 120 + $\left(\dfrac{45 - 42}{4}\right)$ x 10 =

120 + 7.5 = 127.5. The quartiles and percentiles are specific scores.

Quartiles must not be confused with quarters or fourths; the former are

single scores and are counted from the lowest scores upward, whereas the

latter are ranges of scores and are counted from the highest scores down-

ward. The basic formula for the median is used to compute the percentiles

in norms of standardized examinations.

Percentages and proportions of the scores are similar to quarters and

fourths of the scores in a series. They are clusters of scores falling

below or between quartiles.

The Quartile Deviation (Q) is an interval of scores which, when marked

off above and below the median, determines the limits within which fall

the middle fifty percent of the scores. $Q = \dfrac{Q_3 - Q_2}{2}$, whether scores

are ungrouped or grouped. For the data in Table I, $Q = \dfrac{112 - 94}{2} = \dfrac{18}{2}$ = 9.

81

Since the median is 103, the middle fifty percent fall between 94 and 112. The student will note that these limits are identical with Q_1 and Q_3. If these two statistics are known, the Quartile Deviation need not be computed and vice versa.

A counter-part measure of dipersion to the Quartile Deviation is the Standard Deviation, which is based on the mean. The concept involved in the Standard Deviation is the limits within which fall the middle two-thirds of the scores in the series. The standard deviation is based upon the deviations of each of the scores in the series from the mean of the series. For the purpose of illustrating how to compute the standard deviation with ungrouped scores, a series of only six one-digit numbers will be used. Admittedly the scores do not look very realistic as a series, but the objective of this text is to illustrate the steps and computation involved in arriving at the statistics, not to work out problems with data that exists factually. Computations are shown on p. 82. The mean of the series is 5, the standard deviation is 2, therefore, two-thirds of the scores in the series should fall within 2 points above and below the mean, i.e. 3 to 7. Such is the case, for 4 of the 6 scores, viz. 6,6,5, and 3, fall within the limits of 3 to 7, whereas the remaining two scores, 8 and 2, fall beyond the limits of 3 to 7.

The Quartile Deviation and the Standard Deviation serve different functions. The former is more useful to identify individuals who are achieving acceptably, whereas, the Standard Deviation is more useful to identify individuals who are failing in regard to achievement and those definitely above average in achievement.

Computations for Standard Deviation

$X - \bar{X} = X$	x^2	$S = \sqrt{\dfrac{\Sigma x^2}{N}}$
$8 - 5 = 3$	9	
$6 - 5 = 1$	1	$S = \sqrt{\dfrac{24}{6}}$
$6 - 5 = 1$	1	$S = \sqrt{4} = 2$
$5 - 5 = 0$	0	
$3 - 5 = -2$	4	
$2 - 5 = -3$	9	
$6\overline{)30}$	24	
$\bar{X} = 5$	Σx^2	

Research would best use the quartile deviation if the purposes are concerned with individuals who fall within the normal achievement range, but it would best use the standard deviation if purposes are concerned with individuals who fall above and/or below normal achievement. Since many important contemporary problems in education are concerned with gifted individuals on the one hand and the disadvantaged individuals on the other hand, the standard deviation is used more frequently than the quartile deviation. From a more basic research viewpoint also, the standard deviation has advantages as a deviation measure over the quartile deviation. The standard deviation is a more "definite" measure since it reveals the extremes of characteristics and performances; also, it involves absolute values of scores, whereas, the quartile deviation involves ranks.

Another interval measure of dispersion is the Average Deviation, which also identifies the middle fifty percent of the scores in a series. It is based upon the mean and is computed by summing the squares of the deviations from the mean and dividing that sum by the number of scores. Average Deviation has been superseded by the Quartile Deviation which performs the same function.

There are a number of transformations and applications of standard deviation intervals, one of the most important of which are proportions and percentages. For instance, approximately one-third of the scores in a series, or 34.13% of the scores, are included between the mean and one standard deviation above the mean. Likewise 34.13% of the scores are included between the mean and one standard deviation below the mean. Similarly, the standard deviation gives organization to the normal distribution because the second standard deviations above and below the mean each include 13.54% of the cases and the third standard deviations above and below the mean each include the remaining 2% of the cases. This gives the figure below, in which S is the symbol for standard deviation.

NORMAL CURVE

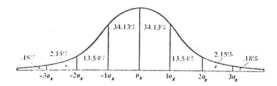

Relationship between distances along the base line and the percent of observations under a normal curve

The extreme standard deviations, three standard deviations above and below the mean, have very few cases. For that reason the normal curve is virtually complete after three standard deviations because they include 99.72% of the cases.

Computations of the Standard Deviation with grouped scores is by means of the formula

$$S = i \sqrt{\frac{\Sigma fx'^2}{N} - \left(\frac{\Sigma fx'}{N}\right)^2}$$

For the data in Table I, the computations are:

Interval	f	x'	fx'	fx'^{2}
150 - 159	1	10	10	100
140-~.149	1	9	9	81
130 - 139	2	8	16	128
120 - 129	4	7	28	196
110 - 119	6	6	36	216
100 ,- 109	17	5	85	425
90 - 99	10	4	40	160
80 - 89	5	3	15	45
70 - 79	2	2	4	8
60 - 69	1	1	1	1
50 - 59	1	0	0	0
	50		244	1360
			fx'	fx'^{2}

$$S = 10\sqrt{\frac{1360}{50} - \left(\frac{244}{50}\right)^2}$$

$$S = 10\sqrt{27.20 - (4.88)^2} = 10\sqrt{27.20 - 23.81}$$

$$S = 10\sqrt{3.79} = 10 \times 1.84 = 18.4$$

The mean of these grouped scores was found to be 103. When we add a standard deviation to it upward, we arrive at 121.1. When we subtract a standard deviation from it, we arrive at 84.9. Within these limits fall the middle two-thirds of the scores.

In addition to giving organization to the normal distribution curve, the standard deviation also serves to transform raw scores into standard scores and into ordinal equivalents which notably facilitate statistical theory and applications.

The standard score known as z-score (small z) is one of the best known of these applications of the standard deviation. A raw score is transformed into a z-score by the formula $z = \frac{X-\overline{X}}{s}$. The mean of the series is subtracted from any score in the series and the differences is divided by the standard deviation. An important advantage of z- scores is that they are all reduced in terms of the standard deviation of the series. Such reduction to standard deviation makes it possible to compare and contrast measures which originally existed in terms of dissimilar criteria and measuring instruments. If a student scores twenty points above the mean in both a reading test and an arithmetic test, he is not necessarily performing equally well in both tests. On the one hand, if he has a score of 120 in reading, if the reading mean is 100, and if the reading standard deviation is 20, the student has a z-score of 1.00 in reading. On the other hand, if he has a score of 100 in arithmetic, if the arithmetic mean is 80, and if the arithmetic standard deviation is 10, he has a z-score of 2.00 in arithmetic. Thus, the student is doing twice as well in arithmetic as in reading. But despite its very real assets as a research concept, the standard deviation also has some short-comings. Most important among these is its lack of discrimination among individuals. Of a student who has an I.Q. of 101, and a student who has an I.Q. of 119, the standard deviation says merely that both are within one standard deviation above the mean. Obviously, this lack of discri-mination between the two students is highly unsatisfactory in view of the difference of eighteen points between them. This lack of power to make distinctions among individual scores has led to several adaptations of the standard deviation that permit making sharper distinctions. These adaptations are summarized in Figure 1. The standard z-score explained above is in fact one such adaptation because although its main focus is on the unitary z-scores of +1, +2, -2, etc., the z-scores also yield

Figure 1

TRANSFORMATIONS AND APPLICATIONS OF THE STANDARD DEVIATION

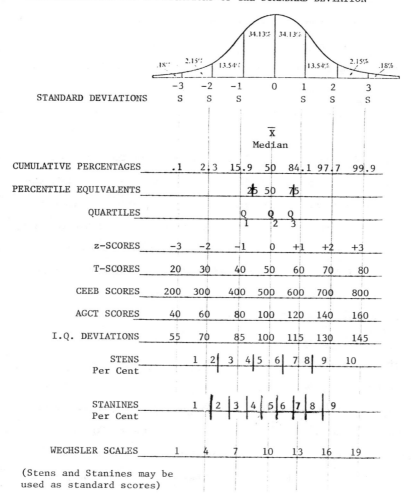

(Stens and Stanines may be
used as standard scores)

decimals. For instance, in a series of I.Q.'s with mean 100 and
standard deviation 20, and individual score of 130 yields a z-score
of $\frac{130 - 100}{20} = 1.5$. This means the score of 130 is midway between the
first and second standard deviations. The z-scores describe individual
scores more specifically than mere standard deviations, but they in
turn have some limitations. Their range is extremely short, and
they include decimals.

Other statistics of the same nature as the z-score have been
developed from the standard deviation to increase its descriptive
power. The T-score combines the z-score with an arbitrary scale
in which the mean is 50 and standard deviation scores are 60, 70, 80,
etc., above the mean and 40, 30, 20, etc., below the mean. The
decimals of z-scores become the units values in the T-scores. The
formula is $T = 50 + \left(\frac{X - \overline{X}}{S}\right) \times 10$. The 10 is introduced into the formula
in order to get rid of the decimal.

The equivalents of the standard deviation in terms of quartiles
and percentiles also help to make it more descriptive of individual
scores. The first standard déviation above the mean is equivalent to
the 85th percentile, whereas the first standard deviation below the mean
is equivalent to the 15th percentile. Likewise, the contrast of the
upper and lower limits of the standard deviation as compared to the
upper (75%) and lower limits (25%) of the quartile deviation, dramatizes
the area occupied by those students who fall beyond the middle half of
the series, but are still within the middle two-thirds.

The concept of the standard deviation is utilized for the standard
scores of the College Entrance Examination Board, which have a mean of
500 and a standard deviation of 100. Similarly, the Army General
Classification Test scores have a mean of 100 and a standard deviation

of 20. Also, I.Q. scores have a mean of 100 and a standard deviation
which is sometimes considered to be 15, sometimes 16, and sometimes
20, depending on the purposes of the researcher or the nature of the
other data involved in the research.

Two more recent adaptations of the standard deviation have
appeared during and since World War II - Stanines and Stens. Both
of these are reactions to the "looseness" of the standard deviation
because of its wide range of points. They seek to remedy this defect
by working with half a standard deviation.

The stanines include 9 half standard deviations with the mean
of the series being the mid-point of the 5th stanine. The 5th stanine
includes 20% of the scores in the series, the 4th and 6th stanines
include 17% each, the 3rd and 7th include 12% each, the 2nd and 8th
include 7%, and the 1st and 9th include the remaining 4% each. The
stanines are also used as a series of standard scores with a mean of
5 and a standard deviation of 2. In this sense, the scores are
classified according to the stanine in which they fall. All of these
scores are then converted to the number of the stanine as a standard
score and then computations proceed with the standard scores. The
advantages of converting raw scores into standard stanine scores is
that much smaller scores are dealt with (all 1 digit scores). In punch-
ing scores on computer cards, only one column is needed for the scores
on any one criterion. A disadvantage, however, occurs no doubt because
raw scores are "compressed" into single digit stanine scores, resulting
in some restriction of dipersion in the data.

Finally, the stens also utilize a half-standard deviation as unit,
but the mean separates the 5th and 6th stens. Approximate rounded percentages of scores in the stens are: 19% in the 5th and 6th, 15% in the

4th and 7th, 9% in the 3rd and 8th, 5% in the 2nd and 9th, and 2% in
the 1st and 10th. The stens are also used as standard scores and
computations carried on in terms of stens rather than standard scores.

The measures of Central Tendency and the Measures of Dispersion
constitute the Descriptive Statistics which may be used to interpret
the data collected in research. Descriptive statistics are just what
their name implies - descriptive. They do not yield any cause-effect
relationships in the data. At most, they reveal concomitances in it.
Causality lies beyond their reach. Nonetheless, descriptive statistics
have wide applications in all forms of descriptive research, and in
historical research. They serve many legitimate research purposes
and frequently reach a wider public than the more technical inferential
statistics. There is a need to research descriptive statistics themselves
to discover more imaginative roles for them in the research process.
The creative use of descriptive statistics is an important aspect of
educational research.

CHAPTER IX. INFERENTIAL STATISTICS

The ultimate purposes of educational research were stated above (Chapter I, p. 9) as understanding and explaining phenomena and processes, controlling forces and events, and predicting outcomes. For the first of these purposes, the descriptive statistics dealt with in the previous chapter are competent. They make it possible for the researcher to des- cribe his data in numerical language as well as in verbal language. But the other two ultimate research purposes are of an inferential nature. The investigator is searching for inferences that can be derived from his data. These inferences are preferably in the form of logical cause and effect principles. The researcher analyzes his data for evidence for or against a hypothesized truth in education.

The term inference is used with two known meanings. One is the sense that inferences are made that findings from a sample are applicable to its universe. But this is the sampling meaning of inference, and not the inductive thinking meaning. In fact, inference is not the issue for this meaning, rather the issue is generalizability of findings; can find- ings from the sample be generalized to the universe? For statistical thinking the term inference should be reserved to mean the process of educing a cause-effect statement from a body of criterion data. Certain statistics objectify this mode of thinking, and such statistics are called inferential statistics. In testing null hypotheses these statistics permit us to infer from the criterion data that one treatment was more effective than another.

The most fundamental concept in the logic of inferential statistics

89

is the Standard Error of a statistic. The standard error of a statistic
is the standard deviation of the distribution of that statistic for
repeated samples drawn from the same universe. A basic formula in inferential statistic is Critical Ratio, which is equal to the difference
between two statistics divided by the standard error of the difference
between the statistics. Thus, the concept of the standard deviation
which was introduced in descriptive statistics is integrated with the
new dimensions of inferential statistics.

There are appropriate formulas for the standard error of various
statistics. The standard error of a mean is $S_M = \dfrac{S}{\sqrt{N}}$. For a sample of
100 I.Q.'s with a standard deviation of 20, $S_M = \dfrac{20}{\sqrt{100}} = \dfrac{20}{10} = 2$. Approximately two-thirds of the time, the mean I.Q. of any sample of 100, drawn
from the same universe from which this sample is drawn, would fall between I.Q.'s 98 and 102. The standard error for a median in terms of the
standard deviation is $S_{Mdn} = \dfrac{1.253\,S}{\sqrt{N}}$, and in terms of the quartile deviation it is $S_{Mdn} = \dfrac{1.858Q}{\sqrt{N}}$. The standard error of the standard deviation
is $S_s = \dfrac{S}{\sqrt{2N}}$. The standard error of the Quartile Deviation is $S_Q = \dfrac{.786\,S}{\sqrt{N}}$
or $S_Q = \dfrac{1.17\,Q}{\sqrt{N}}$. The standard error for the Pearson coefficient of
correlation is $S_r = \dfrac{(1 - r^2)}{\sqrt{N}}$. The standard error of a Spearman rank
correlation coefficient is $S_p = \dfrac{1}{\sqrt{N-1}}$. The standard error of a percentage
is $S = \sqrt{\dfrac{PQ}{N}}$. A statistic similar to the standard error is the probable
error. It is the range within which 50% of the samples drawn from the
same universe would fall for the given parameter. The probable error for
any statistic is .6745 times its standard error. The standard error and
confidence levels are tests of the reliability of different statistics.
The confidence interval at the 95% level is the statistic $\pm$ 1.96 times
its standard error. The confidence interval at the 99% level is the
statistic $\pm$ 2.58 times the standard error.

The standard error is a check on the validity of the data which has been collected. If the standard error is beyond the limits of reliability, it is a warning to the researcher that his measurements are of dubious accuracy and that findings based on them will be inconclusive. If un- reliability of data is revealed by the standard error, the advisable thing to do is to secure new data either with greater precautions for accuracy in the data gathering activities or with different measuring instruments, or with a new sample. The role of the standard error as a check on the validity of the data is vital to the logic of research design, and inductive reasoning, but it does not play a direct role in the interpretation of data. Otherwise, stated, it does not lead to any inferences for theory based on the data. The standard error of the difference between means is later used in inferential statistical computations of the "t" test for means, and the critical ratio of other statistics.

CORRELATION

Correlation as a statistical procedure is included among inferential statistics because it determines the significance or lack of significance of a relationship and thus it makes inferences for the formulation of theory in education. From another viewpoint, correlation is also descriptive in nature. It tells the extent to which two criteria or two groups of individuals are similar to each other. It is especially important to remember that correlation is not an expression of causality. If two criteria have a high coefficient of correlation, we may infer that they are similar, but we cannot infer that one causes the other. There is certainly no objection to using correlation for descriptive research purposes where the purposes of the investigation do not go beyond revealing similarities/dissimilarities in phenomena or situations.

The concept on which correlation is based is the extent to which
things are common to each other. Variables may have several factors in
common with each other, and then the relationship is termed low and may
be positive or negative; or they may be opposite each other on several
factors, and then the correlation is termed high but negative. Because
of this basic concept of correlation, the device for quantifying it is
an arbitrary scale from +1.00 for perfect positive correlation through
0.00 for complete independence from each other, to -1.00 for completely
inverse relationship to each other. For instance, I.Q. scores and
reading scores will be highly positively correlated to each other because both involve ability to generalize, think abstractly, use symbols,
etc. Scores in arithmetic and scores in motor coordination will show
very low coordination because the former demands abilities of a conceptual nature whereas the latter demands abilities of a psychomotor nature.
The correlation between I.Q. score and time taken to complete class assignments will be high but negative because the students who have the highest
I.Q.'s will generally take the least amount of time to complete assignments
whereas conversely, the students with the lowest I.Q.'s will take the
greatest amount of time to complete the assignments.

The concept of correlation can also be expressed in terms of rank
order. Because of the idea of similarity included in correlation, the
scores from highly correlated criteria will be similar to each other:
high in one, high in the other; average in one, average in the other;
low in one, low in the other. As correlation between given criteria
decreases, this similarity in rank order of scores from them is broken up
until finally, for high negative correlation, the rank order of scores
becomes high in one, low in the other, and vice versa. For these reasons corre-

lation is sometimes defined as "extent of change in the same direction", i.e. moving from one score to its counterpart is moving straight across on the same rank level.

The basic concept of correlation lends itself to statistical computation in two ways: 1) in terms of deviation of the scores in a series from the mean of the series, and 2) in terms of rank order. The former is the Pearson Product Moment Coefficient of Correlation r, and the latter is the Spearman Rank Order (rho, ρ).

The Pearson r is not related to the size of the scores or of the mean of each series, but to the size of the deviations of the scores in the series from the mean. Because deviations from the mean may be positive or negative, the correlation is also influenced by the positions of deviations in their sequence. The r may be computed for ungrouped scores and for grouped scores. The r cannot utilize more than two series of scores at the same time. The following computations illustrate ungrouped scores.

X	x	x^2	Y	y	y^2	xy
1	-2	4	6	-2	4	4
2	-1	1	7	-1	1	1
3	0	0	8	0	0	0
4	1	1	9	1	1	1
5	2	4	10	2	4	4
15		10	40		10	10
$\overline{X}=3$		x^2	$\overline{Y}=8$		Σy^2	Σxy

$$r = \frac{\Sigma xy}{\sqrt{\Sigma x^2 \cdot \Sigma y^2}}$$

$$r = \frac{10}{\sqrt{10 \times 10}} = \frac{10}{10} = 1.00$$

In this example, there is perfect correlation between the two series. Although there is a difference of five points between the means of the series, the size of the deviations and the sequence of the deviations from the mean are identical, hence the perfect correlation. When the same scores pair off in different combinations, the means of the series remain the same, the deviations and the squares of deviations also remain the same, but the cross-products change, and hence the correlation coefficient changes. Following are three examples of rearrangement of the same scores and the resultant coefficients:

6		1		2		3	
X	Y	X	Y	X	Y		
2	6	1	9	1	9		
1	7	2	10	2	6		
5	8	3	6	3	8		
3	9	4	7	4	10		
4	10	5	8	5	7		
		r=.60		r=.50		r=.00	

Once the coefficient of correlation has been computed, a table of level of probability can be consulted to determine whether the amount of similarity reflected by the coefficient of correlation r is due to chance factors in the data alone or whether it is due to common factors within the two different variables, common factors which operate consistently and effectively. In order to read the table, we must know the degrees of freedom for the particular set of data. The degrees of freedom is based on the number of independent scores in the series. To arrive at the number of independent scores, we sum all the scores in the series and then as we account for the scores contributing to the sum, we may vary from one to the other save for the last remaining score, which is not free to vary, but is determined by the difference between the sum of the scores accounted for and the total sum of the series. Thus, for any series of scores, the degrees of freedom is one less than the number of scores. In the computations of correlation coefficients there are two

series of scores, so the degrees of freedom is the total number of scores
in the two series divided by 2. Otherwise stated, the degrees of
freedom in a correlation computation is equal to the number of pairs
of scores in the data. Entering a table of significance of the correlation coefficient with 10 degrees of freedom, a coefficient of .576 is
significant at the .05 level. This means that the correlation between
the series of scores would be due to chance alone only 5 times or less
out of a hundred if the coefficient is .576 or greater. From the same
row of the table, we read that a coefficient of .708 is significant at
the .01 level, which means that the correlation is due to chance alone
one time or less out of a hundred when the coefficient is as large or
larger than .708. If the correlation is not due to chance, it is caused
by persisting effective relationships of factors involved in the scores.

Another question arising in the interpretation of the coefficient
of correlation pertains to the size of the coefficient. The question
often takes the form "How important is a correlation of .80 or .50 or
.20?" There is no single answer to these questions. The significance
of the correlation is affected by the reliability of the instruments,
the nature of the variables being correlated, and the size of the sample.
The research purposes for which the coefficient is computed have an
impact on what size is or is not significant. If the tests or other
instruments used for securing data are not reliable, the correlation
coefficient must be large to make allowance for the margin of error in
the scores. As stated above, a smaller correlation coefficient based
on a large sample may be significant whereas a larger coefficient based
on a smaller sample may not be significant. The role of size of the
sample in the interpretation of a correlation coefficient is thus seen

in the table for level of significance, where smaller r's are significant with large degrees of freedom, but not with small degrees of freedom. With these cautions in mind, following are some verbal summations of the importance of correlation coefficients, especially for small and average-size samples:

0.00-0.10   denotes indifferent or negligible relationship;

0.11-0.30   denotes low correlation, present but slight;

0.31-0.50   denotes meaningful correlation;

0.51-0.80   denotes substantial and important correlation;

0.81-1.00   denotes high and very high correlation.

One final caution related to the coefficient of correlation concerns attempting to average out two or more coefficients. Occasionally, it may be in line with the purpose of an investigation to arrive at an overview of correlation of factors pertaining to a field in education. It would be faulty to attempt to do this by averaging several coefficients because of the lack of uniformity in the importance of sizes of coefficients. For the said research purposes either multiple correlation coefficient should be computed or if averaging is desired, first convert the r's to Fischer z's by means of the table for such conversions. These z's may then be averaged because they are scores and the average z reconverted to a Pearson r through the same table.

Computation of r with ungrouped scores is explained above. The r may also be computed with grouped scores, as in the following example.

I.Q.	Achievement 70 - 79	80 - 89	90 - 99	f	y'	fy'	fy'2	fx'	fx'y'
110-119	1	2	3	6	2	12	24		16
100-109	5	10	2	17	1	17	17		14
90-99	8	2	0	10	0	0	0		0
f	14	14	5	33		29	41	(1 x 0)+(2 x 1)+(3+2) 0 + 2 + 6 = 8 (5 x 0)+(10 x 1)+(2x2) 0 +10 + 4 = 14 (8 x 0)+(2 x 1) + (0x0) 0 + 2 + 0 = 2	30
x'	0	1	2					29	24
fx'	0	14	10	24 $\sum$fx'				$\sum$fx'	
fx'2	0	14	20	34 $\sum$fx'2					
fy'	(1 x 2) (5 x 1) (8 x 0)	(2 x 2) (10 x 1) (2 x 0)	(3 x 2) (2 x 1) (0 x 0)	7	14	8	29 $\sum$fy'		
fy'x'	0	14	16	30 $\sum$fy'x'					

$$r = \frac{N(\sum fx'y') - (\sum fx')\ (\sum fy')}{\sqrt{\left[N(\sum fx'2) - (\sum fx')^2\right]\left[N(\sum fy'2) - (\sum fy')^2\right]}}$$

$$r = \frac{(33 \times 30) - (24)\ (29)}{\sqrt{\left[33(34) - (24)^2\right]\left[33(41) - (29)^2\right]}}$$

$$r = \frac{990 - 696}{\sqrt{(1122 - 576)\ (1353 - 841)}}$$

$$r = \frac{294}{\sqrt{546 \times 572}}$$

$$r = \frac{294}{23.37 \times 22.63} = \frac{294}{528.86} = .556$$

Read the scattergram thus: one student had an I.Q. score between

110-119 and achievement scores between 70-79, two students had I.Q. scores

between 110-119 and achievement scores between 80-89, three students

had I.Q. scores between 110-119 and achievement scores between 90-99,

etc. The f, x', fx', fx'^{2} and corresponding y columns have already been

learned from computing the mean from grouped scores. It is in this junc-

ture that if the assumed mean is not placed in the lowest intervals for

x' and y', the computations of the following columns/rows will be

affected by the signs of numbers and become unnecessarily involved.

The fy' and fx' intermediary computations must be performed toward the

fx'y' crossproducts. In those intermediary computations, the frequency

in each box of the scattergram is multiplied by the corresponding

number in the deviation column and these products are summed for that

interval. There are three check points in the computations: $\sum fy'x' = \sum fx'y'$

$\sum fx' = \sum fx'$, and $\sum fy' = \sum fy'$. Replacing in the formula yields the r = .556.

The degrees of freedom is the number of pairs of scores minus 2(N -2) or,

in this case, 33 - 2 = 31. From the table for significance of correlation

coefficients, with 31 df's, an r = .344 is required for significance at

the .05 level, and r = .442 is needed for significance at the .01 level.

This correlation is therefore significant because r = .556.

The correlation coefficient r can also be computed by using un-

grouped raw scores: $$r = \frac{N(\sum XY) - (\sum X)(\sum Y)}{\sqrt{[(N(\sum X^2) - (\sum X)^2][(N(\sum Y^2) - (\sum Y)^2]}}$$

As was indicated previously in explaining the concept of correlation,

the coefficient can also be computed with ordinal data (ranks). The

statistic thus produced is known as ρ (rho), and is referred to as the

rank-order coefficient. The rationale and the computations are credited

to Spearman, for whom the coefficient is also named - Spearman ρ (rho).
An example follows, using the scores for computing r = .60 previously
(p. 94).

		RANK			
X	Y	X	Y	D	D^2
2	6	4	5	-1	1
1	7	5	4	+1	1
5	8	1	3	-2	4
3	9	3	2	+1	1
4	10	2	1	+1	1
					8 D^2

$$\rho = \frac{1 - 6\ D^2}{N\ (N^2 - 1)} \qquad\qquad \rho = 1 - \frac{6 \times 8}{5(25 - 1)}$$

$$\rho = 1 - \frac{48}{5x\ 24} \qquad\qquad \rho = 1 - \frac{48}{120}$$

$$\rho = 1 - .40 \qquad\qquad \rho = .60$$

In this instance the r and ρ come out identical by reason of a small
sample. With large samples, the ρ is usually approximately .05 less than
r. The significance of ρ can be read from the table for r (df = N-2).
The ρ cannot be computed for grouped scores. When criterion data can be
obtained from rankings rather than scores, ρ is very useful. Neither r
nor ρ can be used with more than 2 series of criterion data.

TESTS OF DIFFERENCES BETWEEN MEANS

A widely used inferential statistic involving means is the so-called
Student's t-test. It is named after Gosset, who wrote under the pen name
of "Student", and it tests the null hypothesis of no significant difference
between the means of two series of criterion data. There are two research
situations to which the t-test is applicable: 1) two different groups of

individuals who are given different experimental treatments but measured on the same test, and 2) the same group of individuals who are measured on two different tests. In the first case, the situation is described as involving independent means, and in the second situation as involving correlated means.

$X - \bar{X} = x$	x^2	$Y - \bar{Y} = y$	y^2
$7 - 9 = -2$	4	$0 - 3 = -3$	9
$10 - 9 = 1$	1	$3 - 3 = 0$	0
$\dfrac{10}{27} - 9 =$	$\dfrac{1}{6}$	$\dfrac{6}{9} - 3 = 3$	$\dfrac{9}{18}$

Σx ... $\bar{X}$ 9 ... Σx^2 ... Σy ... $\bar{Y}$ 3 ... Σy^2

$$t = \frac{\bar{X} - \bar{Y}}{\sqrt{\dfrac{\Sigma x^2 + \Sigma y^2}{N_x + N_y - 2}\left(\dfrac{1}{N_x} + \dfrac{1}{N_y}\right)}}$$

$$t = \frac{9-3}{\sqrt{\dfrac{6 + 18}{3 + 3 - 2}\left(\dfrac{1}{3} + \dfrac{1}{3}\right)}}$$

$$t = \frac{9 - 3}{\sqrt{\dfrac{24}{4} \times \dfrac{2}{3}}} = \frac{6}{\sqrt{4}}$$

$$t = \frac{6}{2} = 3.00$$

At this point it is necessary to explain the technique of reading the level of significance of the obtained t from a table of Distribution of t. The table indicates the size of t which could occur by chance factors alone five times out of a hundred (.05), one time out of hundred (.01), and in some tables, a few other levels, for both the one-tailed test and the two-tailed test. The one-tailed test is the research situation in which the sample is made up of homogeneous individuals (such as all gifted or all retarded) and the two-tailed test is the research situation in which the sample is made up of heterogeneous individuals who place along both sides of the mean in a normal distribution.

A series of three relationships must be grasped by the student if he is to read the Table of Distribution of t with comprehension. First, the statistic t is a numerical expression of the differences which exist between the scores in the two series. Secondly, the greater are these differences, the larger is the t which represents them. Thirdly, conversely, however, the larger the t, the less is the probability that the differences which it represents could be due to chance differences only. If the t is as large as or greater than that found in the table for a predetermined level, we declare a statistically significant t and reject the null hypothesis. This is because if the differences are not due to chance, they are attributable to the experimental treatment or other true differences between the groups.

The classical level for declaring a significant t is the .05 and the more desirable level for proof is the .01. These standards, however, are arbitrary, and in recent times researchers are acknowledging other levels, depending upon circumstances related to the research, such as cost, lack of precedents, intangible criteria, etc.

With these clarifications in mind, let us now go back to the t = 3.00 which we obtained in the example above. The degrees of freedom for the t-test is two less than the number of individuals who are in the sample. One degree of freedom is lost from the experimental group and one degree is lost from the control group. Otherwise stated df = N -2; in this case 6 - 2 = 4. Entering the table of distribution of t for the one-tailed test at the row 4 degrees of freedom, we find that a t = 2.132

is significant at the .05 level, and t = 3.747 is significant at .01.

Likewise, for the two-tailed test t = 2.776 is significant at the .05 level

and 4.604 is required for the .01 level. Hence, the t = 3.00 which we

obtained is significant at .05 for both one-tailed and two-tailed tests,

but it is not significant at the .01 level for either tail test. We would

reject the null hypothesis of no significant difference between the two

series of scores because t reached the level for .05. The greater number

of investigations actually performed use heterogenous groups and so the

two-tailed test readings are more frequently made of the table.

The second situation for which the t-test is applicable is that of

correlated means. The correlated means situation is recognizable by the

fact that the same individuals are measured twice, or there is close

matching of different individuals on variables related to the criterion

data. One way to compute the t uses a variation of the formula which is

used for indpepndent means. It is

$$t = \frac{\overline{X} - \overline{Y}}{\sqrt{\frac{\sum x^2 + \sum y^2}{N_x + N_y - 2}\left(\frac{1}{N_x} + \frac{1}{N_y}\right) - 2r\ SE_x\ SE_y}}$$

The term under the radical has the additional $-2r\ SE_x\ SE_y$ factors.

This means the coefficient of correlation must be known and the standard

errors for X and Y must be known. If they are not known, considerably

more involved computations are called for.

Fortunately, there is another approach for the t-test in this situa-

tion which eliminates the complicated computations. Whereas for independent

means one computes for the significance of the difference between the

means, in the correlated means, one computes for the mean of the differences

between the scores in the series. The scores are paired, the difference

between the two scores in each pair is determined, and the mean of these

pair differences is obtained. With the data from the previous t with

ungrouped scores we get:

$$\underline{X} \quad - \quad \underline{Y} \quad = \quad \underline{D} \quad \underline{D}^2$$

7	0	7	49
10	3	7	49
10	6	4	16
		18	114

$$t = \dfrac{\bar{D}}{\sqrt{\dfrac{d^2}{N(N-1)}}}$$

$$\sum d^2 \ = D^2 \ - \ \frac{(\sum D)^2}{N}$$

$$\sum d^2 \ = 114 - \frac{(18)^2}{3}$$

$$\sum d^2 \ = 114 - \frac{324}{3}$$

$$\sum d^2 \ = 6$$

$$t = \dfrac{6}{\sqrt{\dfrac{6}{3 \times 2}}}$$

$$t = \dfrac{6}{\sqrt{1}} \ = 6.00$$

PL.01

From the Table of Critical Values of t, degrees of freedom being number
of pairs of scores minus 1, which gives 2df, a t = 6.00 is significant
at both the .05 and .01 levels of probability. This is different from
t from same scores as independent means. It is clear, therefore, that
correction for the correlation of the means has been made quite accurately
by the procedure involving the mean of the differences of the scores
rather than the difference between the means of the scores.

The Student t-test has long been employed in inferential experimental research. It has some limitations, however. It can accomodate only two series of criterion data simultaneously. This is a serious drawback for much of our contemporary research is concerned with hypotheses which involve relationships among multivariate criterions simultaneously. The other handicap is that the t has only one dimension, differences between groups. Today we also need to investigate differences within groups.

ANALYSIS OF VARIANCE

Probably because of these limitations of the t-test, the more sophisticated F-ratio from the Analysis of Variance has become widely used since World War II. Basically, Analysis of Variance computes the variance between groups, also the variance within groups and computes the ratio of between variance divided by within variance. An example with very small scores from three treatments, A, B, and C, is as follows.

	A	B	C	
	1	4	7	
	2	5	8	
	3	6	9	
$\sum X$	6	15	24	= 45
$\sum X^2$	14	77	194	

1. Total Sum of Squares:
This step squares the individual scores, sums the squares, and subtracts the correction factor $(\sum X)^2 / N$.

$$1 + 4 + 9 + 16 + 25 + 36 + 49 + 64 + 81 - \frac{(45)^2}{9}$$

$$285 - 225 = 60$$

2. Between Sum of Squares:
This step computes $(\not{\xi}X)^2/n$ for each group, sums these values, and subtracts the total correction factor $(\not{\xi}X)^2/N$.

$$\frac{(6)^2}{3} + \frac{(15)^2}{3} + \frac{(24)^2}{3} - \frac{(45)^2}{9}$$

$279 - 225 = 54$

3. Within Sum of Squares:
This step computes $\left[\not{\xi}X^2 - (\not{\xi}X)^2/n\right]$ for each group and sums these values.

$$\left[14 - \frac{(6)^2}{3}\right] + \left[77 - \frac{(15)^2}{3}\right] + \left[194 - \frac{(24)^2}{3}\right] = 2 + 2 + 2 = 6.$$

Also, $60 - 54 = 6$ $\left[\text{total-between} = \text{within}\right]$.

From these sums of squares we can derive the summary table following.

Variation Source	Sum of Squares	df	Mean Square	F	P	P
Between	54	2	27	27.00	.05	.01
Within	6	6	1		(5.14)	(10.92)
Total	60	8				

To read the table of significance for F-Ratio, read degrees of freedom for "between" as the greater mean square, and degrees of freedom for "within" as the lesser mean square. In this case, we enter the table at column 2, row 6. The light-face value is required for the .05 level of confidence, and the bold-face value is required for the .01 level of confidence. The differences among the scores is highly significant. For them to be due to chance less than 5 times in a hundred, an F of 5.14 is required and for them to be due to chance less than 1 time in a hundred, an F of 10.92 is required, but this F-ratio is 27.00. The F, however, does not say which treatment produced the significantly higher scores. To determine this, Schefe's test or Duncan's Multiple Range, or the "Post Mortem" pairing of ANOVA means (FPAIRS, p. 285) can be applied. In the scores above, there was considerably more variation between groups than within groups (27 to 1).

The analysis of variance presented is the one-way classification where one measure is obtained per treatment group. More complicated designs exist in which sub-classifications are established within treatment groups. These statistics permit obtaining F-ratios for interactions among sub-classification groups as the "main effects" criterion data. Whenever these interactions are pursued, the procedure is known as Factorial Analysis of Variance. (Multiple Classification ANOVA).

The procedures for Factorial Analysis of Variance are shown in the following example. (Two-Way Classification ANOVA)

	Treatment (Method) A		Treatment (Method) B			
	Girls	Boys	Girls	Boys		
	11	15	7	10		
	12	9	8	11		
	13	14	9	12		
ΣX	36	38	24	33	=	131
ΣX^2	434	502	194	365		

I. Total Sum of Squares:

This step squares the individual scores, sums the squares, and subtracts the total correction factor $(\Sigma X)^2/N$.

$$121 + 144 + 169 + 225 + 81 + 196 + 49 + 64 + 81 + 100 + 121 + 144 - \frac{(131)^2}{12}$$

II. Between Groups Sum of Squares:

This step computes $(\Sigma X)^2/n$ for each group, sums these values, and subtracts the total correction factor $(\Sigma X)^2/N$.

$$\frac{(36)^2}{3} + \frac{(38)^2}{3} + \frac{(24)^2}{3} + \frac{(33)^2}{3} - \frac{(131)^2}{12}$$

$$[432 + 481.3 + 192 + 363] - 1430.1$$
$$1468.3 - 1430.1 = 38.2$$

III. Between Treatments (Method) Sum of Squares:

     This step combines all treatment groups (Method A, B) into a single group for each treatment. It computes $(\sum X)^2/n$ for each treatment, sums these values, and subtracts the total correction factor $(\sum X)^2/N$.

$$\frac{(74)^2}{6} + \frac{(57)^2}{6} - \frac{(131)^2}{12}$$

$$1454.1 - 1430.1 = 24$$

IV. Between Main Effects (Sex) Sum of Squares:

     This step combines the same main effect across groups (girls, boys) into a single group. It computes $(\sum X)^2/n$ for each main effect group, sums these values, and subtracts the total correction factor $(\sum X)^2/N$.

$$\frac{(60)^2}{6} + \frac{(71)^2}{6} - \frac{(131)^2}{12}$$

$$[600 + 840.2] - 1430.1$$
$$1440.2 - 1430.1 = 10.1$$

V. Interaction Sum of Squares:

     This step computes Between Groups Sum of Squares minus the sum of Between Treatments Sum of Squares plus Between Main Effects Sum of Squares.

$$38.2 - (24 + 10.1) = 38.2 - 34.1 = 4.1$$

VI. Within Groups Sum of Squares:

     This step computes $[\sum X^2 - (\sum X)^2/n]$ for each main effect subgroup and sums these values.

$$\frac{[434 - 432]}{2} + \frac{[502 - 481.3]}{20.7} + \frac{[194 - 192]}{2} + \frac{[365 - 363]}{2} = 26.7$$

Also, Total-Between Groups = Within Groups
$$64.9 - 38.2 = 26.7$$

Summary Factorial Analysis of Variance Table

Source of Variance	Sum of Squares	Degrees of Freedom	Mean Square	F	P
Between Treatments	24	1	24	7.23	.05
Between Series	10.1	1	10.1	3.03	NS
Interaction (TXS)	4.1	1	4.1	1.22	NS
Within	26.7	8	3.3		
Total	64.9	11			

The differences between treatments are significant at the .01 level, but the differences between sexes are not significant at the .05 level and there are practically no differences due to interaction of treatment and sex. The computations of Analysis of Variance are most readily performed if there are equal frequencies within the cells.

CHI-SQUARE

An important nonparametric inferential statistic is Chi-Square. The symbol is Capital Greek X: χ^2. The Chi-Square tests a null hypothesis of no significant difference among frequencies of categories.

The χ^2 for equiprobability tests the null hypothesis for frequencies of categories on a single criterion. Let us assume 160 schools classified themselves as follows:

Urban	Suburban	Inner City	Rural
66	44	27	23

The strictest form of the null hypothesis is that there are exactly the same number of individuals in each category (160/4 = 40). The expected frequency for each cell is 40, under the null hypothesis.

Are the frequencies significantly different (null hypothesis)?

Observed	66	44	27	23
Expected	40	40	40	40
0 – E	26	4	–13	–13
$(0 - E)^2$	676	16	169	289

$$\frac{(0 - E)^2}{E} \quad \frac{676}{40} = 16.9; \ \frac{16}{40} = .4; \ \frac{169}{40} = 4.225; \ \frac{289}{40} = 7.225$$

$$\chi^2 = 16.9 + 0.4 + 4.225 + 7.225 = 28.750$$

Degrees of freedom is one less than the number of groups (4-1) or 3.
From the table of significance of χ^2; $P_{.05} = 7.815$, $p_{.01} = 11.345$, and
$P_{.001} = 16.268$. The χ^2 obtained here indicates that differences in the
frequencies could be due to chance much less than once in one thousand
times. This sample had significant differences as to type of school.

The χ^2 for independence tests whether different categories are
significantly independent when cross-classified according to some other
criterion. Thus, Board Members, Superintendents, and Teachers agree/
disagree with a certain principle or practice.

	Agree $\mathcal{O}$ E	Disagree $\mathcal{O}$ E	Total
Board Members	23 (43)	101 (81)	124
Superintendents	78 (75)	137 (140)	215
Teachers	39 (22)	24 (41)	63
Total	140	262	402

First, the expected frequencies must be computed.

1) $\frac{140 \times 124}{402} = 43.18$ 2) $\frac{262 \times 124}{402} = 80.81$

3) $\frac{140 \times 215}{402} = 74.87$ 4) $\frac{262 \times 215}{402} = 140.12$

5) $\frac{140 \times 63}{402} = 21.94$ 6) $\frac{262 \times 63}{402} = 41.06$

Once observed and expected frequencies are known we compute $\chi^2 = \sum \frac{(0 - E)^2}{E}$

1) $\frac{(43 - 23)^2}{43} = 9.30$

2) $\frac{(101 - 81)^2}{81} = 4.94$

3) $\frac{(78 - 75)^2}{75} = 0.12$

4) $\frac{(140 - 137)^2}{140} = 0.06$

5) $\frac{(39 - 22)^2}{22} = 13.14$

6) $\frac{(41 - 24)^2}{41} = 7.05$

$x^2 = 9.30 + 4.94 + .12 + .06 + 13.14 + 7.05 = 34.61$

Degrees of freedoms is (rows - 1) times (columns - 1) $(r - 1) (c - 1)$, or $2 \times 1 = 2$. Chi-Square is significant at $P_{.001}$, which requires 13.82

For χ^2 - Independence if the χ^2 is not significant, the variables are independent of each other and there is no relationship among them. If the χ^2 is significant there is a relationship. Here, the "higher" careers are more in agreement than the "lower" careers and vice versa. To determine sources of the χ^2. note the difference between observed and expected frequencies in each cell.

MEDIAN TEST

The median test is applicable for independent samples, and it tests the significance of differences between the groups. The two sets of scores are placed in a common rank orger and then a 2 x 2 contingency table is made showing the number of scores above and below the common median, for each group. Then χ^2 is computed, using even split of each group above and below median as expected frequencies.

For example:

	Above	Below	Total	
Sample I	44 (41)	38 (41)	82	This contingency table gives $\chi^2 = 0.20$, which is
Sample II	40 (41)	42 (41)	82	not significant.
Total	84	80	164	

REGRESSION FORMULA

The regression coefficient is a measure of relationship which expresses the rate of change in one variable as compared to change in

another variable. Hypothetically for every change of one score point on
a given variable, individuals may change two score points on another variable.
The regression coefficient, often represented by the letter b, is computed
by the formula: $b = \frac{N(XY) - (X)(Y)}{N X^2 - (X)^2}$. Algebraically, this is equivalent to
$b_y = r_{xy} \frac{S_y}{S_x}$. The regression formula for predicting one variable from another
is basically $Y(\text{predicted}) = r_{xy} \frac{S_y}{S_x} (X - \bar{X}) - \bar{Y}$. If we use the scores
37,17,25,32,18,25,27,36,36 as the predictor variable, and the scores 44,37,
52,58,47,52,50,53,61 as the predicted variable, the formula becomes $Y =$
$.570969 \frac{6.78415}{7.18709} (X - 28.1111) - 50.4444$. Solving this, the regression
formula becomes $Y(\text{pred}) = .538958 (X) - 35.2937$. Any student's score on Y
can be determined by inserting his score on X in the formula and solving.
The predictor variable is called the independent variable, and the predicted
variable is called the dependent variable.

INTRACLASS ANOVA AND CORRELATION

The two-way analysis of variance without replications and the intraclass
correlation are useful for interpreting data in descriptive and in factorial
analysis types of research. For instance, they are applicable to ratings of
items by respondents on an opinion form, or to the ratings of subjects by
a panel of judges. The computer printout on the next page shows the computations for ratings of 25 items (rows) by 14 respondents (columns). The intraclass correlation for rows is a measure of the reliability of ratings of the
items or subjects. The intraclass correlation for columns is a measure of
the reliability of ratings among the respondents. The intraclass correlation
for row averages is an expression of the extent to which similar respondents
would rate similar items. The correlation is enhanced by using the averages
of rows. If an F-ratio is high, the corresponding intraclass correlation will
also be high.

```
1010    DATA  3,2,4,1,4,2,4,5,3,3,5,5,4,4
1020    DATA  2,2,4,2,3,2,4,5,4,5,2,5,4,3
1030    DATA  4,3,2,1,2,5,1,5,5,5,5,5,4,2
1040    DATA  4,3,2,2,4,4,4,2,4,5,4,5,2,4
1050    DATA  5,2,4,2,1,1,4,5,5,4,5,4,4,4
1060    DATA  4,4,3,2,4,5,2,4,5,4,4,5,4,3
1070    DATA  4,3,1,4,3,5,2,4,5,4,5,5,4,2
1080    DATA  4,2,5,4,5,5,4,4,5,5,5,5,4,2
1090    DATA  2,3,2,4,3,2,1,2,5,4,4,2,2,4
1100    DATA  2,2,4,1,2,2,5,5,2,2,5,4,2,2
1110    DATA  2,2,4,2,1,4,4,5,5,4,4,5,3,2
1120    DATA  4,3,5,4,4,5,4,5,5,4,5,5,4,2
1130    DATA  2,2,1,2,1,2,2,2,2,1,4,1,1,2
1140    DATA  4,3,4,2,3,2,4,5,5,4,5,5,4,3
1150    DATA  1,3,2,1,2,4,2,2,2,1,2,1,2,2
1160    DATA  5,3,4,4,4,2,4,5,5,5,4,5,4,2
1170    DATA  3,4,4,2,2,2,4,4,5,1,4,1,2,4
1180    DATA  4,2,4,2,4,5,5,5,5,4,4,5,4,4
1190    DATA  2,4,2,2,3,4,4,2,5,5,4,4,3,4
1200    DATA  4,4,5,4,3,5,4,5,5,5,5,5,4,2
1210    DATA  2,4,2,4,2,2,4,2,5,2,4,1,2,4
1220    DATA  5,4,5,4,5,5,5,5,5,5,5,5,4,4
1230    DATA  2,3,2,4,4,2,4,2,4,4,4,2,1,2
1240    DATA  2,2,4,2,5,5,4,2,4,5,5,5,2,2
1250    DATA  4,3,5,2,4,3,4,5,5,5,5,5,4,1
```

TWØ-WAY CLASSIFICATIØN ANALYSIS ØF VARIANCE
WITHØUT REPLICATIØNS

SUMMARY TABLE

SØURCE ØF VARIANCE	SUMS ØF SQUARES	DEGREES ØF FREEDØM	MEAN SQUARE	F-RATIØ
RØWS	159.298	24	6.63741	6.31089
CØLUMNS	103.5	13	7.96154	7.56988
REMAINDER	328.143	312	1.05174	
TØTAL	590.94	349		

$$\text{INTRACLASS R} = \frac{6.63741 \;-\; 1.05174}{6.63741 \;+\; (\;13\; * \;1.05174\;)} = .275021$$

INTRACLASS CØRRELATIØN CØEFFICIENT FØR RØWS = .275021

R FØR RØW AVERAGES = (6.63741 - 1.05174)/ 6.63741 = .841544

INTRACLASS CØRRELATIØN CØEFFICIENT FØR RØW AVERAGES = .841544

$$\text{R FØR CØLUMNS} = \frac{7.96154 \;-\; 1.05174}{7.96154 \;+\; (\;24\; * \;1.05174\;)} = .208106$$

INTRACLASS CØRRELATIØN FØR CØLUMNS = .208106

CHAPTER X. TYPES OF EDUCATIONAL RESEARCH

The question might be asked: "Why be concerned with types of
research at all since the more basic issue is whether research is
well designed?" The answer to this objection is that both issues are
important. Furthermore, the quality of the design of an investigation
must be judged in terms of the type of research which it is, and in terms
of research purposes. The first thing to be considered when planning
a research design is "What type of research is needed to answer this
question?"

The first issue to be dealt with in distinguishing types of
educational research is to establish a system of categories of research.
Two criteria must be met in elaborating a classification structure.
First, the categories must all be based on the same principle of classification and, secondly, the categories must be mutually exclusive. For
instance, an investigation may be classified as an interview study, after
the tool used to collect the data, or it may be classified as a correlation
study after the statistical procedure used to interpret the data; it may
be classified as a survey after the purpose which it serves in the field
of education, or it may be classified as sociological research after the
field of knowledge within which it falls. Only if a single principle of
classification is adhered to will it be possible to arrive at mutually
exclusive categories. Among the possible bases of classification mentioned
above and of others which can be thought of, the most meaningful from the
view point of research type is purpose which the research serves in the
field of educational research.

112

The other principles of classification are less fundamental.

On the basis of purpose fulfilled, the types of educational research are as follows: 1) Descriptive Research, 2) Historical Research, 3) Factorial Analysis Research, 4) Experimental Research, 5) Predictive Research, and 6) Developmental Research. Any given research design will fall predominantly in one or the other of these types although including some subsidary elements of other types, such as survey of the literature and history of the topic.

DESCRIPTIVE RESEARCH

As pointed out earlier, descriptive research is concerned with establishing the present record for any aspect of education. From the viewpoint of number of research studies, descriptive research may rank first among the types. There are several sub-categories for descriptive research: 1) the Normative Survey, 2) the Continuity (Trend) Study, 3) the Activity Analysis, 4) the Case Study, and 5) the Documentary Study. Each of these types of descriptive research is concerned with establishing the present record for a specific sub-purpose.

The Normative Survey collects the particular facts of who? what? when? where? why? but it does not terminate with collecting and reporting these facts. It pursues the investigation through some form of evaluation of these facts of record so that conclusions can be formulated as to whether the data shows that the status of the variable is good, bad or indifferent. This final phase of the descriptive research raises the issue of criteria for the evaluation. If the data collected is numerical, especially if it consists of test scores or other measurements, it may be already standardized, and these norms serve as criteria for determining the quality level of the subjects surveyed. Frequently in surveys, however, the data collected is not "interval", or "ordinal",

but "nominal," and it becomes the researcher's task to develop conceptual norms for the evaluation of his factual data. These criteria
can be derived from concepts and principles in educational philosophy,
and/or educational research. For example, it is known from principles
of learning theory, supported by research findings that in a good program
for individualizing instruction there is available an abundance of
instructional materials for students at varying levels of development in
each classroom. The survey instrument should have included items designed
to reveal whether such a variety of materials exists in the schools. From
this data it is then possible to evaluate each school on the criterion of
provision of materials for individualizing instruction; also the schools
can be compared with each other as to the extent to which they provide
multi-level instructional materials. Evaluations of this nature are
admittedly subjective, but they lift descriptive studies above the level
of so-called "field reports". Educing normative evaluations from the
data interprets it. There is no implication here, however, to demean the
task of "collecting" data in the first place. It is no sinecure to
construct a good survey instrument which elicits meaningful data accurately and objectively. The fact remains that rising above the sheer facts
to some evaluative generalizations reaches to the higher processes of
descriptive research.

The next type of descriptive research is the Continuity (Trend) Study.
It involves two surveys on the same topic or issue, the second one being
done after a period of time has elapsed. The purpose of the Continuity
Study is to discover trends. Any items of organization, personnel, structure, procedure, etc., which is found in one of the surveys but not in
the other constitutes an element of trend away from a past era or toward
a new era. A classical example of the continuity study is the former

Teacher's Colleges. A survey of these institutions in the early 1950's would have revealed that their student body was predominantly female, that their goals were to prepare teachers and that their curriculum was predominantly the field of Education. A follow-up survey in the middle 1960's would have shown that things were all different. The very names of the institutions were changed frequently to some regional (North, South, East, West) university of the state. The student body was coeducational, maybe predominantly male; the goals had become liberal arts education in the Institution; and the curriculum included majors in all liberal arts fields and one or more professional fields, with degrees offered on the under-graduate and the graduate level, often including the doctoral level. **This type is also called trend analysis.**

The survey tool is a basic concern in this trend-tracing type of educational research. It must be generally the same instrument for the two surveys. A thorough search must be made of the literature on the topic to identify items related to issues that have caused change during the interval of time elapsed. The instrument must be revised to include these issues. The time lapse itself is an issue in the design of the Continuity Study. There is no rule of thumb as to the length of this lapse of time. Traditionally, educational change occurs slowly. However, occasionally the tempo of educational change increases, especially under the pressures of rapid social change. This is what makes the Teacher Colleges such a dramatic topic for **trend analysis.** The transformation of the teachers colleges occurred in the time span of ten years, from 1955-1965. Actually, the decisions, the changes already existed seminally, from 1955-1960. The lapse of time between the two trend detecting surveys is therefore a relative matter. The key to it is for the researcher to be informed and knowledgeable about the topic.

In terms of graduate research, the Continuity (Trend) Study is frequently impractical. Theses and dissertations are conducted under pressures of a time limit for completing the degree. Hence, it is impossible to follow the "survey-time lapse-survey" sequence. This pattern can sometimes be realized by establishing a tandem between a survey of a topic completed by some previous graduate student and a new candidate for a degree. The Continuity research type can fulfill important educational objectives as follow-up studies. There is a dearth of follow-up research, and follow-up lacks a distinctive design of its own. The lead group of the tandem may serve as anchor point for identifying trends, and it may also serve as a norm, at least a comparative norm for evaluating the contemporary group of the follow-up. This adaptation of the Continuity Study for follow-up purposes facilitates planning and program development as well as theory-building in Education.

A third type of descriptive research is the Activity Analysis. In common with the other types of descriptive research, the Activity Analysis seeks to establish the present record of some phase of education, and is also now used to improve performance. Several decades ago, when the activity analysis originated as a research type, its original function was to describe the prototype or model of whatever topic was being investigated. After years of attempting to define the ideal through activity analysis, it was realized that for humans and for human behavior, there is no perfect prototype, model or ideal. There are different patterns of effective behavior and effective individuals seek out their own patterns. Before that conclusion was finally reached, however, numerous persons, actions, and situations had been analyzed and re-analyzed. Ultimately, however, the conviction was reached that the Activity Analysis was chimeric, and it fell into disuse. Since World War II, however, it has been reconceptualized and rehabilitated. The new concept of the Activity Analysis is that it can help meaningfully to improve performance and effectiveness although it admittedly cannot describe perfection. The revised function of the Activity Analysis is therefore to improve effectiveness by reduc'ing time and motion, by utilizing personnel to their fuller capacities, otherwise minimizing cost while maximizing results. The Activity Analysis fulfills this function for roles and processes in education: Administrators, teacher, counselors, pupils. Obviously, the recent development of interaction analysis is a contemporary manifestation of Activity Analysis for it aims at improving effective communication in the classroom.

The re-conceptualization of Activity Analysis has been supported by the creation of a technology to implement it. Data collection remains a problem in Activity Analysis. The most conventional device for doing so has been to deputize and train individuals as observers and recorders of activities and utterances of the subjects whose behavior was being analyzed. With the sophistication of today's technology, cameras and recorders and videotape equipment is utilized to collect the data to be analyzed. The chances are that the computer will be linked to data collecting equipment to deliver instantaneous analysis of the data.

An important task in the design of Activity Analysis is the problem of categorizing the activities. A matrix of classifications must be arrived at. One approach to this task is to attempt to elaborate the system of categories analytically before starting the sorting of behaviors. A second approach is to let the categories build themselves after the activities are recorded. The record is approached without any preset categories and individual items of behavior on sorted into classifications of related activities, leading to subsequent larger

groupings of related sub-classifications. This approach is sometimes

commended as being more scientific, based on the inductive method. It

is also commended for being phenomenological rather than abstract, for

it grows out of the data and does not go beyond it. Criticism of

the procedure of permitting categories to build themselves is that

the procedure is too pragmatic and   lacking in cognitive character.

It is also critized as theoretically deficient, not exhaustive of possible

categories. If some possible categories are not present because there

was no overt evidence of them in the recorded sample of behavior, the

research is deficient because all categories are not included in the

analysis. Conceivably, some of these omitted categories may be very

crucial in terms of interpretation. For instance, if in recording the

behaviors in the classroom of a sample of teachers, none of those teachers

engaged in any form of evaluating their pupils, evaluation activities

would not be involved in the analysis of the behaviors. But is this

to say that evaluating of students is not a teacher behavior, or is it

to say that evaluating students in not an important teacher activity?

The answer to these questions is obviously no. But considerations of

theoretical deficiency do not necessarily prove that a set of dialectically

derived categories is the best. The method of letting categories build

themselves is much more convenient and relevant. Probably it is the

best method if the further safeguards are taken of securing a relatively

representative sample, selecting individuals from a wide variety of set-

tings for the roles. Or possibly, the researcher may let categories

build themselves, but once all the categories present in the record have

been identified, submit this classification scheme to a rigid conceptual

criticism. Presumably, this combination of the inductive approach with the deductive approach will be better than using either of them exclusively.

Once the activities have been recorded and classified into categories they must be evaluated on the basis of some norms or criteria. An example of this phase of the analysis is found in the research that has analyzed activities of classroom teachers. The specific activities were evaluated on the basis of professional preparation needed to perform them successfully. The evaluating criterion became the degree of professionalism of the activity. On the basis of this norm, the research found that more than half of the time of teachers was absorbed performing activities that were judged to be nonprofessional because an under-graduate degree and teacher certification were not necessary to be able to perform them. Likewise, any activity analysis research will need to devise its own criteria for developing a hierarchy of the activities involved, so that the purpose of activity analysis may be limited to a few salient points for a program of action subsequent to the research.

Another type of descriptive research is the Case Study. This category of research establishes the present record with a view to eradicating the disabilities of an individual. Specifically, for Case Studies in education, the predominant concern is to identify and eradicate the learning disabilities of individuals or small groups treated as individual units. Because of this orientation of case studies to the elimination of disorders, and because learning disorders may be rooted in very diverse sources, the file on each individual who is being treated must be very exhaustive; it must include medical, psychological, social, personality, moral, and educational aspects of the individual. Moreover, the examiner who records each aspect of the case must be a professional

person with advanced competencies and experience. It follows from
these inherent traits of the case that a team of several persons each
with advanced specialization in his field is essential to compiling
an accurate record on the individual. Subsequently, in designing therapy, only a team of specialists can prescribe treatment reliably. From
the foregoing considerations, it is obvious that the graduate student on
the master's level cannot measure up to the specifications of the Case
Study. Neither, for that matter, can an experienced educator and
scholar do the job alone. Hence, the Case Study as a research type has
only limited possibilities for graduate research. The research student
in education usually can meaningfully participate in establishing the
case record mainly as a participant rather than as a leader, but there is
the possibility that he may make a greater contribution to devising a
therapy program for the educational factor of the case. Consequently,
where cases of individuals have been established exhaustively, the
educational researcher can hypothesize a program which might be used as
an experimental treatment. But the point must be emphasized that the
existence of the files is pre-requisite for conducting educational research of the Case Study type.

Finally, another type of descriptive educational research is the
Documentary Study. The function of Documentary research is to analyze.
the record on some aspect of education where the record exists in printed
form entirely. This last distinction establishes the difference between
the more Normative Survey and the Documentary Study. Whereas, the
Normative Survey may collect data by the questionnaire, or checklist,
or interview, the Documentary Study does so by close analysis of a written
text. As a result of this distinction, collection of data differs
considerably in the Documentary Study from the Normative Survey. There

are stricter limits to the sources of data in the Documentary Study—
whatever is in the printed record being analyzed. For instance, a
documentary study of state legal provisions pertaining to bus transportation of school children is limited to the text of state statutes
governing bus transportation for its data.

Research utilizing documents as sources of data is relatively
recent and limited, but it can be extended to various other sources.
Documentary investigations of textbooks, curriculum guides, and standardized examinations are obvious possibilities. Not so obvious, but
also rich in research possibilities are minutes of meetings and official
reports of Boards of Education and Commissions or Committees. Important
findings for school operation and administration can be established
through research studies of such records although some safeguards would
have to control access to these documents of governing and/or public
bodies to prevent irrelevant use of them. Documentary research is
closely related to policy-determination and decision-making.

The technique of interpretation in documentary research differs
somewhat from that in other types of descriptive research. As stated
above, the data is already collected in the documentary investigation,
and **the researcher's** role is to analyze related matter and to **categorize**
it. **Then** ultimately, **he** must draw meaning from the data. The nature of
the generalizations which result from documentary research are comparisons
of the status of the variable in varying environments and the establishment of relations of the variable to factors which interact with it, such
as size, administrative style, geographical location, age, etc. Interpretation may also include evaluations of policies or provisions in the
documents, similar to evaluation in the Normative Survey.

The next major type of research is historical research. The history of American Education is as well researched as it will ever be because no new sources will probably ever be available to add to it. This is not to say that the history of American education is well written. On the contrary, adequate records of education were never kept from the beginning, and many of those were lost before the writing of a history of American education was attempted. Herein lies a lesson for contemporary educators to safeguard the records which do exist and to devise record keeping procedures and facilities for the present and the future. Likewise, researchers need to honor more fully the challenges which exist for historical research which can be found in the field today.

The general purpose of historical research is to establish the past record on some phase of education. Among the issues involved in it is the question of how far back is "past". In other words, how do we distinguish between a contemporary survey and a historical study? A good norm for making this distinction is the existence of eyewitnesses to the action, usually human beings not too young at the time nor too old now, to witness meaningfully to events which are to be recorded. In a general sense then, the past record may be said to include events that occurred long enough ago that there are no longer any effective living witnesses of those events.

The first task to be performed in historical research of a topic is to locate sources from which the past record may be reconstructed. For educational research these sources are mainly written or printed documents, and to lesser extent, such sources as buildings and physical remnants.

Sources may be located through bibliographical tools. The articles and books so located, however, will be mainly "secondary" sources, that is they are analyses and reports of original data that was gathered in previous research. Such secondary sources contribute to the survey of the literature and to elaborations of meanings from data that is gathered in the current research. But the data for original historical research must be found in "primary" sources, that is, records and reports before any interpretation is made of them. The sources may have been utilized in some other purposes, but each historical researcher must return to the first hand data for his investigation. The location of such sources involves searching beyond the published bibliographical tools in the library. Primary data exists in records at all levels of school organization. Even in the classroom there are records and data about children and teachers, and so in all offices at the building, district, area, regional, state, and national levels there are data of many types. It is from the facts contained in these primary sources that history is constructed. Fortunately, in the twentieth century, there is an awareness of history, and organizations and administrators make provisions for preserving data so that the record may survive to serve future generations.

Once primary sources have been located, the researcher must evaluate them for accuracy and credibility. This criticism of historical sources is of two types: external and internal. External criticism seeks for evidence to vouch for the authenticity of the authorship and the date of the source. These must be checked against what is known of the contemporaneous record to verify that the date and the author of a source are true. Also, the sources must be criticized internally. Concern in this phase is for the veracity and the competency of the author of the source. Here the criticism is termed internal because it involves searching for internal consistency of the source, appraisal of its language, and evaluation of the thinking and judging revealed in the source. In addition to

completing these evaluations of his sources, the historian must provide
for their physical preservation and their physical accessibility for examination by any of his readers. The location and verification of sources
may be a difficult undertaking in many investigations, but they are
essential because any record of the past is only as good as the sources
from which it is constructed. History at times has to be rewritten when
new sources became available.

Granted that the historian has successfully gathered adequate
sources for his investigation, there are several subsequent processes
in which he must engage. The historian is responsible for sequencing
the events in his sources. He must place them chronologically in
sequence. At times it is debated whether it is the historian's role
to establish causality among events in addition to sequencing them.
Historical cause and effect claims are difficult to substantiate, but
surely the historian is accountable for determining not only what happened,
but also in what order it happened.

A process related to sequencing events which the historical
researcher must perform is to periodize the events he has sequenced.
The task here is to select appropriate turning points of time in the
flow of events which signal the end of a preceding era and the beginning
of a new era. Basically the mental task involved is to group the events
in a significant sector of time around a meaningful force or concept which
unifies the events. Among the discoveries which the mind of the researcher
must make is to identify a factor which predominates over the happenings
of the era and after which the period can be named. This particular
aspect of the task is colored by the fact that the educational researcher
is re-establishing a past record in education and the periods are set
best by their relation to education. Admittedly, military events and

political developments are especially good determiners of turning points in the general history of a people or nation, but in research of their educational history, it may be more desirable to establish historical periods on the basis of more cultural or intellectual criteria. For example, the contemporary American scene is no doubt overshadowed by outstanding economic, military, and political occurrences, but from the viewpoint of American educational history, the period of the 1960's and 1970's could be more meaningfully identified by the Civil Rights Movement, or by the New Role of Federal Government in Education.

The final phase of historical research is writing the report. While the historian is not required to be a literary writer, he must tell the story of the record with some holding power over his readers. His story should attempt to be interesting if not literary. This is helped if his narrative points to lessons for the future based on the past. The historian is not obliged to place praise or blame, for the past, but he should throw light on the future.

The next type of research, Factorial Analysis Research, involves primarily the fields of Psychology and Philosophy. Since the climate of educational research today is empirical and obviously it will remain so for the foreseeable future, it may seem debatable whether philosophical research is justified for inclusion in a text on inductive educational research. As a matter of fact, comparable textbooks on educational research do not usually include philosophical research. This author, however sees the need to emphasize some important concepts of enduring truthfulness concerning deductive thinking as it relates to truth-finding in education. The argument for introducing philosophical research into this textbook is to view deductive inquiry as a counterpoint to inductive inquiry.

Here is precisely the basic concept that the student must recognize,
that philosophical research covers the same territory as psychological
research, but they utilize different approaches. Whereas educational
philosophy utilizes the deductive - intuitive method of thinking, educational psychology utilizes the inductive - empirical method. Both
disciplines however, are concerned with the nature and the relationships
of educational factors; both analyze educational concepts and processes
into their component elements for the sake of securing greater depth of
insight into them. By reason of this analytical process which is
common to them, the term Factorial Analysis can   well be used as the
classification heading for them as single type of educational research
instead of the term Psycho-Philosophical. The term Factorial Analysis
however, would not necessarily identify exclusively with philosophy or
psychology, but would overlap with both fields of knowledge.

Considering philosophy by itself, how does it contribute to
educational research? It can be readily established that philosophical
(deductive) thinking enters into the inductive thinking processes in a
number of ways. At every point where the researcher makes a logical
analysis or a value decision, he is engaging in philosophical thought.
Instances of such thinking are: selecting the research topic, setting
purposes for the investigation, establishing hypotheses, deciding on
criterion data capable of testing the hypotheses, and selecting statistical
procedures appropriate to the nature of educational data to be interpreted
and capable of testing the null hypothesis. All of these appeal to
philosophical thinking within the framework of the inductive method, but
philosophical thinking also enters in many ways into the interpretation
of research data, especially of nominal data. For example, the researcher
who looks for evidences of multi-level materials and individualized

instruction to judge the quality of provisions for gifted students in
schools, is doing philosophical thinking is an empirical setting. Norms
to be applied to such data and evaluations of the data by critical thinking
are prime examples of philosophical thinking. The enumeration above of
the main contact points between philosophical and inductive thinking
should be sufficient to give rebuttal to the misconception that since we
now have the inductive method, the deductive method is henceforth invalidated.
Not only are inductive and deductive thinking not contradictory to each
other, they are complementary and supportive of each other.

The philosophical processes of intuition, abstraction, and deduc-
tion contribute to educational research not only as alternative mental
processes to measurement, description, and induction, but as devices in
themselves for truth---finding and theory--building in education. As
such, they are alternate routes by which the human mind arrives at the
same destination of knowledge via deductive thinking rather than inductive thinking. There is no intent here to attempt to develop a method
of philosophical enquiry, but only a call for recognition of the integrity
of philosophical thought as a viable method for verifying educational
theory and practice in conjunction with the inductive method and even
separately on its own. In this latter case, of course, the practitioner
of "philosophical research" can only be a person well trained in philosophy.
Probably this type of research would find its habitat exclusively in the
Educational Foundations Departments where practitioners of this art are
to be found. At any rate, the beginning graduate educational researcher
should at least be aware of the existence of an alternate method of
truth-finding. This is especially true since research today is increasingly
interested in issues in the affective area of human development,

which are by nature more humanistic. On the other hand, also, philoso-
phers are seeking new patterns of thought processes for their own field
which will accomodate to some data collecting and interpreting techniques
that can be borrowed from other disciplines.

Factorial Analysis research is concerned with the nature and
relationships of human attributes and processes. Typically, for instance,
it is concerned with the conditions of learning. In its concerns, Factorial
Analysis operates by experimental inductive methods. In several ways,
however, it has its own particularities and differences in emphasis in
research design and statistics from other types of educational research.

One of these special emphases for Factorial Analysis is in the
formulation of a topic, the need for clearly defining and precisely limiting
the research topic. In a broad sense, the Factorial Analysis must have
performed the basic task of elaborating a system of classification and
hierarchy of human assets and aspects of the process of education so
that the researcher can place a topic in its exact reference in the field
of education. Relationships are his stock in trade.

The main aspect of research procedures in which Factorial Analysis
has its own particularities from other research types is in the statistics
which are required for the purposes set. Since those purposes are concerned with the nature and relationships of human factors, the correlational-
regression procedures are especially appropriate for these research projects. Whether two variables do or do not have high correlation coefficients between them is of importance to the investigation because the
coefficient is a statement of the extent to which the two variables
involved are alike or different from each other. The statistics of partial
and multiple correlation make it possible to pursue relationships

among variables in greater depth by manipulating some of the subvariables.
A further aspect of statistics that is effective for achieving purposes
of the psychological type of research is regression. This statistical
concept is basically concerned with predicting the future effectiveness
of some variable and there must be a substantial basic correlation between
the predictor (independent) and the predicted (dependent) variables.
The regression coefficient is a statistical expression of the comparative
rate of change on one variable and the rate of change in another given
variable. For instance, the coefficient of regression may indicate
that for every one point of change on I.Q. there are two points of change
on some other variable such as science achievement. Thus, change occurs
twice as rapidly on one variable as on the other. Thus again, the basic
issue is one of nature and relationships of variables. The knowledge of
correlation and of regression analysis which is provided by Factorial
Analysis research is especially pertinent for making choices and valuing.
By means of regression formulas the researcher is able to project a
variable into the future and gain foresight in anticipation of what can
be expected to occur in the future. Regression analysis knowledge also
is basic to the systems approach to program development and evaluation.
Since measures can be obtained of correlations and of regression slopes
for educational variables singly and in groups, it is possible to simu-
late different combinations of programs and program elements, and it is
also possible to predict outcomes of these combinations and simulations.
Thus, decision-making is facilitated and evaluations of personnel needs,
time, and budget can be projected.

In education, the Factorial Analysis type of educational research
associates with Educational Psychology and the field of counseling and
guidance.

In the role of facilitators for problem-solving and decision making, these practitioners need to have basic knowledge of relationships of human variables to each other - likenesses, differences, rates of comparative change -- not in order to give ready-made answers to clients, but that they may give guidance and criticism to individuals who are engaged in making decisions and value choices on their own.

There is one final particularity about the Factorial Analysis type of research in regard to statistics which bears mentioning although it is too advanced to be dealt with in detail in this course. This concept is that the capstone of regression analyses is factor analysis. This branch of research design and statistics involves factors and sub-factors among human characteristics and potentialities. Characteristically, it strives to identify which basic factors are mutually exclusive, which overlap, and which sub-factors can be telescoped into or extracted from others. The statistical devices involved herein are extensive and involved. This level of research design and statistics lies beyond the beginning graduate research course but the student needs to be aware of it.

The most inductive type of educational research is the experimental investigation. This type of study involves collecting empirical data and interpreting it by inductive thinking. In the past it has been commonly referred to as the scientific method of thinking because it was historically in the natural sciences that the collecting of a body of specific instances or facts and deriving generalizations from the uniformities and/or causalities discovered in them first originated as an alternate method of thinking to the deductive method. Subsequently, the application of the "scientific method" as a basic process of thought to non-scientific fields of knowledge gave it a broader identity and today it is more often thought of as simply the inductive process.

The experiment as a research process is based upon the philosophical model of Mill's Cannon of Difference. This model dertifies that
if two phenomena or situations are identical in all variables except
one on which they differ, then any differences in the resolution or
outcomes of the phenomena or situations are attributable to the one variable on which they differ. The implication in the experimental model
possesses the logic of cause and effect relationships. No other type
of educational research rises to this level of certitude and therefore
the experiment is the most powerful type of educational research.

It follows from the model of the research experiment that the most
crucial task in its design is to control the variables other than the
independent variable that can significantly cause outcomes in the
dependent variable(s). Ideally, the independent variable should be the
only element on which the two situations vary. It should exist in the
experimental situation, but in the control situation either it should
be absent or it should be replaced by a competing form of the independent
variable (treatments). If there is not adequate control of variables
then there is no guarantee that different outcomes in terms of the
dependent variables are attributable solely to the independent variable(s)
for the experimental and control situations. Thus, the experimental
model's potential for establishing causality can be destroyed. It is
because of their intermediary role between the independent variables that
these variables are called "control" variables, or "mediating" variables,
or more recently "contaminating" variables.

As a consequence of the above, an initial problem in controlling
variables is to identify factors which can influence the dependent variable.
In this task, logic and common practice may provide some leads, but sound

research design is satisfied only when empirical evidence supports the choice of variables to be controlled. Often previous related research reveals what factors have been proven to affect the dependent variables. If not, it may be necessary to conduct preliminary phases of research, possibly a survey, to identify control variables. These safeguards for controlling variables are especially necessary with topics which are fundamental and relatively unresearched. Today there is a trend toward basic research involving numerous variables and very large samples. This research is made possible by newer, more comprehensive statistical theory and procedures, and facilitated by the fantastic technology of the computer. Hence, the matter of identifying the control variables in the topics which are unfamiliar because of their newness or their comprehensiveness assumes great importance. Some common control variables as aptitude (I.Q.), reading scores, attitude toward learning, socio-economic condition, chronological, age or grade level, and previous knowledge in the topic, may operate differently in new settings. As a consumer of research, the reader should be alert and critical of the control of variables in the more sophisticated research he reads.

The control of variables is the distinguishing characteristic of design for collecting data in an experiment. Other elements are also important to developing a sound design for collecting objective and accurate data: analyzing the topic, purposing, hypothesizing, identifying criterion data, instrumentation for collecting data and objective measurement and evaluation procedures. All of these research processes have been dealt with individually, but it is now appropriate to deal with all of them as a design. The task here is referred to as the "experimental design" of the research. In this book, treatment of this topic permits consideration of only the basic or "true" experimental design, but the student can easily find other sources for information about variations on the true experimental design and of the so-called "quasi experimental" designs. **(cf.** Stanley and Campbell, "Chapter V, Handbook of Research on Teaching, ed. by N.L. Gage. (Chicago: Rand McNally, 1963), pp. **171-246.**

The true experimental design consists of **two or more equal or** — at least equivalent treatment groups which are compared in terms of the independent variable and are controlled on the mediating variables so that differences in outcomes on the dependent variables are attributable to the experimental variable. If the total sample is desired to be representative of any sizable population, it must be drawn from such population by a truly random selection design. If generalizability of results is not particularly desired, a sample which is conveniently available may be used; then population and sample will be coterminous.

On the requirement of equivalence between or among the groups receiving the different treatments, however, there can be no option. There can be no significant differences allowed to exist between or among the treatment groups unless provision is made to "correct" these differences **through statistics .** The random designs referred to in the discussion of sampling apply to random assignment of subjects in the sample. This gives the assurance of equivalence between or among the groups and if further assurance is desired **other** tests of significance of differences between group means may be performed. If these statistical tests show any significant differences, then either new treatment groups should be sought or the researcher should plan to interpret his data by means of analysis of covariance with the significantly different variables as co-variant(s). Covariance will make corrections for the initial differences between or among the treatment groups. The final **remark to make** about

the equivalence of treatment groups in the sample is that matching individuals on the control variables is still possible, but it is so
tedious and time consuming that it is almost never used anymore. Random
assignment to treatment groups, which has replaced it is not free from
error, but there is empirical proof that it works.

It has been the experience of the author, however, in directing
the graduate researchers to encounter two problems which may well be
answered at this point. The first is the question of the single treatment group. The novice in research sometimes fails to see beyond his
experimental treatment group. He sees merit to interpreting effectiveness of an independent variable in terms of differences between pretest
(s) and posttest(s) scores on the dependent variable(s), or in terms of
differences between his posttest scores and standardized norms of his
measuring instruments. The inadequacy in such a "single group" experimental design is that the pretest is too weak and the standardized norms
are too vague as norms against which to evaluate effectiveness of the
independent variable. Neither is it satisfactory to attempt to use
the single group as experimental group for a period of time and then
to use them as a control group in a subsequent period of time, even
immediately following. Under such a pattern it would be inherently
impossible to control the time variables. It remains that the best
strategy for evaluating the change produced by the independent variable
is to set up a control treatment group of individuals who can otherwise
equal the performance of the experimental groups and to test the hypotheses by differences between the groups.

A second idea which arises with beginning researchers is the rotation of the treatment groups. They are impressed with the logic of
showing that the experimental treatment is more effective than the control

treatment even when they exchange groups of subjects to which they are applied. Theoretically, this is true but the increase in certitude that may result from rotating the groups must be weighed in view of the price it costs in added work. There must be posttesting at the point in time just before rotation and then again at the end of the period after rotation. The equivalent amount of work here involved approaches that of repeating the investigation. Experience has shown that the increment in certitude concerning the results because of the rotation is rather minimal. A better experimental design rather than rotating the treatment groups is to add additional control groups, preferably with different treatments, and thus permit the independent variable to prove that it is more effective than other control treatments. Also, prolonging the experiment over a longer period of time is preferable to rotating the groups after short periods of time. The true experimental design is difficult of achievement in educational research, and especially in the atmosphere of the school setting as opposed to the purer atmosphere of a research laboratory, but there is no evidence that any other basic research design is emerging which can better serve the inductive model of thought.

PROGNOSTIC RESEARCH

Yet another type of educational investigation is the Prognostic or Predictive Research. The function of the Predictive Research is to predict the future operation of a variable. The model of independent variable - dependent variable is applicable to this type, with the predictor being the independent variable and the predicted variable being the dependent variable. There are also mediating variables because a predictor can predict an outcome best in a rather singular set of circumstances. Predictions emerge from correlations, and they merge into

regressions. Accordingly, the first steps in a prognostic study consist of identifying factors which can predict the independent variable
reliably. For instance, if I.Q. is used to predict reading, we must
first compute the correlation between I.Q. scores and reading scores
for a given sample of individuals. This correlation coefficient then
becomes the basis for a regression formula which also involves the
means and the standard deviations of the I.Q. scores and the reading
scores. The basic regression formula is $Y' = r \frac{S_y}{S_x} (X - M_x) + M_y$. This
will yield a formula of the type $Y' = bX + C$. In this formula, any
X (I.Q.) can be inserted and yield a predicted reading score (Y').

A very difficult problem in prognostic studies is to know what
factors are good predictors of the given dependent variable. Some
researchers are convinced that no variables are good predictors of
any other variables. For example, intelligence has been used as a
predictor for many variables, but many researchers are convinced that it
is not a good predictor of any variable. A rule of thumb to go by in
predictive studies is that there must be a coefficient at least as
large as .70 between predictor and predicted for any regression formula
to make predictions with accuracy. However, relatively few variables
correlate at the level of .70, and so we proceed to establish some regression formulas with coefficients somewhat lower. For instance, even
a mathematics aptitude test will usually not correlate with the mathematics
achievement scores of the same individuals as high as .70.

An alternative procedure is to use two or more predictors in the
same regression formula. This procedure adds somewhat to the accuracy
of the prediction, but not so much because the prognostic power of two
predictors "overlaps", and a second predictor does not do much predicting
that the first one did not already do. A third predictor in the same

regression formula would add even less on its own to the dimension of
the prediction, so that it is usually advised that regression formulas
involving two predictor variables satisfy most research purposes.

The predicted scores of individuals who were in the group are used
to obtain the Standard Error of the Estimate for the regression formulas.
For these individuals we take their original scores (also called actual
predicted scores), derived by placing the original score in the regression
formula and solving it. In doing so, we turn the regression formula
back upon the scores from which it was derived. Once we have the two
sets of scores from the same individuals, we compute the coefficient
of correlation between them, and for this coefficient, we compute the
standard error of estimate, symbolized by $S_{1.2}$. The formula for this
computation is $S_{1.2} = S_1 \sqrt{1 - R_{1.2}^2}$, where S_1 is the standard deviation
of the actual scores and $R_{1.2}$ is the coefficient of correlation between
actual scores and predictor scores. The standard error of the estimate
is the measure of the margin of error for predicted scores. Thus, if
a regression formula yielded a predicted score of 70 for a given individual,
and the standard error of the estimate were 15 points, this means that
the range of points within which the individuals actual score might fall
would be 70 $\pm$ 15, or from 55 to 85. Difference between actual score
and predicted score is called the residual. This gives an example of
the lack of accuracy of predicted scores, and the assurance of this range
of points is only 68%. If the coefficient of correlation on which the
prediction is based is low, the standard error of the estimate will be larger, and if the original correlation coefficient is greater, the standard
error of the estimate will be smaller. Hence, the accuracy of the prediction
increases or decreases with the size of the original correlation between
the two variables.

The final type of research is the Developmental Research. This type is concerned with the effectiveness of innovations and changes to improve the quality of education. Often the innovation is a new type of curriculum or instruction, but it may pertain to any aspect of education. Developmental research therefore includes two stages: 1) developing the innovation, and 2) testing its effectiveness. Usually, for the innovation which is developed to be worthwhile, it must itself be the fruit of research. For this function, a project in itself may be required, and such project may take the form of factor analysis, factorial analysis of variance, correlation, regression analysis, or surveys. Investigations of this nature provide the researcher with knowledge of causes and effects, and of various relationships among variables which are essential to create innovations that have foundations in empirical evidence.

Once the researcher has developed his innovation, he is ready to test its effectiveness through an experimental investigation. In this experiment, the innovation becomes the independent variable, and its utilization constitutes the experimental treatment. The second stage of the research is a typical experimental investigation as has been discussed earlier.

There may be some question as to whether Developmental Research is in fact a distinct type of research. The second phase experiment is clearly not a distinct type. However, the first stage innovation development has its uniqueness. In terms of the principle of classification in this chapter, the development of an innovation performs a distinctive function which is not found in any other research type presented in this chapter. Whereas descriptive and historical research are concerned with the status of a variable, and the other research types are concerned with the effectiveness and with the prediction of a variable respectively, none of these types is concerned with the creation of a new variable. On the basis of this distinctive function, developmental research is a distinct category of research.

The knowledge of types of research is important to avoid mis-applications of research concepts and statistical procedure. For instance, Chapter III pointed out how the analysis of the topic into the variables subsumed in it has specific adaptation in different types of research. In the experience of the author, beginning researchers can be seriously confused by such variations, and become quite unsure of what they are doing. The same is true of other aspects of research design, and the beginning researcher cannot be too thorough in his mastery of the concepts with which he is dealing in different educational research types.

CHAPTER XI. WRITING THE RESEARCH REPORT

Communication and dissemination of research findings are an integral part of educational research. Hence the need for effective writing of the report of an investigation of whatever type. The report must extend beyond the findings and conclusions; it must encompass analysis of the topic, purposes-hypotheses, sample, criterion data, data collection tools, statistical procedures, and the results. The concern is not with mechanical and physical aspects, for these matters are all adequately dealt with in manuals for writers of reports, but only with the substantive aspects of organizing and writing a research report. The controlling principle in the chapter is that the report should include all the elements necessary for a reader to evaluate the research findings. According to this principle, there may well be three parts in the research report: Part One, dealing with the research topic; Part Two, dealing with the research design; and Part Three, dealing with the data and its interpretation.

The section of the report on the topic should begin with the title and should define the terms in the title which need definition. This means any unusual terms or any usual terms which are defined operationally in the research. The first section of the report should also include an analysis of the variables--independent, dependent, mediating--as applicable to the given topic. This section should place the topic in the field of education by pointing out the issues affected by it, and there should be clarification of any assumptions basic to it. If the research is an experiment, experimental treatments should be clearly described.

Also, the section should effectively report the literature of the field for every topic, especially the research literature. All of this content may be called Chapter I - Analysis of the Topic, because this is the most basic of the functions mentioned above.

The section of the report dealing with research design and procedures may be called Chapter II - Collection of Data. The elements of a research design for a given topic are: purposes, hypotheses, sample, criterion data, and tools and procedures for collecting the criterion data. Since discussion of how to conduct these phases of a research investigation has been the subject of previous chapters, there is no intent to repeat what has already been said. The concern mainly is for an outline for organizing the research report by chapters.

Chapter I - Analysis of the Topic, and Chapter II - Collection of Data have basically standard content applicable to any topic with appropriate adaptations. For instance only experimental research has treatments to report, and the "dependent variable" component in analysis of the topic is replaced by substitute components in various other types of research. A sample outline for an experiment is listed subsequently.

The third section of a research report cannot be standardized so readily. It requires making decisions as to organization which can best be based upon the purposes and hypotheses of the investigation. A variety of patterns of organization of the report giving the data and its interpretation are feasible, and there are no rules of thumb for such organization. Each report is a challenge which must be met by the researcher. The one principle which approaches uniformity is that the body of data of the research cannot all be presented and interpreted in a single chapter of the report. If it can, this could mean that the investigation lacks depth, or it could mean there is lack of analysis of the data in organizing chapters for the body of the report. If the study has the proper dimensions, it will demand two or three chapters, each reporting a broad area of the data and its interpretation. There is also danger of error in the opposite direction. If graduate level research is organized into more than three or four chapters to report and interpret the data, it could be that the study is over ambitious in its purposes. On the other hand, it could be that data are fragmentized so that they are organized into rather truncated chapters in the body of the report. In this case there is a lack of synthesis in the organization of the chapters. The nearest approach possible to standardizing the outline for Part III of the report, is to utilize the purposes in the research design for the chapter organization, one per purpose or purposes. Often for reporting on a chapter a logical pattern can be established which may be repeated in each chapter. As said earlier, it is a challenge to the researcher to develop some functional chapter organization relevant to the topic, and effective for communicating in the research report. For the purposes of a textbook, the author judges that the "stylized" outline based on purposes will be useful to graduate students. It has worked for his own students.

The language and style of a research report are not required to be particularly artistic. The prime criterion is clarity. Not only should the reader be able to gather the researcher's meaning, but he should not be able to mistake the meaning. However, if a research report can be written interestingly also, this is very desirable. Vocabulary in the report should be knowledgeable and as technical as needed for theory-building; but very often it is possible to reduce the level of professional "jargon" in the report. In the past, research reports have tended to be written for a reporting audience that was much too selective and in one's profession. Educational research today commands a much wider public audience, and reports must be written in a more relevant style so as to be meaningful to elements of the non-professional audience. One of the characteristics which this "new reporting" must possess is to be complete enough to be clear, but concise enough to compete for the time of the reader.

The opportunities for publication are great because of modern technology and the knowledge explosion. Even so, the stream of reports is so great that many reach very limited audiences. Fortunately, technology has made available complex systems of retrieval whereby alternate forms of publication are available besides printing. Microfilm, microfische, and other forms of reproduction permit the circulation of a vast body of reported research. Researchers must rise to the challenge of creating a format and style of research reporting which is relevant to media, technology, and the expanded interest of the American public in Educational Research. Mainly this will demand reports written in language with a less technical tone.

The elements of research design and interpretation of empirical data presented in the preceding chapters have been organized in the following suggested composite of an outline for a written research report. The beginning researcher who has imagination and independence of spirit may shy away from borrowing an outline from a textbook, but an individual may at least wish to refer to this composite structure as a checklist for a final review of the contents of his report, to guard against the possibility of important omissions.

STRUCTURE OF A WRITTEN RESEARCH REPORT

CHAPTER I - ANALYSIS OF THE TOPIC

    I. The title. Incomplete sentence. Includes independent variable and identifiers of research setting.

   II. Definitions of terms. New terms and operationally-defined terms.

  III. Assumptions basic to the topic. Especially cause-effect relationships among independent, dependent, and mediating variables.

   IV. The independent variable (s).

    V. The dependent variable (s). This element varies by research type. See Chapter III, Analysis of the Research Topic.

   VI. Control variable (s).

  VII. The experimental treatment. This element applies only for Experimental and Developmental research.

 VIII. Survey of the literature on the topic: conceptual and research backgrounds of the topic.

CHAPTER II- COLLECTION OF DATA

    I. The purposes:

       A. General purpose (s).

       B. Specific purpose (s).

   II. The hypothesis (es):

       A. General hypothesis (es):

          1. Positive form.

          2. Statistical null form.

       B. Specific hypothesis (es):

          1. Positive form.

          2. Statistical null form.

  III. The sample:

       A. Size of the sample; description of the sample.

B. Representativeness of the sample:

    1. Random selection design, or

    2. Stratified selection design.

C. Equivalence of groups in the sample on mediating (control) variables:

    1. Random assignment of individuals to groups.

    2. Equivalence on control variable A.

    3. Equivalence on control variable B, etc.

IV. The criterion data:

A. Scores (observations, measurements) on first criterion.

B. Scores (observations, measurements) on second criterion, etc.

V. Instrument (s) for collecting data:

A. If existing instrument (s) is (are) utilized:

    1. Description and discussion of the instrument (s).

    2. Administration of the instrument.

B. If a special instrument is constructed:

    1. Describe the process of construction.

    2. Administration of the instrument.

CHAPTER III – INTERPRETATION OF CRITERION DATA: PURPOSE (S) I.

I. Presentation of the data:

A. Tables and figures (nominal data); commentary.

B. Series of scores (ordinal, interval data); commentary.

II. Interpretation of the chapter data: findings

A. Through critical interpretation: consistency of the data with criteria for interpretation (philosophy, psychology, research, verified practice, etc.)   AND/OR

B. Through statistics to test relationships or differences between/ among measurements and observations: statistics involve mainly interval data.

III. Chapter conclusions:

Formal statements of generalizations based on data presented and interpreted in this chapter.

CHAPTER IV. - INTERPRETATION OF CRITERION DATA: PURPOSE (S) II.

I. Presentation of the data:

A. Tables and figures (nominal data).

B. Series of scores (ordinal, interval data).

II. Interpretation of the chapter data: (findings)

A. Through critical interpretation: consistency of the data with criteria for interpretation (philosophy, psychology, research, verified practice, etc.), AND/OR

B. Through statistics to test relationships or differences between/among measurements and observations: statistics involve mainly interval data.

III. Chapter conclusions:

Formal statements of generalizations based on data presented and interpreted in this chapter.

CHAPTER V. CONCLUSIONS AND RECOMMENDATIONS.

I. Statements of findings as related to purposes-hypotheses.

II. Statements of conclusions overarching Chapters in the body of the report.

III. Discussion of effectiveness of research design and procedures.

IV. Rationale building with the research findings.

V. Recommendations for future research.

VI. Recommendations for implementation of conclusions in the practitioner setting.

So far this chapter has dealt with writing a research report on the level of organization of the entire report. There are also some points which must be made about writing the report on a more detailed level. It is especially important to provide some answers to the question: "How much should the research report communicate about summary presentations of data (tables, figures), and about statistical computations. Experience shows that these two concerns are a source of bewilderment to many graduate student researchers.

Concerning tables and figures, some remarks have been made previously about how to construct them (supra, pp. 67-69), relative to interpretation. The present connection is with communicating about them so that the reader can readily comprehend them. For this end, several things are definitely required. All tables and figures must have a title. The most important criterion for the title of a table or figure is that it identify the contents of the table. The reader will note that the term used is to identify the contents, not to summarize them. Since tables consist of columns and rows, and figures include areas, the need to identify these items may be met by using more generic terms rather than more specific terms. Thus, although a table may contain a column for vocabulary scores, a column for sentence comprehension, and a column for paragraph comprehension, all three of these columns may be subsumed under the term "reading achievement" in the title of the table, and likewise columns on computations, on concepts, and on problem solving in arithmetic may be subsumed under the term arithmetic achievement. To pursue this illustration further, the rows in the table may consist, not of individual students, but of groups of students, those who have high ability, those who have average ability, those who have low ability, and these rows may be subsumed under the

term "ability level" in the title of the table. For such a table the
measurements reported would not be scores of individual students, but
probably the mean scores of the ability level groups. Hence, for
the students in the experimental group of a project, the title for
the table could read: "Reading and Arithmentic Achievement by Ability
Levels of Students for the Experimental Group." In this title the
identification of contents of the table is accomplished without making
it cumbersome and involved.

In addition to having a title, each table and figure must be
numbered. If there are both tables and figures in the report, tables
may be numbered with roman numerals and figures with arabic numerals
to help prevent confusion that might arise from having a table and a
figure with the same numeral. Numbering of tables and figures must
be continuous throughout the report without re-starting numeration
at the chapter level or any other level of organization. Again, the
reason is to avoid confusion from having more than one table or figure
with the same number in the report. Sometimes the number and title are
placed above tables, but below figures, again to emphasize distinction
between the two series.

Below is the format for the hypothetical table discussed.

Table V. Reading and Arithmetic Achievement by Ability Levels
of Students for the Experimental Group.

	Vocabulary	Sentence Comprehension	Paragraph Comprehension	Total Reading	Arithmetic Computations	Arithmetic Concepts	Applications	Total Arithmetic	
Above Average	M	M	M		M	M	M	M	
Average	M	M	M		M	M	M	M	
Below Average	M	M	M		M	M	M	M	

For clarity in communication, tables should be "introduced" before
they are presented. By introducting a table is meant quoting its
number and describing its content in general terms. The hypothetical
table referred to above could be introduced thus: Table V presents
means of achievement scores by ability levels for the experimental
group. The table should then be presented as soon after its introduction as possible although rather than break a table if there is not
enough room left on the page, the presentation should be   deferred
until the next page.

On a higher congitive level, written reporting of summary presentations of data is concerned with guiding the reader to the more
meaningful items of data in the table or figure. This task is accomplished
by indicating certain characteristics of the data. The researcher may
communicate to the reader as many of the following phenomena as he thinks
important in terms of the purposes and hypotheses: the central tendencies
of data in the table, dispersion, apparent cause-effect connections,
uniformities, consistencies, inconsistencies. The researcher may also

indicate comparisons or contrasts of data of one table with other tables, either previous or subsequent in the report. Most of the details of data, however, are left to be communicated by the table or figure itself, and the reader may search out further relationships of interest to him.

The other concern for communicating about details in the report, as mentioned previously, has to do with statistical computations. Should formulas be reported? How many steps in the computations should be shown? How much elucidation of probability of chance occurence of the statistics according to degrees of freedom should be made? In a written research report in the form of a master's thesis or a doctoral dissertation, it is recommended that the basic formulas be shown in the report, that at least computed values be shown replacing the abstract symbols in the formula, and that probability of chance occurence with degrees of freedom be discussed. The likelihood exists that readers of graduate research reports will mainly be other graduate students. Such detailed reporting will be meaningful to them. However, the recommendations made here for writing a thesis or dissertation are not extended to writing a report for publication in a book or periodical. In these cases the audience of readers is more general, and details of statistical computations are not relevant.

The main criterion of style for an educational research report is clarity. But whereas style as figures of speech and other forms of artistic writing are not the rule, pleasantness in communication achieved through variety in vocabulary, in sentence type, and in sentence structure are desirable. Also, topical sentence construction and placement in paragraphs are important aspects of style in the research report. For the sake of clarity, paragraphs are usually kept relatively short (from half a page to a page), but again paragraph variety in terms of length, and of topical sentence usage will make a report more readable.

Writing the educational research report should not be underestimated; it should receive the same scholarly treatment as the research design and the statistical interpretations with both of which it is integrally united.

CASES AND ANALYTICAL MODELS

I. **REPORTED** EXPERIMENTAL INVESTIGATION

Associated with teaching:

Analysis of the Topic, Purposing, Hypothesizing, Criterion Data, Data Collection, Tools for Collecting Data, Statistical Interpretation of Data.

The reader of research reports must read the research design as well as the research findings. Knowledgeable reading of the design is a tool for evaluative reading of the results of research. Any faults in research design raise doubts about the findings and, vice versa, a pure research design increases the persuasiveness of the findings. This brief points out the elements of research design underlying a written experimental report. The researcher must develop the competency to recognize the meaning in these elements of research design as well as the meaning of research results.

The Influence of Analysis and Evaluation Questions
on Achievement in Sixth Grade Social Studies

FRANCIS P. HUNKINS
Assistant Professor of Education
University of Washington, Seattle

Introduction

QUESTIONS used by teachers in their discourse and those incorporated in instructional materials probably are significant in guiding the development of pupils' levels of knowledge and achievement. Questions reveal the operational objectives which stress, for example, the increase of pupils' knowledge of facts, of understandings, of concepts, and of pupils' skills at interpreting information and ideas.

The classroom teacher devotes a large portion of his time to asking questions, e.g., Adams (1), Aschner (2), Barr (3), Floyd (7), Stevens (9). The usefulness of questions has long been recognized as significant in the teaching-learning interaction. Yet, even with this purported awareness of the importance of questions, little has been done with regard to the effects questions have upon pupils' achievement within the class situation.

This research was concerned with determining the relative effectiveness of knowledge, analysis, and evaluation questions in stimulating achievement in sixth grade social studies. These question types were based on three of the six hierarchical categories of Benjamin Bloom's *Taxonomy of Educational Objectives*, Bloom (4).

Knowledge questions require the recall of ideas, facts, materials, or phenomena. They call for the releasing of certain information stored in the individual's memory. Analysis questions, on the other hand, demand the arrangement and rearrangement of information into elements, relationships, and organizations. The third type of question, evaluation, requires a judgment employing criteria such as accuracy, effectiveness, economic quality, or satisfying quality. These two latter question types subsume knowledge. The evaluation type of question subsumes both knowledge and analysis.

Objectives

This study sought to determine whether a dominant use in social studies text-type materials of analysis and evaluation questions, as defined by Bloom's *Taxonomy*, would effectively stimulate the development of sixth grade pupils' social studies achievement. The overall hypothesis tested, stated in null form was:

Use of text-type materials employing questions requiring "analysis" and "evaluation" will not result in differences in sixth grade pupils' social studies achievement when compared with the use of text-type materials incorporating questions requiring the recall of knowledge in relationship to pupils' (a) reading level, (b) sex, and (c) the interaction between these variables.

General Plan of the Study

The general plan of the study first involved constructing two sets of text-type materials and corresponding answer sheets, one set stressing questions requiring analysis and evaluation (Condition A) and the other stressing questions requiring knowledge (Condition B). Pupils in both treatment conditions were directed to read designated sections of their textbook and to respond in writing to the questions on their worksheets.

For four weeks, pupils used these materials during a thirty-five minute portion of the daily social studies period. For this study, the instructional unit dealt with Africa and Oceania and was based on chapters in the adopted social studies textbook used by the co-operating school system. The general format and directions of the two sets of special materials were identical, the only varying factor being the questions and their emphases. During the experimental period, teachers refrained from actively engaging in teaching but assisted in coordinating the pupils' use of the materials. This lack of active teacher participation was an attempt to reduce their influence on the experimental situation.

Procedure

Subjects

Two hundred and sixty pupils served as subjects in this study. They were enrolled in eleven sixth grade classes in three elementary schools serving the same geographic area of a large suburban public school system in a northeastern Ohio community (population, 47,922, 1960 census). The eleven classes were randomly assigned to one of two experimental treatment conditions, A or B. A total of 127 pupils (67 boys and 60 girls) were assigned to Condition A, while 133 pupils (55 boys and 78 girls) were assigned to Condition B.

Background data were collected and analyzed for both pupils and teachers.

Intelligence quotients were obtained from the *California Test of Mental Maturity*, S Form. The mean IQ for boys in Treatment A was 114.84, SD 16.06 (N = 67). Girls in the same treatment had a mean IQ of 115.80, SD 15.10, (N = 60). In Treatment B, the mean IQ for boys was 112.07, SD 15.38 (N = 55), and the mean IQ for girls was 113.11, SD of 12.65 (N = 78).

Reading test scores were obtained on the subjects from the *Stanford Achievement Test*, Form W. Boys in Treatment A had a mean reading score of 38.90, SD 12.18; girls in the same treatment had a mean reading score of 41.86, SD 11.45. Boys in Treatment B had a mean reading score of 36.45, SD 10.39, while girls in the same treatment had a mean reading score of 39.29, SD 9.74.

Pupils' IQ scores and reading scores were subjected to analysis of variance to determine if significant differences were present. For this analysis, scores were considered across reading levels by treatment and sex.

No significant differences in IQ were revealed between the two treatments, between boys and girls, or their interaction. Thus IQ was eliminated as a possible covariant on subsequent analyses of the criterion data. No significant differences between reading achievement were noted between the two treatments and no significant interaction either. A significant difference between the reading scores of boys and girls was observed. However, this relationship was not considered sufficient reason to use the reading scores as covariants on subsequent analyses of criterion data. Had significant differences in reading achievement existed between treatments, such scores would have been employed as covariants.

Background data on the participating teachers revealed that teachers of classes in both conditions were similar with respect to age and teaching experience.

The mean age for teachers with pupils involved in Treatment A was 35.16, while the mean age for those teachers with pupils involved in Treatment B was 33.20. Experience in teaching was similar, with means of 8.33 years for teachers in Treatment A and 8.80 years for teachers in Treatment B. The Treatment A teachers had slightly more years in teaching the sixth grade, mean 5.66 years, than did the teachers in Treatment B, mean 3.80 years. Ten of the eleven teachers involved had Bachelor degrees. The one teacher without the degree, in Treatment A, had over 24 years of teaching experience. Of the total teacher group, only one teacher had a Master's degree, in Treatment B.

Collection of Data

A criterion test of achievement covering the selected social studies unit was constructed by the investigator. The objective of the test design was to afford a single achievement score in addition to six subscores corresponding to the six categories in Bloom's *Taxonomy*: knowledge, comprehension, application, analysis, synthesis, and evaluation. However, only the total achievement score was of concern in this phase of the investigation.

A total of 59 multiple-choice, four option items was written and submitted to two judges well-acquainted with the *Taxonomy*. With four exceptions, only items having 100 percent agreement among the judges and investigator regarding *Taxonomy* emphasis were selected for the final test which contained 42 items. The test contained seven questions in each of the six Bloom categories. Reliability of the post-test was determined to be .68 using the Kuder-Richardson formula. This reliability is quite low and the reader should bear this in mind when considering the results.

Experimental Material and Procedure

Pupils in both experimental treatments used the regularly adopted social studies text, *The Changing Old World*, by Cooper, Sorensen, and Todd (5).

The unit for study during the experiment was "Africa, Australia and New Zealand." This unit was deemed appropriate, for the investigator felt that the subjects would not bring abundant prior knowledge into the experimental situation.

Experimental pupil materials. For each experimental treatment condition, special materials and answer sheets were constructed. The sets for both conditions were identical in format and directions. Seventeen sets for each condition were developed to correspond to discrete portions of the adopted text. Both treatment groups experienced an identical introductory set to familiarize them with the materials. Condition A materials had 47.53 percent of the total questions in the analysis and evaluation categories: 28.41 percent analysis, and 19.12 percent evaluation. Condition B materials contained a question emphasis on knowledge of 87.38 percent of the total number.

These materials had been submitted to the same judges who served to classify the achievement test items. Every question of each set was categorized by the judges, and, following this, the two individuals met with the investigator to compare results. If a question emphasis could not be agreed upon after discussion, the question was either rewritten until the desired emphasis was obtained or not employed in the final draft of the materials. This procedure was followed in order to ascertain that these question emphases did exist.

A readability analysis, employing the Dale-Chall formula, Dale and Chall (6), was used to determine the reading

level of both the experimental materials and the answer sheets in both Conditions A and B. Results of this analysis revealed that the experimental materials had an average raw score of 5.64, designating a reading level well within the range of fifth and sixth grade pupils. Analysis of the answer sheets revealed an average raw score of 5.65, also designating the material as appropriate for sixth graders.

Working with the materials. Pupils in both conditions were instructed to work independently with the materials. They were given from 30 to 35 minutes each day to work with the experimental sets, reading carefully and writing their answers in the provided spaces. Pupils were provided time to check their work with the answer sheets.

Analysis of Data

The experimental design basic to this study was an analysis of covariance design. Within each treatment condition, data were analyzed according to sex and reading achievement. This resulted in a 2 x 2 x 4 (treatment x sex x reading level) classificatory scheme. Pupils were assigned reading levels according to quartile ranks as determined by their raw scores on the reading achievement test (*Stanford Achievement Test,* Form W). The four levels had the following ranges: Quartile 1, 0-31; Quartile 2, 32-38; Quartile 3, 39-47; and Quartile 4, 48-64.

Results

The post-test achievement scores were subjected to analysis of covariance adjusting for the pre-achievement scores. These results are summarized in Table 1.

No statistically significant differences in achievement between boys and girls were observed, and there were no significant interactions. Condition A pupils achieved more than did Condition B pupils, and better readers obtained higher achievement scores than did poorer readers.

The means for between reading levels were contrasted by a series of t tests, all of which revealed statistically significant differences $(Q_4 > Q_3 > Q_2 > Q_1)$. It appears from these data that whether one can handle high-level questions is related to how well one can read. The higher-level questions usually were more involved with regard to wording than were the knowledge questions. Also, it should be borne in mind that both worksheets and answer sheets placed demands upon pupils' reading skills.

Conclusions

From the analyses conducted, the following conclusions are warranted:

1. The employment of high cognitive-level questions (analysis and evaluation) produced significantly greater scores in social studies achievement than did low cognitive-level questions (knowledge).

2. Better readers in both conditions achieved higher than did poorer readers.

As a result of these significant differences, the major null hypothesis relating to social studies achievement was rejected.

Source of Variation	Original		Adjusted			
	d.f.	S.S.	d.f.	S.S.	M.S.	F
Treatment	1	12.06	1	10.05	10.05	9.85**
Reading level	3	133.55	3	65.02	21.67	21.24**
Sex	1	.92	1	.92	.92	.90
Treatment x reading level	3	.49	3	.23	.07	.06
Treatment x sex	1	.75	1	.26	.26	.25
Reading level x sex	3	2.29	3	.63	.21	.20
Treatment x reading level x sex	3	8.06	3	7.21	2.40	2.35
Within groups	244	269.88	243	247.98	1.02	

** Significant at the .01 level.

Table 1. Summary of Analysis of Covariance of Post-test Scores on Achievement Test

Discussion

Analysis of the data suggests that questions requiring analysis and evaluation stimulated individuals to utilize several viewpoints regarding the information embedded in the task. It seems reasonable that pupils, using such questions, might have been forced to engage in the intellectual activity of considering various aspects of factual knowledge and evaluating the complexity, implications, and applications of such knowledge. Such mental "juggling" may have enabled pupils to know better the information with which they were dealing.

It is assumed that high-level questions will demand of individuals more intellectual activity than would be true with low-level questions. Since the data revealed a significantly greater achievement among the pupils receiving such high-level questions, one might cautiously conclude that the pupils did in fact react more actively with information presented. The evidence seems to suggest, rather than confirm, that pupils were engaged in an interaction with the materials presented. Analysis of the sub-tests of the achievement test, presently being conducted in a second phase of the research, may provide evidence to clarify somewhat exactly how the high-level questions affected various dimensions of achievement.

That the evidence is suggestive rather than confirming should not be cause for alarm. This research is a beginning, not a conclusion regarding the effects of questions. It is premature to make definite statements. These types of questions do have the potential, it seems, to make pupils uneasy, but also to encourage them to probe their knowledge and to discover meanings.

Implications of the Study

Several implications may be drawn from this study regarding the role of questions in relation to social studies achievement in particular and overall school achievement in general. If questions at higher-cognitive levels are capable of stimulating high achievement, then teachers should be using these questions in much greater numbers than they currently do. Teachers, by improving their level of questioning, could very well make information more meaningful for their pupils. In addition, pupils in classrooms where high-level questions are used by teachers should be expected to employ such questions themselves when they engage in class discussions and other class work. Higher-level questions not only should stimulate higher levels of achievement, but also should make pupils better inquirers into the realm of knowledge.

References

1. Thomas Howard Adams. *The Development of a Method for Analysis of Questions Asked by Teachers in Classroom Discourse.* Doctor's thesis. New Brunswick, New Jersey: Rutgers, The State University. 1964. 149 pp.

2. Mary Jane McCue Aschner. "Asking Questions to Trigger Thinking." *NEA Journal* 50 (6); 44-46; September 1961.

3. A. S. Barr. *Characteristic Differences in the Teaching Performance of Good and Poor Teachers of the Social Studies.* Bloomington, Illinois: Public School Publishing Co., 1929. 127 pp.

4. Benjamin S. Bloom, editor. *Taxonomy of Educational Objectives. The Classification of Educational Goals: Handbook I Cognitive*

Domain. New York: David McKay Company, Inc., 1956. 207 pp.

5. Kenneth S. Cooper, Clarence W. Sorensen, and Lewis Paul Todd. *The Changing Old World.* Morristown, New Jersey: Silver Burdett Company, Inc., 1961. 470 pp.

6. Edgar Dale, and Jeanne S. Chall. "A Formula for Predicting Readability." *Educational Research Bulletin* 27: 11-20, 28; January 1948. 27: 37-54; February 1948.

7. William D. Floyd. *An Analysis of the Oral Questioning Activity in Selected Colorado Primary Classrooms.* Doctor's thesis. Greeley: Colorado State College, 1960. 195 pp.

8. Frank M. Gatto. *Pupils' Questions: Their Nature and Their Relationship to the Study Process.* Doctor's thesis. Pittsburgh, Pennsylvania: University of Pittsburgh, 1928. 158 pp.

9 Romiett Stevens: *The Question as a Measure of Efficiency in Instruction.* Teachers College Contribution to Education, No. 48. New York: Teachers College, Columbia University, 1912. 95 pp.

10. Soshichi Yamada. "A Study of Questioning." *Pedagogical Seminary* 20: 129-85; 1913.

I. BRIEF OF AN EXPERIMENTAL INVESTIGATION

Francis P. Hunkins, "The Influence of Analysis and Evaluation
Questions on Achievement in Sixth Grade Social Studies," Educational
Leadership, XXV (January, 1968), 326-332.

I. Topic:

1. This research is an experiment on the topic; the effectiveness
    of using different types of questions in teaching social studies
    in the sixth grade.

2. The topic is important to the science of teaching in the field
    of education.

3. Previous research on the use of questions in teaching has been
    done by Adam , Aschner, Barr, Floyd, and S tevens, but little
    has been done specifically on the effects of types of questions
    on pupils' achievement.

4. Definition of terms:

    a. Knowledge questions: require the recall of ideas.

    b. Analysis questions: demand the arrangement and rearrangement
        of information into elements, relationships, and organizations.

    c. Evaluation questions: require judgement employing criteria
        such as accuracy, effectiveness, economic quality, or satis-
        fying quality.

II. Variables:

1. Independent Variables: the use of different levels of questions.

    a. Treatment A. Analysis and evaluation questions. Students
        studied texttype materials employing questions requiring
        "analysis" and "evaluation".

    b. Treatment B. Knowledge questions. Students studied text-type materials employing questions requiring the "recall" of knowledge.

2. Dependent Variable. Achievement (on a test involving knowledge, comprehension, application, analysis, synthesis, and evaluation) in a unit on Africa, Australia, and New Zealand.

3. Mediating Variables:

    a. Students: I.Q. scores and reading scores, and pretest on the unit.

    b. Teachers: Age, preparation, and years of teaching experience.

    c. These variables were controlled because they could influence the dependent variable.

4. Experimental treatment: Students spent 30 minutes daily studying the unit "Africa, Australia, and New Zealand" in Cooper, Sorensen, and Todd, The Changing Old World. The experimental group (A) answered analysis and evaluation questions on the material and checked their answers. The control group (B) answered rote questions and checked answers. Classroom teachers coordinated pupils' use of the materials. The readability level of all experimental treatment materials was at 5.6, Dale-Chall Formula.

III. Purposes:

    This experiment worked toward some important purposes.

1. General purpose: Will students achieve higher if they study social studies text-type materials with predominantly analysis and evaluation questions that if they study similar materials with predominantly recall questions?

2. Sub-purposes:

    a. Will achievement through analysis and evaluation questions as opposed to recall questions depend upon the pupils' reading level?

    b. Will achievement through analysis and evaluation questions as opposed to recall questions depend upon the pupils' sex?

    c. Will achievement through analysis and evaluation questions as opposed to recall questions depend upon interaction among students' reading level, students' sex, and type of questions used?

IV. <u>Hypotheses</u>:

For each purpose there is a corresponding null hypothesis.

1. General null hypothesis:

There will be no significant difference between the achievement of sixth grade students who study text-type materials with predominantly analysis and evaluation questions and students who study text-type materials with predominantly recall questions.

2. Null sub-hypotheses:

    a. Null sub-hypothesis: reading level:

There will be no significant difference according to reading level between achievement through analysis and evaluation questions as opposed to recall questions.

    b. Null sub-hypothesis: sex of student:

There will be no significant difference according to sex between achievement through analysis and evaluation questions as opposed to recall questions.

    c. Null sub-hypothesis: Interaction:

There will be no significant amount of interaction among type of question, reading level, and sex between the achievement through analysis and evaluation questions as opposed to recall questions.

V. Sample:

1. Size of sample:

The experiment included 11 sixth grade classes in 3 elementary schools.

    a. Total, 260 pupils:

    b. Treatment A: 67 boys + 60 girls = 127.

    c. Treatment B: 55 boys + 78 girls = 133.

2. Representativeness of the sample:

    a. Since the students used in the research were not selected by random design or stratified design, but were used because they were "available," the sample is not representative of any larger universe or population than the 260 students used in the research.

    b. The sample and the "universe" are coterminous.

3. Equivalence of the sub-samples (students in Treatment A and Treatment B):

    a. The classes each as a unit were assigned randomly to Treatment A or Treatment B. This gives basic assurance of equivalence of the students in Treatment A to those in Treatment B.

    b. For greater safeguards, however, sampling statistics were used to test the equivalence of the two sub-samples on I.Q. Score and on Reading Score.

c. Instruments used for collecting data for the sampling statistics were:

    i. California Test of Mental Maturity, S form.

    ii. Stanford Achievement Test, Form W.

d. Equivalence of sub-samples on I.Q.:

    i. Treatment A boys: M-114.84, SD-16.06, N-67.

    ii. Treatment A girls: M-115.80, SD-15.10, N-60.

    iii. Treatment B boys: M-112.07, SD-15.38, N-55.

    iv. Treatment B girls: M-113.11, SD-12.65, N-78.

    v. Analysis of Variance computation for I.Q.scores:

        w. Between Treatment A and Treatment B: no significant difference.

        x. Between boys and girls: no significant difference.

        y. Interaction between treatment and sex: no significant difference.

        z. Hence, I.Q. score was not needed as a covariate in Analysis of Variance of the criterion data (scores on the Unit Test).

e. Equivalence of sub-samples on reading scores:

    i. Treatment A boys: M-38.90, SD-12.18, N-67.

    ii. Treatment A girls: M-41.86, SD-11.45, N-60.

    iii. Treatment B boys: M-36.45, SD-10.39, N-55.

    iv. Treatment B girls: M-39.29, SD-9.74, N-78.

    v. Analysis of Variance computations for Reading Scores:

        w. Between Treatment A and Treatment B: no significant difference.

        x. Between boys and girls: significant difference.

        y. Interaction between treatment and sex: no significant difference.

    z. The significant difference between boys and girls
was not considered influential enough to require
Reading Scores as a covariate in Analysis of
Covariance of criterion data. A significant difference between Treatment A sub-sample and Treatment
B sub-sample would have required Reading Scores as
covariate.

VI. Criterion Data:

1. One total score and 6 sub-scores on a test on Africa, Australia,
and New Zealand, constructed by the researcher. Total score is
the sum of the sub-scores.

2. Criterion data was collected as pretest and as posttest.

VII. Instrument for Collecting Criterion Data:

1. Development of the Unit Test:

    a. Researcher constructed 59 multiple-choice, four-option items
on the unit.

    b. The researcher and two experts on Bloom's Taxonomy served as
a panel of judges to classify the questions into 6 categories:
Knowledge, Comprehension, Application, Analysis, Synthesis,
and Evaluation.

    c. Criterion of classification was 100% agreement among the
judges that a given item belonged in a certain category.
Seventeen items were discarded because this agreement could
not be reached. Four items were retained in the test although
there was not 100% agreement among the judges as to their
classification.

2. Make-up of the Unit Test: Total of 42 items in six sub-sections:

   a. Knowledge, 7 items.

   b. Comprehension, 7 items.

   c. Application, 7 items.

   d. Analysis, 7 items.

   e. Synthesis, 7 items.

   f. Evaluation, 7 items.

3. The reliability of the Unit Test was .68 (Kuder-Richardson
   Formula). This is a low reliability for a standardized test.

VIII. Statistics for Interpreting Criterion Data:

   1. The Criterion Data (total scores on Unit Test) were submitted
       to the statistical Analysis of Covariance, with the pretest
       total unit scores as the covariate.

   2. The Analysis of Covariance model was a 2 x 2 x 4 model (2
       treatments x 2 sexes x 4 reading levels):

   Treatment A   Treatment B

   Boys - Girls   Boys - Girls

   Quartile 1   Quartile 1

   (0 -31)   (0 - 31)

   Quartile 2   Quartile 2

   (32 - 38)   (32 - 38)

   Quartile 3   Quartile 3

   (39 - 47)   (39 - 47)

   Quartile 4   Quartile 4

   (48 - 64)   (48 - 64)

   3. The means of the Total Unit Scores when the students were
       grouped according to reading levels were submitted to t-tests,
       all of which came out significantly different (Q4>Q3>Q2>Q1).

IX. Conclusions:

Analyses of the Criterion Data warrant the following conclusions:

1. The employment of high cognitive-level questions (analysis and evaluation) produced significantly greater scores in social studies achievement than did low cognitive-level questions (knowledge).

2. Better readers in both conditions achieved higher than did poor readers.

3. As a result of these significant differences, the major null hypothesis relating to social studies achievement was rejected.

X. Discussion:

1. Analysis of the sub-tests of the unit test is now being conducted and may provide further evidence of the effects of high-level questions as opposed to low-level questions.

2, There is a cross-over of the treatments because study materials for both groups included questions of the comparison group.

3. A pretest was given to test equivalence of treatment groups, but no report is given as to whether there was a significant difference. This point is interesting because subsequently the pretest score is used as covariate in analysis of covariance.

III. PROPOSAL FOR AN EXPERIMENTAL INVESTIGATION

Associated with teaching:

Analysis of the Topic, Purposing, Hypothesizing,
Data Selection, Data Collection, Tools for Collec-
ting Data, Statistical Interpretation of Data, and
Types of Research.

Before commencing any research activities, the researcher
should have a complete set of plans for his investigation.
These plans are not inexhorable, but they guard against
incomplete or illogical planning. In the course of
research activities, it may prove needful to revise the
details of the plans but the basic structure will invariably
survive from planning to action if the original blue
prints were carefully drawn.

Title: THE INFLUENCE OF TEACHING WITH MULTI-MEDIA ON ACHIEVEMENT
IN SCIENCE AT THE JUNIOR HIGH LEVEL

CHAPTER I. ANALYSIS OF THE TOPIC

The topic is concerned with the impact of the new multi-media
materials on several important factors in teaching-learning.

More specifically, this research will make a contribution to a
theory of teaching science on the junior high level.

Research has been done on the influence of audio-visual materials
on teaching science in the past, and in recent years the new multi-
media have been introduced but little research has been done to evaluate
their effectiveness.

Definitions of terms used in this proposal are as follows:

Multi-media materials: Specifically, loop film casettes, overhead
transparencies, and sound filmstrips.

Science: general science. "Chemistry of the Air," "Water."

Junior high school level: seventh grade.

Achievement: Mastery of knowledge, mastery of processes, teacher
grades, and improvement of attitudes toward science.

The Variables

The independent variable consists of multi-media materials, as
defined above. Treatment **A** The experimental group will be taught
largely with such materials and only a minor part of the time by
traditional classroom lecture and discussion as needed. Treatment
B: The control group will not be taught with any of the above defined
non-printed materials, but will be taught exclusively with printed
materials (textbooks, workbooks, and reference materials.)

The first cognitive dependent variable will be knowledge mastery, as manifested by score on researcher-made tests based on content taught in the experiment. The second cognitive dependent variable will be process mastery as shown by processes in science measured by score on a talent for science test. A general dependent variable will be achievement in school as measured by teacher's grade for the marking period. An affective dependent variable will consist of the student's scores on a researcher-made scale to measure attitude/interest toward science.

The mediating variables involved are: I.Q. of the students, score on the unit pre-test in science, the units taught, score on pre-attitude interest toward science, and teacher qualification. For the first, second, and third mediating variables just mentioned, t-tests will be made of differences between the means of scores of the treatment groups; teaching the same units to both groups will control curriculum; teachers will be matched on degrees, teaching experience, and rating by supervisors.

Survey of the Literature

The new programs in Junior high school science are several years behind the high school programs, but they are now in operation. A typical program is the Intermediate Science Curriculum Study in the 7th, 8th, and 9th grades. The general objective of junior high school science teaching is to give the student an understanding of the nature of science to develop skill in the way scientific knowledge is advanced, and to prepare the student to interpret many of the natural phenomena and much of the technology that confronts him today.[1]

The themes of this particular large-scale project are as follows:

---

[1] Charles E. Richardson and Lawrence E. Oliver, "Intermediate Science Curriculum Study Project as Viewed by Participating Teachers," School Science and Mathematics, LXVIII (December, 1968), 736.

Seventh Grade:

    I. Energy, Its Forms and Characteristics

    II. Measurement and Operational Definitions

Eights Grade:

    I. Matter and Its Composition

    II. Model Building

    III. Open-ended Studies

Ninth Grade:

    To synthesize and extend investigation and knowledge already
gained, and to apply them to problems of practical and
scientific significance.[2]

The new junior high school science curriculum is addressing itself
to the latest curriculum theories as well as bridging the gap in recent
scientific knowledge. For instance, the ISCS seeks to combine the
process approach and the structure approach to curriculum development:
"This program presumes that both of these important aspects of science
can and should be introduced together by allowing concepts to arise out
of student investigation."[3]

The present proposal is not officially associated with the ISCS nor
any other project. However, it is in the mainstream of science education
in junior high school. A more complete description of the status of
science education in Junior High School will be written in the full thesis
from the following sources:

---

[2]Ibid., 787

[3]Ibid., 780

(cf. Education Index, June, 1970 and July, 1969-January, 1970)

I. Science

A. Teaching

1. Junior High Schools

1. N.E. Bingham, "Demonstration of the Role of Science in the Programs of Educationally Deprived Children in Grades 7-9." Science Education, LII (April, 1968), 246-55.

2. A.F. Eiss and G.K. Ofiesh, "Science Education and Educational Technology," Educational Technology, X(January, 1970), 9-69.

3. D.D. Redfield and S.P. Darrow, "ISCS: Intermediate Science Curriculum Study," Physics Teacher, VIII (April, 1970), 170-180.

2. Teaching Aids and Devices

4. E. Selz, "Humanistic Approach to Science Teaching," School Science and Mathematics, LXVIII (December, 1968), 793-806.

5. R.B. Smith and R. Mangum, "Delayed Recall versus Recognition as a Prediction of Higher Level Cognitive Achievement," Psychology in the Schools, VII (April, 1970), 167-171.

6. R.E. Yager, "Critical Thinking and Reference Materials in the Physical Science Classroom," School Science and Mathematics, LXVIII (November, 1968), 743-6.

Experimental Treatment

The experiment will last 10 weeks. The units to be taught are "Chemistry of the Air" (5 weeks) and "Water" (5 weeks). The curriculum guide of the District will be the determiner of content to be included. The same textbook will be used for both groups. Teacher(s) will use only printed materials with control group but a strong emphasis on film casettes, overhead transparencies, and sound filmstrips with the experimental group. The groups will be housed in different junior high schools in the district to prevent cross-over of the experimental treatments. The control group teacher will be the same as the experimental group teacher (the author). All measuring instruments will be administered on the same dates for both groups.

CHAPTER II. COLLECTION OF DATA

The Purposes

This investigation will seek answers to the following questions:

General Purpose: Will students learn science better if taught with
multi-media materials?

Specific Purposes: 1) Will the experimental group learn more in
terms of mastery of knowledge of science (structure)? 2) Will the
experimental group learn more in terms of mastery of processes of science
(talent)? 3) Will the experimental group learn more in terms of
teacher evaluation of achievement (grades)? 4) Will the experimental
group score higher on an attitude/interest toward science scale (affective)?
5) To what extent is there relationship between attitude toward science
and achievement in science (correlation)?

Hypotheses

For each purpose above there is a corresponding hypothesis
expressed in both positive and null forms.

General hypothesis: (Positive) The students taught with multi-
media materials will learn science better than students taught with
printed materials only. (Null) There will be no significant difference
in learning science between the students taught with non-printed multi-
media materials and students taught with conventional printed materials
only.

Specific hypothesis: 1) (Positive) The experimental group will
learn better in terms of mastery of knowledge (structure). (Null) There
will be no significant difference between the scores of the experimental
group and the control group on mastery of knowledge (structure). 2)
(Positive) The experimental group will learn better in terms of mastery

of processes of science (talent). (Null) There will be no significant
difference between the scores of the experimental group and the control
group on mastery of processes of science test (talent). 3) (Positive)
The experimental group will learn better in terms of teacher evaluation
of achievement (grades). (Null) There will be no significant differences
between the evaluation of achievement of the experimental group and
the control group as judged by the teachers (grades). 4) (Positive)
The experimental groups will acquire more favorable attitudes and interests
toward science (affective). (Null) There will be no significant difference
between the scores of the experimental group and the control from a scale to
measure attitude/interest toward science (affective). 5) Achievement
scores of the experimental and control groups will correlate positively
and significantly with their attitude/interest scores (correlation).
(Null) There will not be positive significant correlation between
achievement scores and attitude/interest scores of the experimental group
and those of the control group, nor between the two factors for both
groups combined (correlation).

The hypotheses above are based on research findings which show that
greater science learning occurs from multi-sensory approaches. Also,
the use of multi-media is consistent with the psychology of discovery
learning and inquiry teaching, which are admittedly higher cognitive learning processes.

The Sample

Fifty seventh grade students will be chosen by table of random numbers
from the 400 seventh graders in the school district. The sample will be
representative of the universe of seventh graders in the district. Then
students will be assigned to an experimental group of 25 and a control
group of 25 by the table of random numbers. Random assignment gives as-

surance of the equivalence of the groups. For greater assurance, however, the t-test (pretest) will be made of differences between means as stated under mediating variables. The groups will also be tested for equivalence of their scores on a standardized science test by Educational Testing Service, Cooperative Tests Division, General Science: Cooperative Science Tests, Grades 7-9. Form A. (Princeton, N.J.: Educational Testing Service, 1962-1964). To make these tests of equivalence of the treatment groups, data is organized as follows.

Group Equivalence: I.Q.

Student 1.	Experimental I.Q.	Control I.Q.

Compute Student "t" test

Group Equivalence: Content Pretest

Student 1.	Experimental Pretest	Control Pretest

Compute Student "t" test

Group Equivalence: Pre-attitude

Student 1.	Experimental Attitude	Control Attitude

Compute Student "t" test

Group Equivalence: General Science

Student 1.	Experimental Science	Control Science

Compute Student "t" test

Criterion Data

The criterion data will consist of the posttest scores on all the dependent variables: Structure of knowledge, Process of knowledge, school achievement, and attitude/interest.

Instrument for Collecting Data

1) For specific purpose "knowledge mastery": Researcher-made multiple choice tests on content in the units. 2) For specific purpose process: Science Service, Inc., Science Background: A Science Service Test to Identify Potential Scientific and Technical Talent. Grades 4-9. 1957-1958. Science Service, Inc. 1719 "N" St., N.W., Washington D.C. 20036. 3) For specific purpose school achievement: Teacher grades. 4) For specific purpose attitude: Researcher-made scale to measure attitude toward science. This scale is to be specially constructed. The students will be requested to write essays on their attitudes and interest toward science as a subject. Cues will be drawn from the essays for items in the scale. A Likert-type scale will be constructed (Strong Agreement, Agreement, Uncertain, Disagreement, Strong Disagreement). 5) For specific purpose correlation: The scores on researcher-made unit tests and the attitude scale will provide the data to determine correlation.

CHAPTER III. INFLUENCE ON COGNITIVE ACHIEVEMENT

The measurements from the researcher-made tests, the science talent test, and the teacher grades represent cognitive achievement. Teacher grade is in quality points. Otherwise stated, these data show knowledge mastery of science. The measurements are reported and statistically interpreted in this chapter.

A. Presentation of Data

This section shows tabular organization of the cognitive criterion data.

Table I. Criterion Data of the Experimental Group

Student	Content Test		Process Test		Teacher Grade
	Pre	Post	Pre	Post	
1.	X	X	X	X	X

Table II. Criterion Data of the Control Group

Student	Content Test Pre Y	Post Y	Process Test Pre Y	Post Y	Teacher Grade Y

B. Statistical Computations

This section shows tabular organization and statistical computations for the purposes set in this chapter.

Table III. Significance of difference between the experimental and the control group on the content posttest

Student 1.	Experimental X	Control Y

Compute Student "t" test between X and Y.

Table IV. Significance of difference between the experimental and the control group on the science process posttest.

Student 1.	Experimental X	Control Y

Compute Student "t" test between X and Y.

Table V. Significance of difference between the experimental and the control group on school achievement (teacher's grades).

Student 1.	Experimental X	Control Y

Compute Student "t" test between X and Y.

Table VI. Factorial Analysis of Variance between the experimental and the control group on the content test with the process test as main effect. (2x2 model)

Treatment:	Experimental		Control	
Process:	High	Low	High	Low
Student				
1.	X1	X2	Y1	Y2

Compute two-way Analysis of Variance.

C. Chapter Findings

Statement of findings based on statistical results. Discussion of the findings.

CHAPTER IV.   INFLUENCE ON ATTITUDE

The measurements from the Attitude Scale will be reported and interpreted in this chapter. The chapter will deal with the affective condition of the students toward science study. Interpretation involves statistical analysis of the relationships of these scores to other data as well as difference between the groups on attitude.

A.   Presentation of Data

Table VII.   Scores of the Experimental Group and the Control Group on Attitude Toward Science Scale.

Student	Experimental		Control	
	Pre	Post	Pre	Post
1.	X	X	Y	Y

B.   Statistical Computations

Table VIII.   Significance of Difference between the experimental and the control group on attitude toward Science Posttest

Student	Experimental	Control
1.	X	Y

Compute Student "t" test

Table IX.   Relationship between attitude toward science and content scores for experimental and control groups combined.

Student	Attitude	Content
1.	X	v

Compute Pearson Product-Moment correlation coefficient γ.

Table X.   Relationship between attitude toward science and process scores for the experimental and the control groups combined.

Student	Attitude	Process
1.	X	Y

Compute Pearson Product-Moment correlation coefficient γ.

Table XI.   Relationship between attitude toward science and teacher grades for the experimental and the control groups combined.

Student	Attitude	Teacher Grade
1.	X	Y

Compute Pearson Product-Moment Correlation Coefficient γ.

C. Chapter Findings

Statement of findings based on statistical results. Discussion of the findings.

CHAPTER V. CONCLUSIONS AND DISCUSSION

It is hoped that in this chapter it will be possible to report that the hypotheses will be supported by the data. Findings will be reported in line with the stated purposes.

Discussion will report weaknesses that occurred in the design to control variables, in sampling and in inaccuracies in measurements, effect of limitation of the study in time and numbers. Elements of the research design which proved especially effective will also be reported and discussed.

Conclusions will be formulated, especially those overarching all the data and the entire investigation. Implications of the conclusions for educational theory and practice will be pointed out. Recommendations for application of the conclusions will be made.

BIBLIOGRAPHY

Education Index: Science-Teaching Methods, Science-Tests and Scales

R.R. Carter and M.F. McClellan, "Library-Use Program," Science Teacher, XXXVI (January, 1969), 66-7.

J. Denton, "Audio-Tutorial Instruction in Science," School and Community, LVI (April, 1970), 13+.

W.K. Esler, "Structuring: Inquiry for Classroom Use," School Science and Mathematics, LXX (May, 1970), 454-8.

M.F. Fleming, "S-A-P Approach to Teaching Second Level: Science-As-Process," American Biology Teacher, XXXII (March, 1970), 168-9.

P.B. Hounshell and E.L. West, Jr. "Trends in the Teaching of Science," High School Journal, LIII (January, 1970), 207-15.

L.V. Rasmussen, "Individualizing Science Education," Educational Techonology, X (January, 1970), 53-56.

D.D. Redfield and S.P. Darrow, "ISCS: Intermediate Science Curriculum Study," Physics Teacher, VIII (April, 1970), 170-180.

J. Short, "Writing Criterion Test Items in Science," Educational Technology, X (January, 1970), 46-8.

A.G. Storey, "Versatile Multiple-Choice Item," Journal of Educational Research, LXII (December, 1968), 169-72.

II. REPORTED SURVEY INVESTIGATION

Associated with teaching:

Analysis of the topic, Purposing,

Hypothesizing, Data Selection, Data

Collection, Tools for Collecting Data,

Critical Interpretation of Data,

Statistical Interpretation of Data,

Types of Research, and Written Report.

The survey investigation has a research

design just as the experimental investigation

has a design. Insights into the survey design

are criteria for evaluating the findings of

the study. A sound research design in a survey

is essential to the validity of the details

about the present record as to who? what?

when? where? how? and why?

Oral Questioning Practices of Teachers
in Social Studies Classes

JOHN VANCE GODBOLD *

"QUESTIONS have always been the stock-in-trade of teachers" (Sanders, 1966). The wide use of the question and answer form of class discussion provides questioning with an impact on instruction. The extensive use of questioning as a teaching strategy has caused it to be the focus of a number of recent investigations (Floyd, 1960; Aschner, 1961; Adams, 1964; Hudgins, 1968; Hunkins, 1968; Rodgers, 1968).

Several investigations involving verbal interaction in the classroom have produced evidence concerning the influence of teacher questions in three general areas of the instructional program: student thinking, the social-emotional climate of the classroom, and the mastery of subject matter information (Flanders, 1960; Aschner, 1961; Smith and Meux, 1962; Gallagher and Aschner, 1963; Taba and Elzy, 1964; Bellack, 1966). The growing body of evidence indicating the importance of teacher-questioning in instruction provides a need to identify those factors which influence the nature of such questioning.

The present study hypothesizes that organizational setting (elementary contrasted with secondary), with all that it represents in terms of teacher preparation, instructional program, and the length of a teacher's professional experience (two years or less contrasted with five years or more), may be factors which influence the number and cognitive levels of questions teachers ask. In an effort to describe what relationship exists between the factors mentioned above and teacher-questioning, the present study pro-

poses to describe and compare the questioning practices of elementary and secondary teachers with varying amounts of teaching experience.

Questions for which answers were sought in pursuing this investigation were:

1. What are the questioning practices of teachers during oral class discussion of social studies material?

   a. What are the questioning practices of elementary teachers with two years or less of teaching experience (Elementary Group A) during oral class discussions of social studies material?

   b. What are the questioning practices of elementary teachers with five or more years of teaching experience (Elementary Group B) during oral class discussions of social studies material?

   c. What are the questioning practices of secondary social studies teachers with two years or less of teaching experience (Secondary Group A) during oral class discussions of social studies material?

   d. What are the questioning practices of secondary social studies teachers with five or more years of teaching experience (Secondary Group B) during oral class discussions of social studies material?

2. Is there a difference between the questioning practices of elementary teachers and those of secondary teachers during the oral class discussion of social studies material?

*John Vance Godbold, Assistant Professor of Education, East Texas State University, Commerce

3. Is there a difference between teachers with two years or less of teaching experience (Group A) and teachers with five years or more of teaching experience (Group B) in regard to their questioning practices during oral class discussion of social studies material?

4. Does the difference between the oral questioning practices of elementary teachers and those of secondary teachers during class discussions of social studies material vary in regard to the length of teaching experience?

Procedures

Sample. A "purposive sampling" design (Mouly, 1963) was used to select the subjects of this study from the teaching staffs of four junior high schools and four elementary schools in a large metropolitan school district in a populous Southeastern state. A total of 32 teachers, divided equally into four groups, participated in the study.

"Elementary Group A" consisted of eight teachers who were currently teaching in grades four, five, or six. In addition, they shared the following characteristics: (a) held a state teaching certificate in elementary education; (b) graduated from an undergraduate program in elementary education; and (c) had two years or less of teaching experience in the elementary school and no experience teaching in secondary school. The teachers in this group were deployed across the three grade levels as follows: two in grade four and three each in grades five and six.

"Elementary Group B" consisted of eight teachers who were currently teaching grades four, five, or six. They shared the same certification and undergraduate teacher preparation characteristics as the "Elementary Group A" teachers. Each of the teachers in "Elementary Group B" had five years or more of elementary school teaching experience and no secondary school teaching experience. The teachers in this group were deployed across the three grade levels as follows: three in grade four, two in grade five, and three in grade six.

"Secondary Group A" consisted of eight teachers who were currently teaching social

studies in grades seven, eight, or nine. They shared the following characteristics: (a) held a state teaching certificate in secondary social studies; (b) graduated from an undergraduate program in secondary education with subject matter specialization in social studies; and (c) had two years or less of teaching experience in secondary social studies and no elementary school teaching experience. The teachers in this group were deployed across the three grade levels as follows: three in grade seven, four in grade eight, and one in grade nine.

"Secondary Group B" consisted of eight teachers who were currently teaching social studies in grades seven, eight, or nine. They shared the same certification and undergraduate preparation characteristics as the "Secondary Group A" teachers. Each of the teachers in "Secondary Group B" had five years or more of experience teaching social studies in secondary school and no experience teaching in elementary school. The teachers in this group were deployed across the three grade levels as follows: four in grade seven and two each in grades eight and nine.

Collection of Data. Data for this investigation were derived from audio-tape recordings of social studies class discussions directed by the participating teachers. Fifty minutes of taped material was obtained for each teacher. Such material was obtained during one or more taping sessions for each teacher.

Administrative personnel in each school supervised the production of tapes. Printed material entitled *Suggested Taping Procedures* was distributed to ensure that taping procedures would conform to the needs of the study. The following statement contained in the above material represents the instructions given to participants concerning the type of class activity to be taped: "The class activity taped should be one in which the teacher is directing a class discussion in social studies."

Each tape was analyzed in terms of the questions asked by the teacher. For this purpose an instrument was developed for classifying and noting sequencing of questions.

The system of question classification used in the instrument was developed by Norris Sanders (1966). Sanders (1966) states that his "taxonomy of questions" is an application of the ideas presented in the *Taxonomy of Educational Objectives*, edited by B. S. Bloom.

As the "taxonomy of questions" was not developed exclusively for an analysis of oral questioning, a pilot tape revealed that an instrument for analyzing oral questioning would need an additional category, "routine." The inclusion of the "routine" category in the instrument used in this investigation provided for the recording and classification of such questions as: "Will you repeat that?" "Does anyone know where the chalk is?" The eight cognitive categories included in the instrument were memory, translation, interpretation, application, analysis, synthesis, evaluation, and routine.

Each question asked was noted on the instrument in regard to its classification and order of occurrence. Questions which were repeated verbatim in response to a request for clarification or in the process of continuing discussion were noted only once. Such a procedure was needed, since the total number of questions asked is one of the major considerations of this study.

Each tape was analyzed independently by two observers. A comparison was made between the two reports of each tape. Where differences occurred, that portion of the tape was reviewed jointly by the two observers in an effort to identify explanations for the differences. Where consensus regarding the disputed question could not be reached, a third qualified observer was secured to participate in a jury to review the tape and make a decision.

Statistical comparisons were made between varying combinations of the four teacher groups to determine the degree to which teacher-questioning practices in terms of the number of questions asked and the cognitive level of questions asked were related to the factors of organizational setting and length of teacher experience. The use of chi square made possible the determination of the degree of difference between groups in regard to the distribution of questions asked among the observational categories. Differences at the .05 level were considered to be significant.

To determine the degree of variability among the teachers within each group, a test of "difference in population proportions" using the Z statistic as described by Wyatt and Bridges (1967) was employed. For these statistical comparisons, the categories of "memory" and "interpretation" were used, as they accounted for the major portion of questions asked by every teacher. Differences at the .05 level were considered to be significant.

Findings

Four questions were posed concerning the relationship between teacher-questioning and organizational setting and length of teaching experience. Questioning practices of teachers were described in terms of the

	Category of Question								
	Memory	Translation	Interpretation	Application	Analysis	Synthesis	Evaluation	Routine	Total
Total number[a] of questions asked	423	41	118	2	0	13	7	20	624
Mean number[b] of questions asked	52.88	5.10	14.75	.25	0	1.63	.88	2.5	78
Percentage of the total number of questions asked	67.78	6.57	18.91	.32	0	2.08	1.12	3.20	99.98

[a] By the eight teachers during a total of 6.66 hours of class discussion.
[b] By an individual teacher during 50 minutes of class discussion.

Table 1. Analysis of Questions Asked by Elementary Group A
(Two or Less Years of Teaching Experience)

			Category of Question						
	Memory	Translation	Interpre-tation	Appli-cation	Analysis	Synthesis	Evalua-tion	Routine	Total
Total number[a] of questions asked	393	32	135	2	0	5	6	14	587
Mean number[b] of questions asked	49.12	4	16.88	.25	0	.63	.75	1.75	73.38
Percentage of the total number of questions asked	66.95	5.45	22.99	.34	0	.85	1.02	2.38	99.98

[a] By the eight teachers during a total of 6.66 hours of class discussion.
[b] By an individual teacher during 50 minutes of class discussion.

Table 2. Analysis of Questions Asked by Elementary Group B
(Five or More Years of Teaching Experience)

number and cognitive level of questions asked.

Question 1. Question 1 asks for a description of the questioning practices of each of the teacher groups representing differences in organizational setting and length of teaching experience. Tables 1, 2, 3, and 4 describe the questioning practices of each of the four groups. Table 5 presents a compilation of the questions asked by all the participating teachers.

The questioning practices of the groups of teachers identified for this investigation differed in varying degrees in both the number and cognitive level of questions asked. Two statements concerning questioning practices hold true for all four groups. At least 54 percent of the questions asked by each of the four groups fell into the "memory" category. Second, those categories above "interpretation" were the most neglected. For example, no questions were asked in the "analysis" category.

All of the groups were characterized by some degree of variation among individuals in the number and distribution of questions asked as revealed by difference in proportion Z statistic. However, within each of the groups, one or more fairly tight patterns involving varying members of the group were identified. The less experienced secondary group appears to be the most internally consistent.

Question 2. Question 2 concerns the differences between the questioning practices of elementary teachers and the questioning

practices of secondary teachers. When compared without regard to experience, elementary teachers asked 33.66 percent more questions and were significantly different beyond the .001 level from secondary teachers in the distribution of questions among the cognitive level categories.

Among the less experienced teachers, the elementary teachers asked 59.18 percent more questions and were significantly different beyond the .001 level from secondary teachers in the distribution of questions among the cognitive level categories.

When the more experienced teacher groups were compared, the elementary teachers asked 14.2 percent more questions and were significantly different at the .001 level from secondary teachers in the distribution of questions among the cognitive level categories.

Among both the less and the more experienced teachers, the elementary teachers asked more questions in the memory and translation categories and fewer questions in the categories above interpretation than did the secondary teachers.

Question 3. Question 3 explores the relationship between teacher-questioning practices and the length of teaching experience. When the two elementary groups were compared, the less experienced elementary teachers asked 6.59 percent more questions than did the more experienced elementary teachers. There was no significant difference between the two elementary groups in the distribution of questions asked.

The more experienced secondary teachers asked 31.12 percent more questions than did the less experienced secondary teachers. In regard to the distribution of questions asked, the two secondary groups were significantly different.

Perhaps it should be noted at this point that comparisons of distribution of questions across organizational setting lines produced differences that were significant beyond the .001 level. The same comparisons made across experience group lines within the elementary and secondary settings produced no significant difference in the elementary group and a difference which was not significant beyond the .05 level in the secondary group.

Question 4. Question 4 asks if the differences between elementary and secondary teachers vary with a shift in the length of teaching experience. The differences between the less experienced elementary and secondary groups are represented by the elementary group's asking 59.18 percent more questions than the secondary group, and a difference in the distribution of questions which is significant beyond the .001 level. The differences between the more experienced elementary and secondary groups are represented by the elementary group's asking 14.2 percent more questions than did the secondary group, and a difference in the distribution of questions which is significant beyond the .001 level.

As a shift is made from the less to the more experienced groups, the difference between elementary and secondary teachers in terms of the total number of questions asked decreases. However, both the less and the more experienced elementary teachers are significantly different beyond the .001 level from secondary teachers of like experience in the distribution of questions asked.

Conclusions

1. Questions requiring direct recall of information are the most common type found in oral teacher-questioning during class discussions of social studies material.

2. Among the teachers participating in this study, elementary teachers differed from secondary teachers in the number and cognitive level of questions asked during oral discussions of social studies material.

3. The results of this investigation do not indicate a clear-cut relationship between teacher-questioning practices during social studies class discussions and length of teaching experience. A significant difference was noted, however, for the experienced secondary group.

Discussion

There is a growing body of evidence which indicates that teacher-questioning has an influence on pupil thinking, social-emotional climate of the classroom, and pupil mastery of subject matter material. Can some indication be gained from the results of this study as to what changes are needed in the questioning practices of teachers?

A look at the questioning practices of

	Category of Question								
	Memory	Translation	Interpretation	Application	Analysis	Synthesis	Evaluation	Routine	Total
Total number[a] of questions asked	215	17	124	19	0	7	12	8	392
Mean number[b] of questions asked	26.88	.88	15.5	2.38	0	.88	1.5	1	49
Percentage of the total number of questions asked	54.84	1.78	31.63	4.84	0	1.78	3.06	2.09	99.97

[a] By the eight teachers during a total of 6.66 hours of class discussion.
[b] By an individual teacher during 50 minutes of class discussion.

Table 3. Analysis of Questions Asked by Secondary Group A
(Two or Less Years of Teaching Experience)

	Category of Question								
	Memory	Translation	Interpre-tation	Appli-cation	Analysis	Synthesis	Evalua-tion	Routine	Total
Total number [a] of questions asked	312	27	126	19	0	7	16	7	514
Mean number [b] of questions asked	39	3.38	15.75	2.38	0	.88	2	.88	64.25
Percentage of the total number of questions asked	60.7	5.25	24.51	3.69	0	1.36	3.11	1.36	99.98

[a] By the eight teachers during a total of 6.66 hours of class discussion.
[b] By an individual teacher during 50 minutes of class discussion.

Table 4. Analysis of Questions Asked by Secondary Group B
(Five or More Years of Teaching Experience)

the teachers participating in this study indicates a need for programs intended to help teachers increase the number of questions asked at higher cognitive levels. If one of the objectives of social studies instruction is the development of thinking skills, it is reasonable to assume that students should be called upon to respond to questions at varying cognitive levels. Sanders (1966) states that a minimum of one-third of the time allotted to questioning should be devoted to levels above memory. Most of the teachers observed in the course of this investigation asked at least half of their questions in the memory category. Those levels above interpretation were particularly neglected.

There is no clear implication from this investigation as to whether the elementary or the secondary teachers have the greater need for a program to increase the number of questions asked above memory. Though the elementary teachers asked a larger propor-

tion of their questions in the memory category, the actual number of questions asked above it was approximately the same for both elementary and secondary groups.

However, there is some evidence that the secondary teachers explored the higher cognitive levels to a greater degree than did the elementary teachers. The secondary teachers asked approximately twice as many questions in the application through evaluation categories. This circumstance is somewhat mitigated by the consideration for variability among individuals. One of the factors which may contribute to such variability is the precise nature of the social studies content being considered.

Three limitations should be kept in mind when considering the possible implications of this investigation:

1. The questioning practices of the teachers in each of the groups were characterized by a degree of individual variation.

	Category of Question								
	Memory	Translation	Interpre-tation	Appli-cation	Analysis	Synthesis	Evalua-tion	Routine	Total
Elementary									
Number [a]	816	73	253	4	0	18	13	34	1,211
Percent	67.38	6.02	20.89	.33	0	1.48	1.07	2.80	99.97
Secondary									
Number [a]	527	34	250	38	0	14	28	15	906
Percent	58.16	3.75	27.59	4.19	0	1.54	3.09	1.65	99.97
Total									
Number [b]	1,343	107	503	42	0	32	41	49	2,117
Percent	63.43	5.05	23.76	1.98	0	1.51	1.93	2.31	99.97

[a] Questions asked by 16 teachers during a total of 13.33 hours of class discussion.
[b] Questions asked by 32 teachers during a total of 26.66 hours of class discussion.

Table 5. Analysis of Questions Asked by Participating Teachers

2. Care must be exercised when generalizing from the sample in this investigation to other teacher groups.

3. Though this investigation produced a statistically significant relationship between organizational setting and teacher-questioning practices, this does not necessarily indicate a cause and effect relationship.

This investigation did not formally consider issues relating to the relative instructional value of questioning other than the number and cognitive level of the questions employed. However, in the process of the investigation the author concluded that questions at the same cognitive level varied in their overall instructional value as a result of the content students were asked to consider. In the author's view, efforts intended to improve teacher-questioning practices must include concern for the number and cognitive level of questions asked and the potential contribution of question content to instructional objectives.

More research is needed to determine the most desirable questioning practices for stimulating pupil thinking, establishing a supportive climate in the classroom, and enhancing pupil mastery of subject matter information. When more precise information of this nature is available, the differences in the questioning practices of elementary and secondary teachers may have more significance.

References

Thomas H. Adams. "The Development of a Method of Analysis of Questions Asked by Teachers in Classroom Discourse." Doctor's thesis. New Brunswick: Rutgers, The State University, 1964. Abstract: *Dissertation Abstracts* 25: 2809; 1964.

Mary Jane McCue Aschner. "An Analysis of Verbal Behavior in the Classroom." In: Arno A. Bellack, editor. *Theory and Research in Teaching.* New York: Bureau of Publications, Teachers College, Columbia University, 1963.

Mary Jane Aschner. "The Language of Teaching." In: B. O. Smith and R. H. Ennis, editors. *Language and Concepts in Education.* Chicago: Rand McNally & Company, 1961.

Arno A. Bellack and others. *The Language of the Classroom.* New York: Teachers College Press, Teachers College, Columbia University, 1966.

Benjamin S. Bloom, editor. *Teaching Early Adolescents To Think.* Danville, Illinois: Interstate Printers and Publishers, 1960.

Ned A. Flanders. *Teacher Influence, Pupil Attitudes, and Achievement.* U.S. Department of Health, Education, and Welfare, U.S. Office of Education Cooperative Research Project No. 397. Minneapolis: University of Minnesota, 1960.

William D. Floyd. "An Analysis of the Oral Questioning Activity of Selected Colorado Primary Classrooms." Doctor's thesis. Greeley: Colorado State College, 1960. Abstract: *Abstracts of Field Studies for the Degree of Doctor of Education* 22: 48; 1960.

J. J. Gallagher and Mary Jane Aschner. "A Preliminary Report on Analysis of Classroom Interaction." *Merrill-Palmer Quarterly* 9: 183-94; July 1963.

Bryce B. Hudgins and William P. Ahlbrand, Jr. "Teachers' Demands and Students' Thinking." *Educational Leadership* 25: 583-89; March 1968.

Marie M. Hughes. "Utah Study of the Assessment of Teaching." In: Arno A. Bellack, editor. *Theory and Research in Teaching.* New York: Bureau of Publications, Teachers College, Columbia University, 1963.

Francis P. Hunkins. "The Influence of Analysis and Evaluation Questions on Achievement in Sixth Grade Social Studies." *Educational Leadership* 25: 326-32; January 1968.

G. L. Miller. "The Teacher and Inquiry." *Educational Leadership* 23: 550-55; April 1966.

George J. Mouly. *The Science of Educational Research.* New York: American Book Company, 1963.

Frederick A. Rodgers. "Effects of Classroom Questions on the Selection of Resources and Responses by Undergraduate and Sixth-Grade Students." *Educational Leadership* 26: 265-74; December 1968.

Norris M. Sanders. *Classroom Questions: What Kinds?* New York: Harper & Row, Publishers, 1966.

B. O. Smith and Milton Meux. *A Study of the Logic of Teaching.* U.S. Office of Education Cooperative Research Project No. 258 (7257). Urbana: University of Illinois, 1962.

Hilda Taba and Freeman Elzy. "Teaching Strategies and Thought Processes." *Teachers College Record* 65: 524-34; March 1964.

Woodrow W. Wyatt and Charles M. Bridges, Jr. *Statistics for the Behavioral Sciences.* Boston: D. C. Heath & Company, 1967. □

BRIEF OF A SURVEY INVESTIGATION

(Associated with teaching Analysis of Topic, Purposing,
Hypothesizing, Data Selection, Data Collection, Tools
for Collecting Data, Statistical Interpretation of
Data, Types of Research and Written Report)

John Vance Godbold, "Oral Questioning Practices of
Teachers in Social Studies Classes, "Educational
Leadership," XXVII (October, 1970), 61-67.

I. Analysis of the Topic.

This topic deals with the use of questions and
answers as a form of class discussion. It seeks
evidence of conditions under which oral questions are
effective in teaching.

A. Review of Literature.

Research has been done on oral questioning
strategy by Floyd, Aschner, Adams, Hudgin, Hunkins, and
Rodgers. Research findings have been reported by
Flanders, Aschner, Smith and Neux, Gallagher and Aschner,
Taba and Elzy, and Bellach, that verbal interaction in
the classroom influences student thinking, social-
emotional climate of the classroom, and mastery of
subject matter information. There is need for further
research to identify factors that influence the effectiveness of questioning in teaching.

B. The Topic Variables.

1. Independent Variable: The independent variable
surveyed is the use of questions and answers as
teaching strategy.

2. Descriptive Variables: The dimensions in terms of which oral questioning is described in the investigation are: the types, i.e. , categories of questions utilized, and the frequency of their usage. The categories of questions included are: memory, translation, interpretation, application, analysis, synthesis, evaluation, and routine. Frequencies involved are frequencies by type of question, and total frequencies.

3. Mediating Variables: The mediating variables which affected the independent variable in the survey included grade level, years, and level of teaching experience, and professional preparation. The combinations of levels of education and years of teaching experience are different environments in which the present record of use of questions is established. The social studies limits the study of questioning to that field of knowledge.

II. Collecting the Data.

A. Purposes: The purposes of the investigation are clearly stated.

1. General Purpose: What are the questioning practices of teachers during oral class discussion in the field of the social studies?

2. Specific Purposes:

2.1 What are the questioning practices of elementary

school teachers with 2 years or less experience?

2.2 What are the questioning practices of elementary school teachers with 5 years or more
experience?

2.3 What are the questioning practices of secondary school teachers with 2 years or less
experience?

2.4 What are the questioning practices of secondary school teachers with 5 years or more
experience?

2.5 Are there differences between questioning
practices of elementary school teachers
and those of secondary school teachers?

2.6 Are there differences between questioning
practices of teachers with 2 years or less
experience and those with 5 years or more
experience?

B. Hypothesis: The hypotheses are easily identified.

1. General Hypothesis: There are differences in oral
questioning practices of elementary, and secondary
school teachers who have varying years of teaching
experience.

2. Specific Hypotheses:

2.1 (Positive). Questioning practices of elementary

school teachers with five or more years of teaching experience differ significantly from those of elementary school teachers with two or less years of teaching experience.

2.1 (Null). There are no significant differences between the questioning practices of elementary school teachers with five or more years of teaching experience and those of elementary school teachers with two or less years of teaching experience.

2.2 (Positive). Questioning practices of secondary school teachers with five or more years of teaching experience differ significantly from those of secondary school teachers with two or less years of teaching experience.

2.2 (Null). There are no significant differences between the questioning practices of secondary school teachers with five or more years of teaching experience and those of secondary school teachers with two or less years of teaching experience.

3.1 (Positive). The questioning practices of all elementary school teachers differ significantly from those of all secondary school teachers.

3.1 (Null). There are no significant differences between the questioning practices of all elementary school teachers and those of all secondary school teachers.

3.2 (Positive). The questioning practices of all teachers with five or more years of teaching experience differ significantly from those of all teachers with two or less years of teaching experience.

3.2 (Null). There are no significant differences between the questioning practices of all teachers with five or more years of teaching experience and those of all teachers with two or less years of teaching experience.

C. Sample. There were four groups of eight teachers each, two groups on the elementary level and two groups on the secondary level. On the elementary level eight teachers had taught two years or less in grades 4,5,6, and eight had taught five years or more. All sixteen of these teachers had an elementary certificate, had graduated in elementary education, and had no teaching experience on the secondary level. On the secondary level, eight teachers had taught two years or less in grades 7,8,9, and eight had taught five years or more. All sixteen of these teachers had a secondary certificate in social studies, had gradua-

ted in secondary education, and had no teaching experience on the elementary level.

D. <u>Criterion Data</u>. The criterion data - types and frequencies of questions- was derived from audio-tape
recordings of 50 minutes of social studies class
discussions directed by each of the participating
teachers. The tapes were analyzed to obtain tallies
of how many of each of the following categoties of
questions were utilized: memory, translation, interpretation, application, analysis, synthesis, evaluation, and routine. These tallies yielded subtotals
by cognitive level of questions, and total questions
asked. The tallies and totals for each teacher
constitute the criterion data in the survey.

E. <u>Tool for Collecting Data</u>. The basic tool for
collecting data was the audio tape recorder, but
the principal tool was the taxonomy of categories
of questions listed above.

F. <u>Statistical Interpretation of Criterion Data</u>. The
Z statistic, which is a test of difference in population proportions was computed for the categories
"memory" and "interpretation" questions. These two
accounted for the major portion of questions asked
by every teacher.

III. Findings and Conclusions.

    A. Findings.

        The findings can be reported according to questions set forth as purposes. The first four specific questions asked for factual reports on the oral questioning practices of each category of teacher. Each question is answered by a table reporting the facts for each category of teachers, and a fifth table gives a total summary of the previous four tables.

        Question 5 asks if elementary teachers differ from secondary teachers in oral questioning practices. As to total amount of questions, elementary school teachers asked significantly more questions in both the less experienced and the more experienced teacher types than secondary school teachers. As to cognitive level of questions asked, the elementary school teachers asked more lower level of questions, and the secondary school teachers asked significantly more higher level questions.

        Question 6 asked if there are differences between less experienced teachers and more experienced teachers. More experienced elementary school teachers did not ask more questions than less experienced elementary school teachers. More experienced secondary school teachers, however, asked significantly more questions than less experienced secondary school teachers.

As to level of questions asked, there was no significant difference between less experienced and more
experienced elementary school teachers, but more
experienced secondary school teachers asked higher
level cognitive questions than less experienced secondary school teachers.

B. Discussion.

The purposes and hypotheses of this investigation
were more thoroughly and clearly stated than in most
research reports.

The sampling technique used is not a representative procedure. There is no research evidence that
the 32 teachers represent any universe greater than
themselves. The findings cannot be generalized with
any assurance beyond the 32 classes involved.

The taping of lessons and analyzing them by the
taxonomy of questions is commendable and well done.

The use of the Z statistic which his source
(Wyatt and Bridges) terms a difference in population
proportions is an application of the Student-t-test to
differences between proportions instead of between
means. This is a valuable contribution to analyzing
descriptive research data, for there are not many
such statistical procedures. The researcher also

applies Z computations to the "distribution of questions" as testing differences among more than two population proportions. This however, is really the Chi square procedure worked out with proportions rather than frequencies. The same results could have been obtained with frequencies, computing Chi square for equi-probability and for independence of factors.

The researcher had a good design for collecting and interpreting data. His written report of findings is well organized around his purposes, but he could state the strength of each finding with greater clarity. Sometimes he indicates level of significance, but sometimes he doesn't.

XII. PROPOSAL FOR A SURVEY INVESTIGATION

Associated with teaching:

Analysis of the Topic, Purposing, Hypothesizing,

Data Selection, Data Collection, Tools for Collecting

Data, Critical Interpretation of Data, Statistical

Interpretation of Data, Types of Research.

PROPOSAL FOR SURVEY RESEARCH

Multi-Media Utilized in Teaching Seventh Grade Science

(Associated with teaching analysis of the Topic, Purposing, Hypothesizing, Data Selection, Data Collection, Tools for Collecting Data, Critical Interpretation of Data, Statistical Interpretation of Data, Types of Research).

CHAPTER I. ANALYSIS OF THE TOPIC:

The topic is concerned with the use of new multi-media materials in teaching science at the seventh grade level. This research will help to establish the present record (who, what, when, why, where, how) for using multi-media in teaching science in junior high school.

Research has been done on trends in teaching junior high school science by Hounshell and West, on the new science curriculum by Redfield and Darrow, and on teaching junior high school science by Esler, Fleming, and Rasmussen. Denton has researched audio-tutorial instruction, but no research has directly surveyed the use of multi-media materials in teaching science in junior high school. Eiss and Ofiesh, and Przekop have reported the use of various media and materials in teaching science. Newport and McNeill have researched the effectiveness of Science - A - Process Approach. Finally, Vitrogan has done research and development in teaching science to the socially disadvantaged.

Definitions of terms used in this proposal are as follows:

Multi-media materials: materials which involve two or more sensory

approaches in learning - visual, audio,
tactile sensory impressions.

Teaching science: planning and guiding the learning activities
of students to increase their knowledge of
science.

Seventh grade: 8th year in school whether as part of K-8,
middle school, or junior high school.

Analysis of this topic includes: the independent variable, the
descriptive variables, and mediating variables.

Independent Variable: The independent variable is multi-media
materials, a factor which may improve the learning of children. In
this survey, the media include: 1) motion pictures, 2) filmstrips,
3) slides, 4) 8mm loop film casettes, or reels, 5) audio casettes or
records, 6) overhead transparencies; graphics: charts, graphs, diagrams,
plates, 7) manipulables: models, mock-ups, reproductions, 8) specimens,
9) laboratory experiments, 10) field trips, 11) videotapes, 12) television.

Descriptive Variables: The descriptive variables are the functions
inherent in teaching science. In this survey they are: 1) developing
in students mastery of science concepts (structure of science), 2) developing in students mastery of mental processes in science (processes of
science), and 3) developing in students an interest in learning science
(motivation for science). These are the dimensions of teaching science
for which this investigation will attempt to determine which of the
above multi-media materials are being used.

Mediating Variables: The mediating variables are the factors
which have a causal relationship to the independent variable. In the
descriptive investigation, mediating variables have the roles of providing the structure for stratifying the survey sample, and providing

the structure for organizing the data with a view to interpreting it.
They are different environments in which the independent variable is
surveyed. In the survey of multi-media used in teaching seventh grade
science, the mediating variables are: type and size of school, size and
social economic level of community, and demographic location of the
community: urban, suburban, rural. The school may influence the use
of multi-media materials in teaching science according as it is small,
intermediate size, large, and as organized as K-6, Middle, or Junior
High School. The characteristics of the science teacher which may
affect the use of multi-media are: whether the teacher is male or
female; his/her number of years of teaching experience; also, whether
the teacher has a Bachelor's Degree, Master's Degree, Sixth Year
Certificate, Doctoral Degree; also, years of experience as a science
teacher; and finally whether the teacher has had preservice or in-service
preparation in using multi-media materials. The students may influence
the use of multi-media materials according as they are below average,
average, or above average in ability. Finally, the school's community
environment may be related to use of multi-media according as it is:
rural, suburban, urban-disadvantaged, urban blue collar, urban white
collar, urban advantaged. Information on these mediating variables will
be solicited as general information on the instrument for collecting
the data in the survey.

Survey of the Literature

The focus in junior high school science teaching today is on new
curriculum materials and the use of multi-media in teaching science is
receiving exposure in the literature of the field. The research reported
reveals use of multi-media in teaching science. One of the sources on

which this remark is based surveyed the use of instructional resources, broadly considered, in 35 randomly selected Missouri high schools.[1] Part of the investigation surveyed the use of "instructional media." The data are set forth in the table partially reproduced below. The table also represented a break down of the data for rural, urban, and suburban schools.

Table IV. Number and Per Cent of Science Teachers Who Used Various Instructional Media During the Classroom Observations. (N=90)[2].

Media	N	%
Textbooks	43	47.8
Reference Books	5	5.6
Periodicals	2	2.2
Workbooks	18	20.0
Bulletin Board	22	24.4
Graphics (Graphs, Diagrams, etc.)	17	18.9
Three Dimensional Models	8	8.9
Film Strips	3	3.3
Slides	1	1.1
Overhead Transparencies	6	6.7
Standard Motion Picture	7	7.8
Single Concept Continuous Cartridge	0	0.0
Records	0	0.0
Tape Recordings	0	0.0
Television (Commercial)	1	1.1

--------------------------------(cont)

[1]Donald W. McCurdy, "Are Science Teachers Making Adequate Use of Their Instructional Resources?" School Science and Mathematics, 69 (April, 1969), 323-330.

[2]Ibid., p. 323

Television (Educational)	0	0.0
Teaching Machines	0	0.0
Programmed Textbooks	0	0.0

McCurdy paraphrases his table as follows:

The number and percent of science teachers who used various
instructional media during the classroom observations is presented in Table IV. Obviously, the textbook is still the
favorite tool of most teachers since 47.8% of the ninety
instructors observed referred at least once to the text
during their presentation. One-fifth of the teachers employed
a workbook of some sort and approximately one-fourth of the
group took advantage of the bulletin board as a mode of
presenting materials. In the realm of audio-visual aids,
graphics, diagrams, models, and the standard motion picture
projector were widely used. Several of the teachers (approximately seven per cent) were observed using the overhead projector on the other hand, not one of the ninety visits yielded
any use of single concept films, recordings, radio, educational
or closed circuit TV, or programmed learning materials of any
kind. Only slight use of reference materials, film strips,
slides, and commercial television was noted.[3]

A possible explanation of why there was so little activity in
using multi-media materials in teaching junior high school science as
late as 1968 is that educators at this level were then preoccupied with
an even more basic issue ,revisions of curriculum content.

---

[3]Ibid., p. 327

New programs in junior high school science are several years behind
the high school programs, but several are now in operation. An
outstanding one is the Intermediate Science Curriculum Study (ISCS),
for grades 7, 8, and 9. The general objective of junior high school
science is to give the student an understanding of science, to develop
skill in the way scientific knowledge is gathered, and to prepare the
student to interpret many of the natural phenomena and much of the
technology that confronts him today.[4]

The curriculum themes of this large-scale project are as follows:

Seventh Grade: I. Energy, Its Forms and Characteristics

                  II. Measurement and Operational Definitions

Eighth Grade: I. Matter and Its Composition

                  II. Model Building

                 III. Open-ended Studies

Ninth Grade: To synthesize and extend investigative experience
and knowledge already gained, and to apply them
to problems of practical and scientific significance.

The new junior high school science curriculum is implementing
the latest curriculum theory as well as bridging the gap in recent
scientific knowledge. For instance, the ISCS project combines the
process approach and the structure approach in curriculum development:
"This program presumes that both of these important aspects of science
can and should be introduced together by allowing concepts to arise out
of student investigation."[5]

---

[4]Charles E. Richardson and Lawrence E. Oliver, "Intermediate
Science Curriculum Study Project as Viewed by Participating Teachers,"
School Science and Mathematics, LXVIII (December, 1968), p. 786.

[5]Ibid., p. 786.

A more complete description of the background curriculum and
the use of media in science teaching will be written from sources
listed in the bibliography at the end of this proposal, especially
such as the comprehensive report of Eiss and Ofiesh. (Index classifications headings under which sources can be found are: Science-
Teaching-Junior High School). There is a need to investigate the
status of utilization of multi-media in teaching science because of
the intense activity in developing and disseminating them.

CHAPTER II. COLLECTION OF DATA

This chapter is concerned with the design for collecting data
that is objective, accurate, and of sufficient amount to support
valid conclusions. The elements of design involved are: purposes,
hypotheses, the sample, criterion data, and the instruments for collecting
data.

Purposes: The general purpose of this normative survey is to
discover what multi-media are being used in teaching seventh grade
science, for what objectives are they being used, and to what extent
are they being used. The investigation will seek to determine whether
differences in usage are statistically significant.

This general purpose includes several specific purposes which
give depth and show relationships for the data. The first such purpose
is: What media materials are used most in teaching structure content
of science?

The second such purpose is: What media materials are used most
in teaching process content of science?

The third such purpose is: What media materials are used most
in motivating students to learn science?

The fourth such purpose is: Is usage of media materials related
to teacher characteristics? Is it related to the sex of the teacher?
to the teacher's years of teaching experience? to the teacher's
years of teaching experience at the junior high school level? to the
professional degree(s) which the teacher has earned?

The fifth such purpose is: Is usage of media materials related
to characteristics of the pupils? Is it related to the student's I.Q.
level? to the student's level of achievement in science? to the
student's interest in learning science?

The sixth such purpose is: Is usage of media materials related
to characteristics of the school as an administrative unit? Is it
related to whether the seventh grade is part of a school organized
a K-6, or middle school, or junior high school? Is it related to
whether the seventh grade is part of a school which has an enrollment
less than 200, 200-500, 500-1000, above 1000?

The seventh such purpose is: Is usage related to characteristics
of the community in which the school is located? Is it related to
whether the community is rural, suburban, urban regular, or urban
disadvantaged? Is it related to the racial composition of the school,
as all or mainly black, integrated, all mainly white, or predominantly
ethnic groups?

Whereas content structure of science, content process of science,
and motivation to learn science are the dimensions in terms of which
the use of multi-media will be described (descriptive variables),
characteristics of teachers, of students, of the school, and of the
community are factors which can facilitate or hinder the utilization of
multi-media in teaching science (mediating variables).

Hypotheses: Hypothesizing findings of this survey is based on
the rather limited knowledge provided by the survey of the literature
and along the lines of the purposes decided upon in the previous section.
The general hypothesis is that relatively few multi-media are being used
and those are either the older, well-established varieties, or lend
themselves to close usage with the textbook in teaching. Other, specific
hypotheses are as follows:

1) Utilization of multi-media is related to some teacher characteristics, especially professional degrees.

2) Utilization of multi-media is related to some student characteristics, especially when they are used with low ability students.

3) Utilization of multi-media is not related to type of school
organization.

4) Utilization of multi-media is related to socio-economic characteristics of the community; especially media are used in the affluent community.
The justification of this last hypothesis is that only the affluent
community can afford multi-media materials for its schools, and the
affluent school can offer salaries and working conditions that will attract
more experienced, better prepared teachers who are likely to utilize
multi-media.

Criterion Data: The criterion data needed to answer the purposes
and test the hypotheses in this survey are basically the responses of
the teachers as to what multi-media materials they use to teach structure
of science, process of science, and motivation to learn science. These
responses will be given in the part of the questionnaire title Criterion
Data. The other information related to supporting data needed for
sampling and interpretation procedures will be collected in the part of
the questionnaire title General Information.

Multi-Media Utilized in Teaching Seventh Grade Science

Part I. General Information

Directions: Please check the following categories which best describe

         your school.

1. Is your school organized as:

    a) K-6_____   Middle School_____   Junior High____

2. What is the enrollment in your school?

    a) Less than 200_____   b) 200-500_____

    c) 500-1000_____   d) More than 1000_____

3. In what socio-economic environment is your school located?

    a) rural_____   b) urban ghetto_____

    c) urban regular_____   d) suburban_____

4. Please check the following characteristics which best apply to you.

    sex: M_____ F_____   Total years teaching experience_____

    Years teaching experience at junior high level_____

    Professional degrees earned: Less than Bachelor's_____

    Bachelor's Degree_____   Master's Degree_____

    6th year degree_____   Doctoral Degree_____

5. Please check the following characteristics which best describe

    your students as a group. Please check only one trait in each

    sub-group, and to do so, think of the best single term which

    applies best to the majority of your students.

    (a). I.Q. level: Above average - average - below average-

    (b). Level of achievement in science: above average - average -

        below average

    (c). Level of interest in studying science:

        Somewhat interested - interested - Very interested

Part II. Criterion Data

Directions:

This part of the questionnaire asks what multi-media you are using
in teaching various outstanding concepts from Earth Science, which is
assumed to be seventh grade science content in this survey. The multi-
media materials included in this survey are: (1) motion pictures,
(2) filmstrips, (3) slides, (4) 8mm. loop films or reel-to-reel,
(5) audio-cassettes or recordings, (6) overhead transparencies and
graphics, (7) manipulables, (8) specimens, (9) laboratory experiments,
(10) field trips, (11) videotapes, (12) television. Please check as
many media as you use for each content or motivation item. In responding
to each item in the questionnaire, remember to indicate what you
do in your own teaching. Do not be concerned with giving a right or
wrong answer or with whether other teachers teach as you do.

Content Item	Media Materials											
A. Structure of Earth Science:	1	2	3	4	5	6	7	8	9	10	11	12
1. <u>Earth and Sun:</u>												
(a) Planet earth												
(b) Earth Science												
(c) Earth Fields												
(d) Sources of Energy												
(e) Changes below earth surface												
(f) Changes above earth surface												
(g) Changes at earth interfaces												
(h) Interfaces and heat												
(i) Interfaces and kinetic energy												
(j) Interfaces and materials												
2. <u>Earth Cycles:</u>												
(a) Transfer of mass and energy in atmosphere												
(b) Transfer of mass and energy in hydrosphere												
(c) Transfer of mass and energy in lithosphere												
(d) Unsolved problems												
3. <u>The Earth's Past:</u>												
(a) Relationships of time												
(b) Organic evolution												
(c) Organisms at the interfaces												
(d) Unsolved Problems												

Content Item	Media Materials											
	1	2	3	4	5	6	7	8	9	10	11	12
4. Earth and the Universe:												
(a) Dynamics of distance												
(b) Speed and motion												
(c) Mass												
(d) Temperature												
(e) Composition												
(f) Euclidean geometry and space												
(g) Non-Euclidian geometry and space												
B. Process of Earth Science												
1. Recognizing ancient environment by fossils												
2. Incompleteness of the record												
3. How we know												
4. Resolving conflicting theories												
5. Logical and systematic development of conclusions from observations.												
6. Use of Models												
7. Maximum possible error												
8. Accuracy and experimental error												
9. Relative and percentage error												
10. Significant figures												
11. Tabulating and graphing data												
12. Investigation unsolved problems												
C. Motivating to Learn:												
1. Importance of knowing												
2. Realizing how much we don't know												
3. Difficulty of experimental verification												
4. Student action in learning science												
5. Studying science as housework												

The Sample .. The sample for this normative survey of utilization of multi media materials in teaching seventh grade science will be the seventh grade science teachers in 50 schools selected at random from all K-8 and junior high schools in the County of a large metropolitan area. The random sampling design will be to identify all such schools from the Illinois School Directory, assign a random number to each one, and then to select 25 by means of the table of random numbers. The universe will be the seventh grades in the County. Random selection is being relied upon to guarantee representativeness of the sample in terms of type of administrative organization as well as size of enrollment and socio-economic environment of the community.

Chapter III. Media Utilization for Teaching
Structure, Process, and Motivation

The first part of this chapter will report the responses to the
questionnaire in tabular form. Tabular structure will follow the format
of the questionnaire for grand total tabulations and also for sub-total
tabulations (by type of teacher, by type of school, etc.). Responses
for each item in the questionnaire will be given as a frequency and
as a proportion of the responses to that item. The bulk of the
responses will be reported in the tables and not otherwise mentioned,
but certain items showing central tendencies, dispersion, uniformity,
etc. will be singled out for verbal paraphrase in commentary on the
tables.

The interpretation of the data will consist of a conceptual analysis
of the evidence in order to arrive at some normative judgments about
the status of utilization of media. To do such evaluative thinking with
the data it is necessary to arrive at some criterion principles to
serve as norms for making judgements about the data. In this survey
the principle will be:

1. Is there evidence in the data that the media utilized
   supplement the curriculum?

2. Is there evidence in the data that the media utilized
   facilitate inquiry teaching and learning?

3. Is there evidence in the data that the media utilized
   facilitate individualizing instruction?

Applying the logic of these criterion principles to the frequencies by columns and rows will give an estimate of whether the media utilized facilitate, are indifferent to, or handicap the teaching of science in the seventh grade.

Statistical Interpretation: In this plan of chapter organization, the data will be presented in tabular form and then the tables will be verbally commented upon. Following such presentation of the data, its meanings will be analyzed in greater depth by means of statistics.

For each row of the responses in the questionnaire, a null hypothesis of no significant differences among the frequencies for the various media will be tested. The statistic for this purpose will be the Chi-square for equiprobability of use of media. The formula is $\chi^2 = \sum \dfrac{(fo - fe)^2}{e}$. This Chi-square will reveal whether any one of the media is being used significantly more extensively to teach a given item of content. For each column of the questionnaire (each media) the total frequency will be tallied. The total frequencies for the 12 media will then be submitted to the Chi-square test to determine whether some media predominate over the others in teaching science.

Also, the sub-total frequencies for each media will be tallied for each section of the questionnaire: Structure Content, Process Content, and Motivation. These frequency tallies will show usage of each media for each purpose of teaching science. The organization of the data in this fashion will be as follows:

Media	Structure Frequency	Process Frequency	Motivation Frequency
1			
2			
3			
4			
5			

- -

12

These frequencies will then be treated by the Kruskal - Wallis One-Way Analysis of Variance for ranked data by the formula:

$$H = \left[\frac{12}{N(N+1)} \right] \left[\sum \frac{ER_j^2}{N_j} \right] -3(N+1).$$

These statistics will tell whether different media predominate in teaching for structure, process, and motivation.

The chapter will terminate with a summary statement of findings.

CHAPTER IV.   RELATION OF UTILIZATION TO TEACHER AND PUPIL CHARACTERISTICS

The data frequencies of utilization of media will be reported in tables showing frequencies by sex, by total years of teaching experience, by years of experience teaching junior high school, and by professional degrees.   These frequencies will be used to rank the usage of media. These ranks will then be used to compute Spearman Rank Correlation Coefficient as follows:

1. for male - female ranks

2. for less than 5 years - More than five years teaching

3. for less than 5 years - More than five years junior high teaching

4. for less than M.A. - M.A. degree or more

For frequencies of utilization by types of students taught, the same procedures will be used to arrive at Spearman Coefficients of Correlation as follows:

1. for below average - average and above (ability)

2 . for below average - average and above (achievement)

The chapter will end with a summary statement of findings.

CHAPTER V. MEDIA UTILIZATION BY SCHOOL AND COMMUNITY CHARACTERISTICS

Procedures similar to those in Chapter IV will lead to Spearman correlation coefficients as follows:

1. for rural - urban ghetto schools

2. for rural - urban regular schools

3. for urban ghetto - urban regular schools

4. for urban regular - suburban schools

Also, by organization type, Spearman coefficients will be obtained thus:

1. for K-6 - middle and junior high schools

2. for less than 500 - more than 500 schools

The chapter will end with a summary statement.

CHAPTER VI. SUMMARY AND RECOMMENDATIONS

This chapter will bring together findings for the survey as a whole overarching Chapter summaries. Discussion of the research design and quality of the data will be made. Insights will be sought to improve the utilization of multi-media in teaching seventh grade science.

BIBLIOGRAPHY

Hans O. Anderson, Readings in Science Education for the Secondary
School. New York: Macmillan, 1969.

E.F. Baldwin, "USDA Science Study Aids," Science and Child, VIII
(September, 1970), 17.

N.E. Bingham, "Demonstration of the Role of Science in the program
of Educationally Deprived Children in Grades 7-9," Science Education,
LII (April, 1968), 246-55.

R.R. Carter and M.F. McClellan, "Library-Use Program," Science
Teacher, XXVI (January, 1969), 66-7.

J. Denton, "Audio-Tutorial Instruction in Science," School and
Community, LVI (April, 1970), 13.

A.J. Eiss and G.D. Ofiesh, "Science Education and Educational
Technology," Educational Technology, X (January, 1970), 9-69.

W.K. Esler, "Structuring: Inquiry for Classroom," School Science
and Mathematics, LXX (May, 1970), 454-8.

M.F. Fleming, "S-A-P Approach to Teaching Second level: Science-
As-Process" American Biology Teacher, XXII (March, 1970), 168-9.

P.B. Hounshell and E.L. West, Jr., "Trends in the Teaching of
Science," High School Journal, LIII (January, 1970), 207-215.

J. Kane, "Learning Science With Video-Tapes," The Instructor,
LXXXIX (October, 1969), 126-7.

J.F. Newport and K. McNeill, "Companion of Teacher-Pupil Verbal
Behaviors Evoked by Science - A Process Approach and by Textbooks,"
Journal of Research in Science Teaching, VII (No. 3, 1970), 191-5.

L.R. Przekop, "8mm. Filmloop in Science Instruction," Educational Technology, X (March, 1970), 9-10.

L.V. Rasmussen, "Individualizing Science Education," Educational Technology, X (January, 1970), 53-6.

D.D. Redfield and S.R. Darrow, "ISCS: Intermediate Science Curriculum Study," Physics Teacher, VIII (April, 1970), 170-180.

Charles E. Richardson and Lawrence E. Oliver, "Intermediate Science Curriculum Study Project as Viewed by Participating Teachers," School Science and Mathematics, LXVIII (December, 1968), pp. 785-90.

E. Selz, "Humanistic Approach to Science Teaching," School Science and Mathematics, LXVIII (December, 1968), 793-806.

J. Short, "Writing Criterion Tests Items in Science," Educational Technology, X (January, 1970), 46-8.

R.B. Smith and R. Mangum, "Delayed Recall versus Recognition as a Prediction of Higher Level Congitive Achievements," Psychology in the Schools, VII (April, 1970), 167-171.

A.G. Storey, "Versatile Multiple-Choice Item," Journal of Educational Research, LXII (December, 1968), 169-72.

D. Vitrogan, "Scientific Literary and the Socially Disadvantaged Youth: A Laboratory Demonstration Project, " School Science and Mathematics, LXIX (October, 1969), 618-23.

Helen M. Walker and Joseph Lev, Elementary Statistical Methods, Revised edition, New York: Holt, Rinehart and Winston, 1958.

Woodraw W. Wyatt and Charles M. Bridges, Jr., Statistics for the Behavioral Sciences. Boston: D.C. Heath and Company, 1967.

R.E. Yager, "Critical Thinking and Reference Materials in the Physical Science Classroom," School Science and Mathematics, LXVIII (November, 1968), 743-6.

III. REPORTED FACTORIAL ANALYSIS INVESTIGATION

Associated with teaching:

Analysis of the topic, Purposing,

Hypothesizing, Data Selection, Data

Collection, Tools for Collecting Data,

Critical Interpretation of Data,

Statistical Interpretation of Data,

Types of Research, and Written Report.

The factorial analysis investigation explores the
nature and relationships of factors. It is applicable
to numerous types of data: cognitive, affective, social.
Its predominant statistical procedures are correlation
and regression (regression analysis). The factors whose
relationships to the independent variable are **invest**igated
are called correlate variables.

Educational Leadership / RESEARCH SUPPLEMENT

COORDINATED BY FREDERICK A. RODGERS

Volume 6   **December 1972**   Number 2

CONTENTS

Reproduced with the permission of Educational Leadership and
F. K. Heussenstamm

Black, White, and Brown Adolescent Alienation

F. K. HEUSSENSTAMM*
RALPH HOEPFNER

ALIENATION may exist whenever society, being composed of dominant and subdominant societal groups, creates feelings of anxiety, rootlessness, isolation, and apathy; and this represents the actual condition of life for many contemporary young people. Alienation is a multidimensional construct taken to mean conscious rejection or repudiation by an individual of expected roles representing the values of his society.

Infinite variations of alienation can be described in response to the four questions which follow:

1. Focus: Alienated from what?

2. Replacement: What replaces the old relationship?

3. Mode: How is the alienation manifested? and

4. Agent: What is the agent of the alienation?

Types of alienation include a sense of cosmic outcastness, developmental estrangement, historical loss, and self-estrangement.

It would seem vital to those who engage in direct contact with junior and senior high school students, and to those who are preparing teachers for these institutions, to have an understanding of the internal dynamics of members of the student body and their feelings about the educational experiences in

* *F. K. Heussenstamm, Associate Professor, Teachers College, Columbia University, New York City; and Ralph Hoepfner, Director, Evaluation Technologies Program, Center for the Study of Evaluation, Graduate School of Education, University of California at Los Angeles*

which they are engaged. The major question involved in this study, based on cultural stereotypes, was: What demographic characteristics differentiate among young people and correlate with their levels of alienation?

Instrument Development

In a pilot study, a preliminary version of the *Adolescent Alienation Index* (Heussenstamm, 1971) was designed and tested to determine the existence and extent of alienation as manifested by in-school adolescents. The Rotter I-E Scale was selected for use in the pilot study. Because it had been validated almost entirely with adults, and inasmuch as the language was somewhat staid and formal for younger adolescents, it was utilized to supply criteria for assessing the concurrent validity of the *Adolescent Alienation Index*. The latter consisted originally of 47 forced-choice items written largely to include Seeman's five dimensions of alienation: normlessness, meaninglessness, powerlessness, self-estrangement, and social isolation. The items were written to translate Seeman's dimensions into operational terms and to make them comprehensible to adolescents. For example:

NORMLESSNESS:

———I don't pay much attention to school rules.
———I try to follow school rules.

MEANINGLESSNESS:

———I have a clear idea of why I am in school.
———I have never been sure of what we students were really in school for.

POWERLESSNESS:

———It doesn't do any good to vote in school elections, since the student government has no real voice in running the school.
———It is important to vote in school elections, because student government has a voice in running this school.

SELF-ESTRANGEMENT:

———I spend a lot of my free time moving around, looking for something to do.
———I usually know what I want to do in my spare time.

SOCIAL ISOLATION:

———I don't like most people.
———I can usually find some good in everyone.

	N	Mean	S.D.	K-R Rel.
1. Suburban Caucasian HS students	134	10.83	5.47	.797
2. Black Job Corps enrollees	55	13.42	7.91	.890
3. Urban high school students	681	11.89	5.24	.754
4. Urban Jr.-sr. high students	221	14.17	5.48	.750
5. Rural Mexican American HS students	137	12.45	5.55	.781

Figure 1. Descriptive Statistics for Five Youth Groups on the Experimental Measure of Alienation

The pilot version was completed by 75 lower division college students. The Rotter I-E Scale was also administered to these subjects. Nondiscriminating items were eliminated from the *Adolescent Alienation Index*, which condensed it to 41 items. Upon application of the Kuder-Richardson Formula 20, a reliability coefficient of .78 was estimated. The correlation between the total score and the Rotter Scale score was $+.61$.

Procedure

Five groups of adolescents were examined by means of their responses to a demographic questionnaire and the *Adolescent Alienation Index*. Group 1, a sample of 134 Caucasian males and females, was drawn from a suburban lower middle class four-year Los Angeles County high school. Group 2 consisted of 55 males, all black voluntary enrollees in a Job Corps Center for Men in California. Group 3, 681 males and females, came from a predominantly middle class black south-central Los Angeles high school. Group 4, 221 males and females, came from junior and senior urban high schools selected as the target population for a Coro Foundation teacher education project. Group 5, composed of 137 males and females, all low income Mexican Americans, was evaluated in a rural California school district.

Items suggested in the literature as probably relevant to feelings of alienation in adolescents included sex, age, number of hours of weekly employment, grade point average, socioeconomic status, transiency and stability of family parental approval of friends, solidarity with peers and marital status of parents.

Hypotheses involved relationships between these demographic variables and scores on the measure of alienation. The 11

- 223 -

hypotheses and findings relevant to them are described. Supporting statistical data are found in Figures 1, 2, and 3.

Results

1. *Sex.* Due to differentially applied pressures of society on adolescent males and females, males are more likely to experience alienation than females in school settings. This hypothesis was supported in groups 1 and 4, and indicated, but not significantly, in groups 3 and 5.

2. *Age.* Alienation has often been described as progressive; therefore, the older the subjects, the greater the degree of alienation once the process has begun. This hypothesis was not supported.

3. *Employment.* Hours at work outside of the school setting indicate a focus into the larger community. The greater the number of hours of work, the greater the alienation. This hypothesis was supported and highly significant only for group 3, from a predominantly middle class black high school. We might speculate that rising aspirations when compared with work opportunities strengthen feelings of alienation in black adolescents.

4. *Academic Achievement.* Students' estimates of their grade point average proved to be highly significantly related to alienation scores. The hypothesis, that the higher the grade point average the less the alienation, was supported in all five groups.

Demographic Characteristic	1	2	3	4	5
Sex	−.21*	—	.06	−.14*	−.04
Age	.12	—	.07	.00	.02
Hrs. of work/week	.02	.12	.14**	−.02	.04
Estimate of GPA	−.32**	−.25	−.23**	−.25**	−.32**
Father's education	−.21*	−.38**	.05	.03	−.10
Time at present residence	.11	−.06	.08*	.10	.04
No. of moves in past 5 years	−.16	−.03	−.06	−.16*	.06
Parental approval of friends	−.30**	.06	−.13**	−.29**	−.21
Solidarity with peers	−.33**	.32*	.00	−.19**	−.08
Marital status of parents	−.15	.04	−.17**	−.06	−.14

* Significant at .05 level. ** Significant at .01 level.
— Coefficient not computed, as sample was homogeneous on the characteristic.

Figure 2. Correlations Between Demographic Characteristics and Scores on the Experimental Measure of Alienation

December 1972

Groups 1	2	3	4	5
1.	2.22*	2.06*	5.56**	2.41*
2.		1.41	0.67	0.93
3.			5.43**	1.08
4.				2.86**

* Significant at .05 level. ** Significant at .01 level.
All tests are two-tailed, nondirectional tests.

Figure 3. Z Ratios (Z Tests) Between Groups of Youths on Scores on the Experimental Measure of Alienation

5. *Socioeconomic Status.* Using the father's educational attainment as a measure of societal position, it was hypothesized that the higher the position, the less the alienation. Findings were mixed; the hypothesis was supported and significant only for groups 1 and 2.

6. *Residential Status.* Length of residence at a given address may facilitate the development of family solidarity; therefore, the less the transiency, the less the alienation. This hypothesis was not supported.

7. *Transiency.* The number of changes of residence may also be an indicator of the involvement of the family cohesiveness with the community. Therefore, the less the family transiency, the less the alienation. Findings were significant only for group 4, but trended toward the hypothesis in three other groups.

8. *Parental Approval of Friends.* It was hypothesized that the greater the approval of friends, the less the alienation. The hypothesis was supported in four groups still enrolled in public school. For Job Corps enrollees, all aged 19 or older, the parental-approval variable is no longer significantly related to alienation.

9. *Solidarity with Peers.* The relationship of adolescents to their friends and confidants has been emphasized at length in both sociological and psychological literature. Therefore, the hypothesis was that the greater the cohesiveness with peers, the less the alienation. Findings were inconsistent.

10. *Marital Status of Parents.* As an indicator of family stability, two-parent families may be better able to provide support needed by the adolescent during this critical phase of his development. Therefore,

243

the greater the family stability as indicated by nonfractionated experience, the less the alienation. The hypothesis was significantly supported for group 3; indicated, but not significantly, for groups 1, 4, and 5; but reversed for group 2. Once again, the older Job Corps enrollees exhibit attitudes not typical of younger peers.

Conclusions

Those demographic characteristics of adolescents that proved to be most highly significant in relationship to alienation are grade point average, parental approval of friends, and solidarity with peers. Achievement, as validated by rewards from school staff in the form of average or above average grades, reflects approval from significant others—in this case, teachers. Such validating messages received on a regular basis serve to counter or prevent alienation, as measured by the *Adolescent Alienation Index.*

Supportive reinforcement by parents instead of criticisms of youthful selection of cohorts apparently helps prevent alienation. Attack by parents on a major factor of the adolescent's world, specifically his friends, may be interpreted as an intolerable attack on his person and may negatively influence performance on the *Adolescent Alienation Index.* Another approach to the assessment of the importance of the position of friends in the adolescent's life is measurement of his solidarity or cohesiveness with his peers. In this study, the feeling of being valued by agemates served to distinguish those low in alienation when compared with those individuals whose scores indicated more marked separation from the system.

Mixed findings on other possible related variables, such as the number of hours of work outside the school, socioeconomic status, and family stability, indicate the need for further exploration of the differences between groups.

References

F. K. Heussenstamm. *Adolescent Alienation Index.* Los Angeles: Monitor Press, 1971.

F. K. Heussenstamm. "Creativity and Alienation: An Exploration of Their Relationship in Adolescence." *California Journal of Educational Research* 21 (3): 140-46; May 1970.

J. B. Rotter. "Generalized Expectancies for Control of Reinforcement." *Psychological Monographs,* Vol. 80, No. 1; 1966.

M. Seeman. "On the Meaning of Alienation." *American Sociological Review,* Vol. 24; 1959. □

BRIEF OF A FACTORIAL ANALYSIS
INVESTIGATION

F.K. Heussenstamm and Ralph Hoepfner, "Black, White, and Brown
Adolescent Alienation," Educational Leadership, Vol. 30, (December, 1972),
pp. 241-244.

I. Topic of the Investigation: This investigation is concerned with
alienation among adolescents. The topic arises from the fact that
society is composed of dominant and subdominant groups, causing some
to feel outcast.

The investigation makes a contribution to education for personal
and social development in the curriculum.

Alienation is a multidimensional construct taken to mean conscious
rejection or repudiation by an individual of expected roles representing
the values of his society. Subconcepts related to alienation are:
1. Focus: alienation from what? 2. Replacement: What replaces the
old relationship? 3. Mode: How is the alienation manifested? and
4. Agent: What is the Agent of the alienation?

II. Analysis of the Topic:

1. Independent Variable:

The factor being investigated is alienation among adolescents;
this is the independent variable. The manifestations of alienation in
the investigation are: 1. Normlessness, 2. Meaninglessness, 3. Powerlessness, 4. Self-Estrangement, and 5. Social Isolation.

2. Correlate Variables:

The factors whose relationships to alienation are investigated
are demographic factors: 1. Sex, 2. Age, 3. Hours of work per week,
4. Estimate of grade point average, 5. Father's education, 6. Time
at present residence, 7. Number of moves in past five years, 8. Parental

approval of friends, 9. Solidarity with peers, and 10. Marital
status of parents. All of these factors are associated with alienation.

3. Mediating Variables:

Mediating variables are factors which are extrinsic to the
independent variable, but which influence it. They are a set
environments for testing the hypothesis. In this investigation, the
mediating variables are the different groups of adolescents participating in the investigation: 1. Suburban lower Middle class
Caucasians, 2. Black Job Corps Enrollees, 3. Middle class black urban,
high school students, 4. Junior High and Senior High students of a
school in an urban teacher education project, and 5. Low income rural
Mexican Americans.

III. Purposes:

General Purpose:

The investigation seeks to answer the general question:
Is alienation related to demographic factors in various groups of
adolescents?

Specific Purposes:

Included in the general purpose are the specific questions:

1. Do various groups of adolescents differ significantly in
alienation? and

2. What is the direction and the level of correlation between
alienation and selected demographic characteristics in various groups of
adolescents?

IV. Hypotheses:

General Hypothesis: In response to the general purpose, the general hypothesis is: Alienation is related to some but not all demographic factors in adolescent youth.

Specific Hypotheses: Included in the general hypothesis are the following:

1. Groups that are black or predominantly black will be more alienated than others because it is harder for them to succeed in society.

2. There should be some significant negative correlations because these groups are generally low on social success, consequently high on alienation.

3. A hypothesis is formulated for each of the ten demographic factors in reporting results.

V. Criterion Data:

According to the purposes of the investigation, measurements are needed on the one hand on the alienation factor and on the other hand on the demographic factors. It is not reported how Parental Approval of Friends, Solidarity with Peers, and Marital status of Parents were quantified.

VI. Instruments for Collecting Criterion Data:

Alienation scores are measurements from the Adolescent Alienation Index by the author. He based this instrument on the Rotter I.E. Scale. Reliability of the AAI was .78 and correlation of AAI with Rotter I.E. was .61. Several Demographic factors are quantified mostly by frequency tallies of incidence of the factor.

VII. Statistical Interpretation of Data:

1. The purpose concerned with differences between groups was achieved by use of the z test of differences between pairs of groups. The z test equals difference between the means of the groups divided by

the standard error of the difference between the means. This is an algebraic transformation of the Student-t-test; it is sometimes referred to as the Critical Ratio of the two groups.

2. The purpose concerned with the level of correlation between alienation and demographic factors was achieved by computing a Pearson r between alienation and each factor for each group. Significance of correlation was read from the table of probability of chance occurrence.

VIII. Findings of the Investigation:

A detailed statement of findings is given in the article. Findings were sometimes significant and sometimes not for both purposes.

Specifically, a significant negative correlation was found between alienation and academic achievement for all groups, and between alienation and employment for blacks. The older job corps group exhibited attitudes different from their younger peers.

IX. Discussion of Research Design:

1. The correlate variables represent an interesting set of factors which are newcomers to educational research.

2. It is not clearly established whether the samples (groups) were chosen randomly and represent any further universe than themselves.

3. Statistics used are direct and effective for the purposes.

4. More specific purposes and findings would result if the investigation had concerned itself with correlations among the ten demographic correlates and the five manifestation of alienation: 1. Normlessness, 2. Meaninglessness, 3. Powerlessness, 4. Self-Estrangement, and 5. Social Isolation. Such computations, however, would be possible only if it were possible to get sub-scores on the 5 alienation manifestations from the Adolescent Alienation Index.

XIX-A. PROPOSAL FOR A FACTORIAL ANALYSIS INVESTIGATION

   Associated with teaching:

   Analysis of the Topic, Purposing, Hypothesizing,

   Data Selection, Data Collection, Tools for Collecting

   Data, Critical Interpretation of Data, Statistical

   Interpretation of Data, Types of Research.

PROPOSAL FOR FACTORIAL ANALYSIS RESEARCH

Relationships of Study Habits and Attitudes to
Achievement and Career Interests

(Associated with teaching analysis of the Topic, Purposing, Hypothesizing, Data Selection, Data Collection, Tools for Collecting Data, Critical Interpretation of Data, Statistical Interpretation of Data, Types of Research).

CHAPTER I.   ANALYSIS OF THE TOPIC:

This chapter explores the importance and the meaning of the topic.

Selection of the Topic

The role of attitudes, habits, and interests in the education of children and youth is crucial. Their importance can be inferred from the well-known phenomenon that some students with apparently high scholastic aptitude do poorly in school whereas other students with only average ability do much better. It can be inferred that study habits and attitudes are the answer to the challenge posed by this unexpected outcome.[1] For their part, measured interests are strong indicators of what a person likes to do or wants to be. A positive correlation between measured interests and career satisfaction has been reported in research studies.[2]

---

[1]W.H. Holtzman and W.F. Brown, "Study Habits and Attitudes in the Prediction of Academic Success," American Psychologist, 8 (1953), 369.

[2]G.G. MacRae, "The Relationships of Job Satisfaction and Earlier Measured Interests," Ph.D. dissertation, University of Florida, 1959.

In view of the contemporary emphasis in the schools on both academic achievement and career preparation, it is evident that the relationships among these two affective areas needs to be investigated. If the assumption is made that the student succeeds academically in school will also be effective in a career, then it can be presumed that strong predictors of academic success (study habits and attitudes) will be related to strong predictors of career success (general interests). This line of reasoning is the basis for selecting relationships among study habits and attitudes on one hand, and general interests of students on the other.

Analysis of the Topic

In a factorial analysis investigation analysis of the topic is concerned with the independent variable(s), the correlate variable(s), and the mediating variable(s).

Independent Variable

The variable investigated in this research includes factors constituting study habits and attitudes. Specifically, in this investigation, those factors consist of: delay avoidance, study methods, teacher approval, education approval, study orientation. These are the factors included in the Survey of Study Habits and Attitudes which is being used in the study.

Correlate Variables

There are two general variables whose relationship to study habits and attitudes is being investigated: academic achievement and career interests.

Specifically, academic achievement is limited to vocabulary, reading comprehension, total reading score, mathematics computation, mathematics concepts, and total mathematics score.

The subfactors constituting career interest are: outdoor, mechanical, computational, scientific, persuasive, artistic, literary, musical, social service, and clerical. These are the factors in the Kuder General Interest Survey which will be used in this study.

Mediating Variables

This investigation will explore the relationships among the independent variable and the correlate variables and subfactors of both independent and correlate variables among eighth grade students in an inner-city school, in an urban school, in a suburban school, and in a rural school. These are the different environments within which the relationships among the variables will be investigated. Sex of the student is also a mediating variable affecting relationships of the independent and correlate variables studied. It is assumed that differences among these environments could be supportive of or suppressive of the relationships.

There is a fairly abundant literature on the field of relationships among study habits and attitudes with intellectual achievement. Evidence to this fact is found in the numerous entries on this topic in bibliographic indexes, and in the fact that the "Survey of Study Habits and Attitudes"[3] is a topical classification heading in the Education Index.

---

[3]W.F. Brown and W.F. Holtzman, Survey of Study Habits and Attitudes. (New York: The Psychological Corporation, 1967).

Research involving the non-intellective correlates of intellectual achievement was especially active in the period from the mid-sixties to the mid-seventies.

An overview of the literature on study habits and attitudes as related to intellectual achievement shows several categories of investigations: 1) instrumentation for measuring study habits and attitudes, 2) investigations of the relationships of study habits and attitudes as correlates of intellectual achievement among students below the college level, 3) investigations of the relationships of study habits and attitudes as correlates of intellectual achievement on the college level, and 4) experimental-type investigations concerned with developing/modifying study habits and attitudes as well as their relationships as correlates of intellectual achievement.

Scale Development

Worthy of note in the first category of research literature, in addition to the Brown, Holtzman development of the instrument mentioned above, are the work of Roark and Harrington[4] of Zimmerman, Michael, and Michael,[5] and of Goldfried and D'Zurilla.[6]

---

[4]Albert A. Roark and Scott A. Harrington, "Survey of Study Habits and Attitudes: A Review," Journal of Educational Measurement, Vol. 6 (No. 2, 1969), pp. 120-122.

[5]Wayne S. Zimmerman, Joan C. Michael, and William B. Michael, "The Factored Dimensions of the Study Attitudes and Methods Survey Test Experimental Form," Educational and Psychological Measurement, Vol. 30 (1970), pp. 433-436.

[6]Marvin R. Goldfried and Thomas J. D'Zurilla, "Prediction of Academic Competence by Means of the Survey of Study Habits and Attitudes," Journal of Educational Psychology, Vol. 64 (No. 1, 1973), pp. 116-122.

Roark and Harrington point out the limitation of SSHA as a self-rating instrument with the possibility of manipulating answers as a hazard, but they evaluate it as a well constructed instrument suitable for many regression analysis research studies. Goldfried and D'Zurilla review some validation studies of SSHA. They question the use of achievement as a criterion for validating a measure that surveys effective behavior. Pursuing their analysis further, these two authors validate SSHA against self-ratings and peer ratings of effective behavior in situations related to academic achievement. The self and peer ratings of effective behavior correlated more highly with study habits than with study attitudes. The self and peer ratings did not correlate significantly with aptitude scores, just as SSHA scores do not correlate significantly with aptitude scores. In the study, SSHA did not correlate significantly with grade point average though other research found that it does. As a general conclusion, Goldfried and D'Zurilla hold that self and peer ratings of study habits and attitudes are a valid alternative to measuring factors by the SSHA scale alternative to measuring factors by the SSHA scale technique.

Zimmerman, Michael, and Michael developed a scale of their own comparable to the Survey of Study Habits and Attitudes, and they entitled their scale "Study Attitudes and Methods Survey Test."[7]

---

[7]W.B. Michael, J.J. Michael, and W.S. Zimmerman, Study Attitudes and Methods Survey. (San Diego, Ca: Educational and Industrial Testing Service, 1969).

Their "survey" includes ten psychological dimensions which were shown
by previous research to be significantly correlated with measures of
academic success. The factors are: 1) general achievement drive, 2)
method and system, 3) positive mental health - freedom from exhibition
of neurotic behavior patterns as well as the manifestation of self-
confidence, 4) academic affective value - pleasure in studying, 5) con-
formity to teacher and institutional expectations including persevering
behavior, 6) positive versus negative attitudes toward teachers and the
educational institution, 7) perception of one's own ability, 8) self-
orientation vs. orientation toward others, 9) "conning the teacher" -
political sensitivity and manipulation, and 10) risk-taking behavior
patterns associated with creative endeavor. The survey includes five
scales of twenty-five items each. In 1970, activities were under way
to establish the reliability and empirical validity of these scales and
to refine their validity relative to selected criteria of academic
achievement.

Investigations below College Level

A study by Robert L. Williams[8] grew out of the results of
other investigations, especially that by Jackson and Getzels, that
scholastic attitudes are significantly related to personality variables
but not to ability and achievement indices.[9] Williams first concerned
himself with securing a more normal sample distribution and measurements
from standardized instruments with national norms. He attempted to
delineate ability, achievement, and personality variables which differentiate students having positive attitudes toward school from those with
negative attitudes. In constituting the attitudinal groups, the experi-
menter administered the "California Study Methods Survey"[10] to students
in three public high schools. Fifty-six students who scored at least
1.3 standard deviations above the national mean on the attitudes toward
school scale constituted the positive group, and sixty-five who scored
at least 1.3 standard deviations below the normative mean constituted
the negative group. The findings indicate that students who were dissatis-
fied with school obtained significantly lower scores on all ability,
achievement, and personality variables than students of positive orientation.
Williams is careful to point out, however, that his hypothesis would be
supported only in schools where competitive evaluation policies prevail,

[8]Robert L. Williams, "Personality, Ability, and Achievement Correlates
of Scholastic Attitudes, " The Journal of Educational Research, Vol. 63
(May-June, 1970), pp. 401-403.

[9]P.W. Jackson and J.W. Getzels, "Psychological Health and Classroom
Functioning: A Study of Dissatisfaction with School among Adolescents,"
Journal of Educational Psychology, Vol. 50 (1959), pp. 295-300.

[10]H.D. Carter, California Study Methods Survey (Los Angeles: California Test Bureau, 1958).

and the three schools in his study were so selected.

S.B. Khan conducted what is probably the best designed and convincing study of effectiveness of the psychological corporation's SSHA
to discover relationships among non-intellective and intellectual factors
and to predict academic achievement from study habits and attitudes.[11]

He administered the SSHA to 509 male and 529 female students in
Florida junior high schools. This data was his affective data. His
intellective data was: verbal and mathematical scores on the School and
College Ability Test, and on Metropolitan Achievement test scores on
reading, language, arithmetic computation, problem solving, social studies,
and science.

The factor, "Attitude toward Teachers," correlated significantly
with achievement criteria for males but not females, and conversely,
the factor, "Study Habits," correlated significantly with achievement
criteria for females, but not for males. The factors "Achievement Anxiety"
and 'Need Achievement" correlated significantly with achievement criteria
for both females and males. When multiple correlations of affective
factors were combined with aptitude, greater correlations with achievement
criteria were obtained. Correlations were usually higher for females
than for males.

Affective predictors yield higher correlations with standardized
tests than with teacher grades. Also, subscores as compared to overall
score are useful and suggest that attitudes, motivation, and study habits
cannot be represented unidimensionally.

---

[11]S.B. Khan, "Affective Correlates of Academic Achievement," Journal
of Educational Psychology, Vol. 60 (No. 3, 1969), pp. 216-221.

The Khan study is quite convincing that relationships among affective/intellective factors are valid, and that predictions are possibly among them.

A similar but less extensive study to that of the Florida junior high schools was also conducted by Khan in Ontario, Canada.[12] His cri-- terion data consisted of scores on SSHA as affective data, scores on the Canadian Academic Aptitude Test as the ability factor, and scores on the Dominion Group Achievement test (vocabulary, arithmetic computation, and spelling). The subjects in the study were 240 eighth grade students in four schools.

Significant correlations were obtained among attitude toward teacher, need achievement, work methods, and academic achievement. Correlations among remaining factors and achievement criteria are negligible. Stepwise regression formulas which included one or more predictor factors beyond the two most highly correlated to achievement did not add to the accuracy of the prediction.

At the sixth grade level, a factorial analysis investigation was made of SSHA scores and achievement in reading and mathematics.[13] There were sixteen boys and ten girls in the study at a private institution in Jamaica Estates, New York. Arithmetic was measured by the Iowa Tests of Basic Skills, and reading achievement by the Metropolitan Reading Achieve- ment Test.

---

[12]S.B. Khan and Dennis M. Roberts, "Relationships among Study Habits and Attitudes, Aptitude and Grade 8 Achievement," *Educational and Psycholo- gical Measurement*, Vol. 29 (1969), pp. 951-955.

[13]Florence P. Shepps and R. Ronald Shepps, "Relationships of Study Habits and School Attitudes to Achievement in Mathematics and Reading," *The Journal of Educational Research*, Vol. 65 (October, 1971), pp. 71-73.

Only the Study Attitudes subtest was a satisfactory predictor

of reading achievement. Total SSHA (SO) was a good predictor of reading

for boys and of arithmetic for girls.

College Level Studies

There are probably as many or more factorial analysis investigations

of correlation and regression among non-intellective factors and achieve-

ment variables on the level of higher education as on the secondary and

elementary school level. Several are listed here, but not reported on

because this sample proposal for a factorial analysis investigation does

not intend to be exhaustive. Among such studies are:

[14]Donald F. McCausland and Nancy E. Stewart, "Academic Aptitude,
Study Skills, and Attitudes and College GPA," The Journal of Educational
Research, Vol. 67 (April, 1974), pp. 354-357.

[15]Donna Corlett, "Library Skills, Study Habits and Attitudes, and
Sex as Related to Academic Achievement," Educational and Psychological
Measurement, Vol. 34 (1974), pp. 967-969.

[16]Yi-Guang Lin and Wilbert J. McKeachie, "Aptitude, Anxiety, Study
Habits, and Academic Achievement," Journal of Counseling Psychology,
Vol. 17 (July, 1970), pp. 306-309.

Other References

Related bibliographical references may be found in the literature

on this topic. For instance two experimental-type sources are:

[17]Mary B. Harris and Fred Ream, "A Program to Improve Study Habits
of High-School Students," Psychology in the Schools, Vol. 9 (July, 1972),
pp. 325-30, and

[18]Richard D. Briggs, Donald J. Tosi, and Rosemary M. Morley,
"Study Habit Modification and Its Effect on Academic Performance:
A Behavioral Approach," The Journal of Educational Research, Vol. 64
(April, 1971), pp. 347-350.

On the other hand, references of a general supportive nature to

factorial analyses could include:

[19] James A. Grob, "Reading Rate and Study-Time Demands on Secondary Students," *Journal of Reading*, Vol. 13 (January, 1970), pp. 285-8.

From the preceding survey of some of the literature on this topic several generalizations can be reached.

Generalizations

1. Non-intellective factors (study habits and attitudes) measure factors which are related to achievement but are different from aptitude factors.

2. The correlation between non-intellective factors and achievement is not high, and the greatest effectiveness results from combining non-intellective factors (study habits and attitudes) with intellective factors (aptitude) in a multiple correlation to provide the basis for predicting achievement. The multiple correlation coefficients combining non-intellective with intellective factors in relation to achievement are higher than correlation coefficients of either type of factors alone in relation to achievement.

3. The achievement of girls seems to be more predictable than the achievement of boys and different non-intellective factors are related to achievement among girls than among boys.

4. Factors which are psychologically "achievement-oriented" (motivation, anxiety, achievement need, *etc.*) correlate more highly with intellectual achievement than factors which are more "mechanical" (study habits). The more psychological factors are better predictors of achievement generally, although study habits predict intellectual achievement fairly well among girls.

5. The learning environment in which the relationship between non-inte-

lectual factors and intellectual achievement is investigated seems

to have a role promoting or hindering the correlation and prediction.

An atmosphere which provides supportive feedback for all students re-

gardless of ability and achievement would most likely not produce a

significant correlation between non-intellective factors and intellectual

achievement whereas a typical competitive milieu, according to a

classical conditioning model, produce more positive relationships

between these variables. The learning environment must be taken into

consideration when interpreting the data collected in factorial analyses

of non-intellective variables and intellectual achievement variables.

In summary, non-intellective factors such as study habits and

attitudes are invalid correlates of intellectual achievements and the

investigation of this issue has begun, but much research still needs to

be done in this field.

CHAPTER II. COLLECTION OF THE DATA:

This chapter is concerned with the general research design for investigating the topic analyzed in chapter one. This general research design involves the following elements of a research design: purposes, hypotheses, the sample, the criterion data, and instruments for collecting the criterion data. These elements constitute the safeguards which are taken to assure that measurements and observations are valid, accurate, objective, and sufficient to help establish generalizations – such safeguards must be effective to enable the inductive model of thinking to be operational in an investigation. There can be no substitute for the validity, the accuracy, and the objectivity of the measurements and observations which are interpreted in the study. No sophistication of statistical analyses or technology of computer services can lend truthfulness to conclusions based on data that was invalid or drawn from an unrepresentative sample by means of tests or scales which do not measure what they are supposed to measure. In an educational research investigation there must be as much concern given to the procedures by which the data is collected (research design) as to the analysis and statistical interpretation of the data once it has been collected.

The Purposes

General Purpose

The general purpose of this investigation is to discover the level and direction of the correlations among the independent and the correlate variables, and to explore the accuracy of predictions among them based on these correlations. Answers will be sought to this general question in the four separate environments identified as mediating variables (inner city, urban, suburban, rural).

Specific purposes included within the general purpose include
the following specific questions:

1. What are the study habits, attitudes, achievement levels, and career
   interests of students at the eighth grade level?

2. What are the level of correlation (size of the r) and direction of
   the correlations among the total independent and correlate variables,
   and the direction (positive/negative) of those correlations?

3. Are there differences among the measurements and their relationships
   for the independent and correlate variables by socio-economic
   environment in which they exist (inner city, urban, suburban, rural)?

4. Are there differences among the measurements and their relationships
   for the independent and the correlate variables according to the
   sex (female, male) of the students?

5. Can predictions be made among the independent and correlate variables,
   and how accurate are the predictions from such regression formulas?

The Hypotheses

For all of the purposes set forth above there are corresponding
hypotheses answering them.

General Hypothesis

In general it is hypothesized that valid measures can be obtained
of the independent and the correlate variables, and there will be significant correlations among them.

Specific Hypotheses:

As to specific purposes listed above, the following hypotheses may
be advanced.

1. Independent and correlate variables are amenable to valid measurements and observations.

2. The null hypothesis will be tested that correlations among the independent and correlate variables will not be significantly different from zero.

3. In null form, there will be no significant differences among the measurements and their relationships between the independent and the correlate variables according to the socio-economic environments in which they exist.

4. In null form, there are no significant differences among the measurements and their relationships for the independent and the correlate variables according to the sex of the students.

5. Statistically significant predictions can be made among the independent and the correlate variables.

The Sample

For each of the socio-economic environments which are the mediating variables, a random sample of thirty eighth graders (15 girls and 15 boys) will be selected from one school in each environment. The random design utilized will be the table of random numbers. Thus, by selecting the sample by a random design, there will be assurance that the sample(s) are representative of the populations from which they are selected.

Instruments for Collecting Data

The instrument for collecting the measurements on study habits and attitudes is a scale: William F. Brown and Wayne H. Holtzman, Survey of Study Habits and Attitudes (New York: The Psychological Corporation, 1967), Form H. There are four basic factors in the scale: delay

avoidance, work methods, teacher approval, and education acceptance.
The first two factors are summed to give a different subscore called
study habits; and the last two are summed to give yet a further subscore
called study attitudes. Finally, the study habits subscore and the
study attitudes subscores are summed to give a seventh score, called
study orientation. The survey has been validated, standardized (normed),
and has been extensively used in factorial analytical studies of
non-intellective and intellective factors. Form H is to be used on the
junior and senior high school level.

The instruments to obtain the measurements on academic achievement
are standardized achievement tests. In this study the test used will
be the California Achievement Tests in Reading and in arithmetic.

The instrument used to obtain the measurements on career interests
will be the G. Frederic Kuder General Interest Survey (Chicago: Science
Research Associates, 1963), Form E, Grades 6-8. The survey has been
normed and standardized, and extensively used in research and counseling.
The range of subfactors involved in career interests is: outdoor,
mechanical, computational, scientific, persuasive, artistic, literary,
musical, social service, and clerical. The survey responses are in the
format of forced-choice technique. The items in the survey are based
on the assumption that there are differences between expressed interests
and measured interests; measured interests tap only affective responses-
likes, dislikes, and preferences.

CHAPTER III.   RELATIONSHIPS AMONG STUDY HABITS AND ATTITUDES AND
              ACHIEVEMENT

Report the scores on Survey of Study Habits and Attitudes as raw

scores and the Reading and Mathematics scores as standard scores or grade

equivalents.

1. Present the measurements on the SSHA scale by socio-economic groups

    and by sex (tables). Also, present the measurements on achievement

    by subject, socioeconomic group, and sex. (Tables).

Table_____.   Scores on the Survey of Study Habits and Attitudes
                    of Inner-City Students

SS	Delay Avoidance		Work Methods		Study Habits		Teacher Approval		Education Acceptance		Study Attitudes		Study Orientation	
	Pre	Post	Pre	Post	Pre	Post	Pre	Post	Pre	Post	Pre	Post	Pre	Post
Girls 1. etc.														
Boys 1. etc.														

Comments on the table:

Highest scores, lowest scores, central tendencies among the scores,

dispersion, logical consistencies, inconsistencies, unexpected results.

Overarching comments on the table: Level of scores in total table,

comparisons of scores of girls and boys, comparisons of scores by subtest,

comparisons of pretest and posttest scores.

Table_____.   Scores on the Survey of Study Habits and Attitudes of
                    Urban Students

SS	Delay Avoidance		Work Methods		Study Habits		Teacher Approval		Education Acceptance		Study Attitudes		Study Orientation	
	Pre	Post	Pre	Post	Pre	Post	Pre	Post	Pre	Post	Pre	Post	Pre	Post
Girls 1. etc.														
Boys 1. etc.														

Comments on the table:

Highest scores, lowest scores, central tendencies among the scores, dispersion among the scores, logical consistencies among the scores, inconsistencies, unexpected results. Overarching comments on the table: Level of scores in the total table, comparisons of scores of girls and boys, comparisons of pretest and posttest scores, comparisons of subtest scores.

Table_____. Scores on the Survey of Study Habits and Attitudes of Suburban Students

SS	Delay Avoidance		Work Methods		Study Habits		Teacher Approval		Education Acceptance		Study Attitudes		Study Orientation	
	Pre	Post	Pre	Post	Pre	Post	Pre	Post	Pre	Post	Pre	Post	Pre	Post
Girls 1. etc. Boys 1. etc.														

Comments on the table:

Highest scores, lowest scores, central tendencies among the scores, dispersion among the scores, logical consistencies among the scores, inconsistencies, unexpected results. Overarching comments on the table. Level of the scores in the total table, comparisons of scores of girls and boys, comparisons of pretests and posttests, comparisons of scores on subtests.

Table_____. Scores on the Survey of Study Habits and Attitudes of Rural Students

SS	Delay Avoidance		Work Methods		Study Habits		Teacher Approval		Education Acceptance		Study Attitudes		Study Orientation	
	Pre	Post	Pre	Post	Pre	Post	Pre	Post	Pre	Post	Pre	Post	Pre	Post
Girls 1. etc. Boys 1. etc.														

Comments on the table:

    Highest scores, lowest scores, central tendencies among the
scores, dispersion among the scores, logical consistencies among the
scores, inconsistencies, unexpected results. Overarching comments on
the table: Level of the scores in the total table, comparisons of
scores of girls and boys, comparisons of pretests and posttests, comparisons of scores on subtests.

Table_____. Achievement Scores in Reading and Mathematics of Inner-
City Students

SS	Vocabulary		Comprehension		Total Reading		Mathematics Concepts		Mathematics Computations		Total Mathematics	
	Pre	Post	Pre	Post	Pre	Post	Pre	Post	Pre	Post	Pre	Post
Girls 1. etc. Boys 1. etc.												

Comments on the table:

    Highest scores, lowest scores, central tendencies among the scores,
dispersion among the scores, logical consistencies among the scores,
inconsistencies, unexpected results. Overarching comments on the table:
Level of the scores in the total table, comparisons of scores of boys
and girls, comparisons of pretests and posttests, comparisons of scores
on subtests.

Table_____. Achievement Scores in Reading and Mathematics of Urban
Students

SS	Vocabulary		Comprehension		Total Reading		Mathematics Concepts		Mathematics Computations		Total Mathematics	
	Pre	Post	Pre	Post	Pre	Post	Pre	Post	Pre	Post	Pre	Post
Girls 1. etc. Boys 1. etc.												

Comments on the table:

Highest scores, lowest scores, central tendencies among the scores, dispersion among the scores, logical consistencies among the scores, inconsistencies, unexpected results. Overarching comments on the table: Level of the scores in the total table, comparisons of scores of girls and boys, comparisons of pretests and posttests, comparisons of scores on subtests.

Table_____. Achievement Scores in Reading and Mathematics of Suburban Students

SS	Vocabulary		Comprehension		Total Reading		Mathematics Concepts		Mathematics Computations		Total Mathematics	
	Pre	Post	Pre	Post	Pre	Post	Pre	Post	Pre	Post	Pre	Post
Girls 1. etc. Boys 1. etc.												

Comments on the table:

Highest scores, lowest scores, central tendencies among the scores, dispersion among the scores, logical consistencies among the scores, inconsistencies, unexpected results. Overarching comments on the table: Level of the scores in the total table, comparisons of scores of girls and boys, comparisons of pretests and posttests, comparisons of scores on subtests.

Table_____. Achievement Scores in Reading and Mathematics of Rural Students

SS	Vocabulary		Comprehension		Total Reading		Mathematics Concepts		Mathematics Computations		Total Mathematics	
	Pre	Post	Pre	Post	Pre	Post	Pre	Post	Pre	Post	Pre	Post
Girls 1. etc. Boys 1. etc.												

Comments on the table:

Highest scores, lowest scores, central tendencies among the scores, dispersion among the scores, logical consistencies among the scores, inconsistencies, unexpected results. Overarching comments on the table: Level of the scores in the total table, comparisons of scores of girls and boys, comparisons of pretests and posttests, comparisons of scores on subtests.

2. Compute the correlations of the total scores and subscores of SSHA with the Achievement scores (compute Pearson coefficient r).

Table_____. Coefficients of Correlations among SSHA Scores and Achievement Scores of Girls in an Inner City School.

To compute these correlations, use all possible pairs of inner-city girls' scores on all SSHA measurements and on all their achievement measurements. Organize all of the correlation coefficients into the following matrix.

	DA	WM	SH	TA	EA	SA	SO	Voc	Comp	Read	Conc	Compu	Math
DA	–												
WM	–	–											
SH	–	–	–										
TA	–	–	–	–									
EA	–	–	–	–	–								
SA	–	–	–	–	–	–							
SO	–	–	–	–	–	–	–						
Voc	–	–	–	–	–	–	–	–					
Comp	–	–	–	–	–	–	–	–	–				
Read	–	–	–	–	–	–	–	–	–	–			
Conc	–	–	–	–	–	–	–	–	–	–	–		
Compu	–	–	–	–	–	–	–	–	–	–	–	–	
Math	–	–	–	–	–	–	–	–	–	–	–	–	–

Mark with * all coefficients significant at P $<$.05

Mark with ** all coefficients significant at P $<$.01

Table_____. Coefficients of Correlations among SSHA Scores and
Achievement Scores of Boys in an Inner-City Schools

To compute these correlations, use all possible pairs of inner-city boys' scores on all SSHA measurements and on all their achievement measurements. Organize all of the correlation coefficients into the following matrix.

	DA	WM	SH	TA	EA	SA	SO	Voc	Comp	Read	Conc	Compu	Math
DA	–												
WM	–	–											
SH	–	–	–										
TA	–	–	–	–									
EA	–	–	–	–	–								
SA	–	–	–	–	–	–							
SO	–	–	–	–	–	–	–						
Voc	–	–	–	–	–	–	–	–					
Comp	–	–	–	–	–	–	–	–	–				
Read	–	–	–	–	–	–	–	–	–	–			
Conc	–	–	–	–	–	–	–	–	–	–	–		
Compu	–	–	–	–	–	–	–	–	–	–	–	–	
Math	–	–	–	–	–	–	–	–	–	–	–	–	–

Mark with * all coefficients significant at P $<$.05

Mark with ** all coefficients significant at P $<$.01.

Table_____. Coefficients of Correlation among SSHA Scores and
Achievement Scores of Girls in an Urban School

To compute these correlations, use all possible pairs of urban

girls' scores on all SSHA measurements and on all their achievement

measurements. Organize all of the correlation coefficients into a

matrix as in the preceding table.

Table_____. Coefficients of Correlation among SSHA Scores and
Achievement Scores of Boys in an Urban School

To compute these correlations, use all possible pairs of urban

boys' scores on all SSHA measurements and on all their achievement

measurements. Organize all of the correlation coefficients into a

matrix as in the preceding table.

Table_____. Coefficients of Correlation among SSHA Scores and
Achievement Scores of Girls in a Suburban School

To compute these correlations, use all possible pairs of suburban

girls' scores on all SSHA measurements and on all their achievement

measurements. Organize all of the correlation coefficients into a

matrix as in the preceding table.

Table_____. Coefficients of Correlation among SSHA Scores and
Achievement Scores of Boys in a Suburban School

To compute these correlations, use all possible pairs of suburban

boys' scores on all SSHA measurements and on all their achievement

measurements. Organize all of the correlation coefficients into a

matrix as in the preceding table.

Table_____. Coefficients of Correlation among SSHA Scores and
Achievement Scores of Girls in a Rural School

To compute these correlations, use all possible pairs of rural
girls' scores on all SSHA measurements and on all their achievement
measurements. Organize all of the correlation coefficients into a
matrix as in the preceding table.

Table_____. Coefficients of Correlation among SSHA Scores and
Achievement Scores of Boys in a Rural School

To compute these correlations, use all possible pairs of rural
boys' scores on all SSHA measurements and on all their achievement measurements. Organize all of the correlation coefficients into a matrix as
in the preceding table.

3. <u>Compute regression formulas for predicting some/all of the achievement factors (dependent) from some or all of the SSHA factors
(independent). Compute the standard error of the estimate to test
the accuracy of these predictions. This regression analysis is
relatively sophisticated and should be used with selected topics
where prediction is relevant. The more highly an independent
variable correlates with a dependent variable, the more accurately
will the independent variable predict the dependent variable.</u>

Table_____. Regression Formula for Predicting Reading Score from
Study Orientation Score in an Inner-City School

To compute this formula, use the total reading score of girls
and boys combined, and their study orientation score combined. Compute
the regression formula:

Reading (pred.) = regression coefficient (SO score) $\pm$ constant

Table_____. Regression Formula for Predicting Mathematics Score
from Study Orientation Score in an Inner-City School

To compute this formula, use the total mathematics score of girls
and boys combined, and their study orientation score combined. Compute
the regression formula:

Mathematics (pred.) = regression coefficient (SO score) $\pm$ constant

Table_____. Regression Formula for Predicting Reading Score from
Study Orientation Score in an Urban School

To compute this formula, use the total reading score of girls
and boys combined, and their study orientation score combined. Compute
the regression formula:

Reading (pred) = regression coefficient (SO score) $\pm$ constant

Table_____. Regression Formula for Predicting Mathematics Score
from Study Orientation Score in an Urban School

To compute this formula, use the total mathematics score of girls
and boys combined, and their study orientation score combined. Compute
the regression formula:

Math (pred.) = regression coefficient (SO score) $\pm$ constant

Table_____. Regression Formula for Predicting Reading Score from
Study Orientation Score in a Suburban School

To compute this formula, use the total reading score of girls and
boys combined, and their study orientation score combined. Compute the
regression formula:

Read (pred.) = regression coefficient (SO score) $\pm$ constant

Table_____. Regression Formula for Predicting Mathematics Score from Study Orientation Score in a Suburban School

To compute this formula, use the total mathematics score of girls and boys combined, and their study orientation score combined. Compute the regression formula:

Mathematics (pred.) = regression coefficient (SO score) $\pm$ constant

Table_____. Regression Formula for Predicting Reading Score from Study Orientation Score in a Rural School

To compute this formula, use the total reading score of girls and boys combined, and their study orientation score. Compute the regression formula:

Read (pred.) = regression coefficient (SO score) $\pm$ constant

Table_____. Regression Formula for Predicting Mathematics Score from Study Orientation Score in a Rural School

To compute this formula, use the total mathematics score of girls and boys combined, and their study orientation score combined. Compute the regression formula:

Math (pred.) = regression coefficient (SO score) $\pm$ constant

The formula for Standard Error of the Estimate is $S_{1.2} = S_1\sqrt{1-R^2_{1.2}}$, where S_1 is the standard deviation of the actual scores and $R_{1.2}$ is the coefficient of correlation between actual scores and predictor scores.

4. <u>Compute one-way analyses of variance of indpendent factors/subfactors for socioeconomic groups (F-ratio).</u>

Table_____. One-Way Analysis of Variance on Delay Avoidance
Scores for Four Socio-Economic Groups

To compute this F-Ratio, organize the data as follows:

Delay Avoidance: Data

SS	Inner-City	Urban	Suburban	Rural
Girls:				
1.	-	-	-	-
etc.	-	-	-	-
Boys:				
1.	-	-	-	-
etc.	-	-	-	-

Compute the one-way analysis of variance among the four socio-economic groups on delay avoidance. The summary table is as follows:

Summary Table

Source	Sum of Squares	DF	Mean Square	F
Between				
Within				
Total				

This same pattern of organization and computations serves for computing the one-way analysis of variance among the four socio-economic groups on any SSHA factor or sub-factor or on any achievement test or sub-test.

5. Compute two-way analyses of variance of indpendent factors/sub-factors, and of correlate factors/subfactors by socio-economic group and sex as main effect. (F-ratio rows and for columns).

Table_____. Two-Way Analysis of Variance on Delay Avoidance
Scores for Four Socio-Economic Groups, by Sex

If the two-way analysis of variance by socio-economic group and sex

is computed for any factor, there is no need to compute the one-way

analysis of variance by socio-economic groups with both sexes combined

because the F-Ratio for "rows" in the summary table is "F" for one-way

Anova

Delay Avoidance: Data

Inner-City		Urban		Suburban		Rural	
Girls	Boys	Girls	Boys	Girls	Boys	Girls	Boys
1.	1.	1.	1.	1.	1.	1.	1.
etc.	etc.	etc.	etc.	etc.	etc.	etc.	etc.

The summary table for this two-way analysis of variance is as

follows:

Summary Table

Source	Sum of Squares	DF	Mean Square	F
Rows(groups)				
Columns(sexes)				
Interaction (group & sex)				
Within				
Total				

This same pattern of organization and computations serves for

computing the two-way analysis of variance for any SSHA factor or

sub-factor or on any achievement test or sub-test.

6. Chapter Summary. Findings derived from points 1,2,3,4,5 above in

   this chapter. State findings based on correlation coefficients,

   or regression coefficients, and F-Ratios individually. Also try to

   establish generalizations based on combinations of these statistical results , whether of the same type, or across types. Be alert to establish generalized relationships.

CHAPTER IV. RELATIONSHIPS AMONG STUDY HABITS AND ATTITUDES AND
             CAREER INTERESTS

The data for measurements on the Survey of Study Habits and

Attitudes have already been presented in Chapter III, and need not be

repeated here. The data for measurements on the General Interest Scale

must be presented in this chapter, but a caution must be observed. The

scores for General Interest Scales are given only as percentiles in the

norms. Since percentiles are ordinal data, they are not compatible

with the SSHA scores, which are interval data, at least to compute the

one-way and the two-way analysis of variance. This problem can be solved

by expressing the data proportion which the raw score for a scale is

of the total points in that scale. Thus, the score of a student on

the Outdoor Scale is the raw score divided by the highest score in the

norms for Outdoor. To avoid data expressed as decimals, the proportion

is multiplied by 100. Hence, the formula used is:

$$\text{Score} = \frac{\text{Student Raw Score}}{\text{Highest Possible Raw Score}} \times 100$$

1. <u>Present the measurements on the General Interest Survey by socio-
   economic group and sex. (tables).</u>

The scales in the Kuder Survey are: Outdoor, Mechanical, Compu--

tational, Scientific, Persuasive, Artistic, Literary, Musical, Social

Service, and Clerical

Table_____. Scores on the Kuder General Interest
Survey of Inner-City Students

SS	Outd		Mech		Compu		Sci		Pers		Art		Lit		Mus		Soc Ser		Cler	
	Pre	Post	Pre	Post	Pre	Post	Pre	Post	Pre	Post	Pre	Post	Pre	Post	Pre	Post	Pre	Post	Pre	Post
Girls																				
1.																				
etc.																				
Boys																				
1.																				
etc.																				

Comment on the table:

Highest scores, lowest scores, central tendencies among the scores, dispersion among the scores, logical consistencies among the scores, inconsistencies, unexpected results. Over-arching comments on the table: Level of the scores in the total table, comparisons of scores of girls and boys, comparisons of pretests and posttests, comparisons of scores on the various scales.

Table_____. Scores on the Kuder General Interest Survey of Urban Students

Organize this table in the same format as the preceding table.

Table_____. Scores on the Kuder General Interest Survey of Suburban Students

Organize this table in the same format as the preceding table.

Table_____. Scores on the Kuder General Interest Survey of Rural Students

Organize this table in the same format as the preceding table.

2. Compute the correlations among the total scores and subscores of SSHA with the scores on general career interests (compute Pearson coefficient r).

Follow the format and procedures for this analysis of SSHA and General Interest scores as were used for SSHA and Achievement scores as were used for SSHA and Achievement scores in Chapter III.

3. Compute regression formulas for predicting some/all of the general career interest factors (dependent) from some or all of the SSHA factors (independent). Compute the standard error of the estimate to test the accuracy of these predictions.

Follow the format and precedures for this analysis of SSHA and General Interest scores as were used for SSHA and Achievement scores in Chapter III. Select several General Interest Scales that correlate the highest with Study Orientation and compute the regression formulas for predicting the scales from Study Orientation.

The formula for Standard Error of the Estimate is $S_{1.2} =$

$S_1 \sqrt{1 - R_{1.2}^2}$, where S_1 is the standard deviation of the actual scores
and $R_{1.2}$ is the coefficient of correlation between actual scores and
predictor scores.

4. Compute one-way analyses of variance of independent factors/
   subfactor, and of correlate factors/subfactors for socioeconomic
   groups. (F-ratio).

   Follow the format and precedures for this analysis of SSHA and
General Interest scores as were used for SSHA and Achievement acores in
Chapter III.

5. Compute two-way analyses of variance of independent factors/subfactors,
   and of correlate factors/subfactors by socioeconomic group and sex
   as main effect. (F-ratio for rows and for columns).

   Follow the format and procedures for this analysis of SSHA and
General Interest scores as were used for SSHA and Achievement scores in
Chapter III.

6. Chapter summary from points 1-5 above. State findings based on
   correlation coefficients, or regression coefficients, and F-Ratios
   individually. Also, try to establish generalizations based on
   combinations of these statistical results, whether of the same type
   or across types. Be alert to establish generalized relationships.

CHAPTER V. CONCLUSIONS AND DISCUSSION

Establish generalizations over-arching all of chapter III and all of chapter IV, or overarching parts of chapter III and parts of chapter IV.

Make recommendations for application of findings to school practices: administration, curriculum, instruction, guidance, evaluation, etc.

Organize generalizations and recommendations around the purposes of the investigation:

1. What are the study habits and attitudes, achievement levels, and general career interests of eighth grade students?

2. What are the size and direction of correlations among independent and correlate variables/subvariables by socio-economic background for girls and for boys?

3. To what extent are there differences among independent and correlate variables/subvariables according to socio-economic backgrounds of the students?

4. To what extent are there differences among independent and correlate variables/subvariables according to socio-economic backgrounds and sex of the students?

5. To what extent can predictions based on the independent variable/ subvariables be made of correlate variables/subvariables? Include in this final chapter a discussion of the topic and your procedures in terms of researchability, design, and statistics.

BIBLIOGRAPHY

Bodden, J.L. and Others, "Value of a Study Skills Inventory for Feedback and Criterion Purposes in an Educational Skills Course," Journal of Educational Research, 65: 309-11 March, 1972.

Briggs, R.D. and Others, "Study Habit Modification and Its Effect on Academic Performance: A Behavioral Approach: RSQ3R," Journal of Educational Research, 64: 347-50, April 1971.

Corlett, D. "Library Skills, Study Habits and Attitudes, and Sex as Related to Academic Achievement," Educational and Psychological Measurement, 34: 967-9 Winter, 1974.

Draayer, D.R. and J.W. McClure. "Comparison of Student Study Habits and Attitudes on Traditional and Modular Scheduling," North Central Association Quarterly, 46: 348-59 Winter, 1972.

Entwistle, N.J. and J.D. Wilson, "Personality, Study Methods and Academic Performance," University Quarterly, 24: 147-56 Spr. '70.

Entwistle, N.J. and Others, "Prediction from Scales of Motivation and Study Methods," British Journal of Educational Psychology, 41: 258-67 November, 1971.

Goldfried, M.R. and T.J. D'Zurilla, "Prediction of Academic Competence by Means of the Survey of Study Habits and Attitudes," Journal of Educational Psychology, 64: 116-22 Feb. 1973.

Grob, J.A. "Reading Rate and Study-Time Demands on Secondary Students," Journal of Reading, 13: 285-8 Ja '70.

Harris, M.B. and F. Ream, "Program to Improve Study Habits of High School Students," Psychology in the Schools, 9: 325-30 July 1972.

Huque, A.O. "Studying Science Effectively," Science Education, 54: 87-90 January 1970.

Khan, S.B., "Affective Correlates of Academic Achievement," Journal of Educational Psychology, 60(No. 3, 1969), 216-221.

Khan, S.B. and D.M. Roberts, "Factorial Stability of Academically Relevant Affective Characteristics," Measurement and Evaluation in Guidance, 3:209-12 Winter 1971.

Khan, S.B. and D.M. Roberts, "Relationships among Study Habits and Attitudes, Aptitude and Grade 8 Achievement," Educational and Psychological Measurement 29: 951-5 Winter 1969.

Lin, Y. and W.J. McKeachie, "Aptitude, Anxiety, Study Habits, and Academic Achievement," Journal of Counseling Psychology, 17: 306-9 July, 1970.

Lin, Y. and W.J. McKeachie, "Student Characteristics Related to Achievement in Introductory Psychology Courses," British Journal of Educational Psychology. 43: 70-6 February, 1973.

McCausland, D.F. and N.E. Stewart, "Academic Aptitude, Study Skills, and Attitudes and College GPA," Journal of Educational Research, 67: 354-7 April, 1974.

Martin, L.W. and R.N. Sawyer, "Specialized Study Skills, Developmental Reading Instruction and Counseling," Journal of Experimental Education. 37: 52-6, Sum. '69.

Moskovis, L.M. "Studying Study Habits," Business Education Forum, 27: 24-6 Oct. 1972.

Page, L.T. "Reading and Study Skills," Reading Improvement, 6: 41-2, Fall '69.

Pauk, W. "Study Skills! That's the Answer!" Reading Improvement, 10: 2-6 Winter 1973.

Roark, A.E. and S.A. Harrington, "Survey of Study Habits and Attitudes: Review," Journal of Educational Measurement 6: 120-2 Sum '69.

Shepps, F.P. and R.R. Shepps, "Relationship of Study Habits and School Attitude to Achievement in Mathematics and Reading," Journal of Educational Research, 65: 71-3 October, 1971.

Williams, R.L. "Personality, Ability, and Achievement Correlates of Scholastic Attitudes," Journal of Educational Research, 63: 401-3 May, 1970.

Zimmerman W.S. and Others, "Factorial Dimensions of the Study Attitudes and Methods Survey Test; Experimental Form," Educational and Psychological Measurement, 30: 433-6 Summer, 1970.

IV. REPORTED HISTORICAL INVESTIGATION

Associated with teaching:

Analysis of the Topic, Purposing,

Hypothesizing, Data Selection, Data

Collection, Tools for Collecting Data,

Critical Interpretation of Data,

Statistical Interpretation of Data,

Types of Research, and Written Report.

The historical investigation is relatively infrequent today. The dimensions along which the independent variable is investigated are called descriptive variables. Hypothesizing plays a role in historical investigation. Location and evaluation of sources is the unique challenge of historical investigations.

Benjamin Franklin and William Smith
Their School and Their Dispute†

By Melvin H. Buxbaum*

THE LONG and acrimonious battle between Benjamin Franklin and William Smith, Provost of the College of Philadelphia, has excited a good deal of scholarly interest. Two articles on the troubles between the men have appeared recently. The earlier of these, by Ralph Ketcham,[1] argues that Smith's pamphleteering in behalf of Thomas Penn, the proprietor of Pennsylvania, was the major cause for the break in friendship with Franklin, who supported the Quaker Assembly against the proprietor. The second article, by James H. Hutson,[2] suggests that a chief reason for the final rupture between the provost and the philosopher had to do with more personal matters.† Because of the political antagonisms and a personality clash between them, Smith tried to prevent Franklin from being awarded an honorary doctorate from Oxford. The latter in turn responded by striving to undermine Smith's efforts to raise money for the College of Philadelphia. And the provost, according to Hutson, retaliated by spreading the word that William Franklin was illegitimate. Smith hoped that this information would make it impossible for the son to be appointed governor of New Jersey. Thus he tried to strike back at the father by ruining William's political career at the outset. No doubt both articles present good reasons for the bitterness between Smith and Franklin; however, neither gets at what I take to be the heart of the problem. It was more than personal pettiness or than even the Assembly's battles with the

---

†See also Bruce R. Lively, "William Smith, the College and Academy of Philadelphia and Pennsylvania Politics, 1753-1758," *Historical Magazine of the P.E.C.,* XXXVIII, No. 3 (Sept., 1969) , pp. 237ff.—*Editor's Note.*

*Dr. Buxbaum is Professor of English, University of Illinois at Chicago Circle.—*Editor's Note.*

[1]Ralph Ketcham, "Benjamin Franklin and William Smith: New Light on an Old Philadelphia Quarrel," *Pennsylvania Magazine of History and Biography,* LXXVIII (1964) , 142-63.

[2]James H. Hutson, "Benjamin Franklin and William Smith: More Light on an Old Philadelphia Quarrel," *Pennsylvania Magazine of History and Biography,* XCIII (1969) , 109-13.

proprietor and his friends that caused Franklin to undermine an institution so close to him and of which he himself was the chief founder. There seem to be other and at least equally important reasons, and these are also related to the political situation in Pennsylvania.

Franklin was at first delighted that Smith accepted the offer to head the Academy of Philadelphia, for the young man seemed to him a liberal-minded scholar. Although he had some reservations about Smith's tendency toward censoriousness and advised him to be more cautious, he still expressed his "great Esteem"[3] for his young friend. This regard did not diminish when Smith took orders in England, since Franklin had a genuine respect for bright and liberal Churchmen. Though a deist, he could live comfortably with Anglicanism that stressed morality rather than the rigid orthodoxy or the extreme piety that Calvinist ministers, according to their theological position, insisted on. We would do well to remember that although he stopped attending Presbyterian services while still a young man in Philadelphia, Franklin did later take out a pew in Christ Church. And it is further true that one of his favorite authors and moralists was Archbishop Tillotson, a man whose works Franklin wanted read by Academy students.[4] He therefore took Smith's ordination in stride even though he realized that many people would resent it.[5] Then, too, until about 1756 he was confident that he would be able to guide the younger man and keep a benevolent but firm hand on the reins that would give direction to the Academy. He was, after all, at least half serious when he referred to Smith as "my Pupil" to whom he had been trying to teach his "Philosophy."[6]

Such a relationship, however, existed only in the mind of the master. Smith was an inveterate politician with as much ambition as Franklin. His naturally conservative outlook on government and social order, coupled with his gratitude to Thomas Penn for endowing a chair for him at the Academy, logically placed him in the proprietary camp and thus, as Ketcham points out, made him an opponent of Franklin and the Assembly. Moreover, Penn had become an Anglican, and Smith hoped to use this situation and his friendship with the Archbishop of Canturbury to improve his secular and church positions. From Penn he looked forward to financial gain

[3]*The Papers of Benjamin Franklin*, ed. Leonard W. Labaree *et al.* (12 vols.; New Haven: Yale University Press, 1959-) , IV, 475-76.
[4]*Papers*, I, 329; II, 90; and IV, 107.
[5]*Ibid.*, V, 331.
[6]*Ibid.*, V, 263.

and political prominence, and from Canterbury he desired the pair of "lawn Sleeves" that would proclaim him the first Bishop of America. The best of both worlds was what he wanted, and it is not without reason that his Quaker detractors referred to him as the "Pope." Not only did Smith use his effective pen in behalf of the proprietor, but he used his position at the school, which was intended by Franklin and supposedly everyone else to be nonsectarian, to promote the interests of the Church of England. For a man in Smith's place to become involved in such affairs was dangerous; and to make matters more complicated, politics and religion, as Carl and Jessica Bridenbaugh have noted, were largely inseparable in colonial America.[7]

The proprietary party with which Smith aligned himself was made up of about half the Anglican church in Philadelphia and eventually, as the wealthy and influential Presbyterian, Chief Justice William Allen, wrote to Thomas Penn, the Presbyterians "to a man."[8] Smith's efforts in behalf of the Penn family, then, were often serviceable to the Dissenters. In 1755, for example, he wrote *A Brief State of the Province of Pennsylvania*, a piece designed to wrest power from the Quaker Assembly by attacking the group's principle of nonviolence which, Smith charges, made the Friends unfit to protect a province threatened by the Catholic French and their Indian allies. The many pleas for help from the frontier have been ignored by the Assembly, for the Quakers are willing to let the settlers die in order to retain both their principle and their political power.[9] Smith further argues that the frontiersmen, the great majority of whom are Germans and Scotch-Irish Presbyterians, far outnumber the Friends; however, the Assembly makes certain that they have no political influence. By working on the fears of the ignorant Germans, who suffered in Europe because of vicious landlords, the Quakers turn them against the kind and generous Penn family and are thus assured of German support in all elections. The provost appeals to the Germans to unite with their Presbyterian neighbors and fellow sufferers against the Assembly, the common enemy of both groups.

[7]Carl and Jessica Bridenbaugh, *Rebels and Gentlemen: Philadelphia in the Age of Franklin* (New York: Reynal & Hitchcock, 1942), pp. 13-19.

[8]William Allen to Thomas Penn, October 21, 1764, Penn Official Correspondence, IX. The manuscript is in The Historical Society of Pennsylvania. The Penn Official Correspondence will hereafter be referred to as POC, and The Historical Society of Pennsylvania will be abbreviated as HSP.

[9][William Smith], *A Brief State of the Province of Pennsylvania* . . . (London: R. Griffiths, 1755), pp. 16, 26. This piece appears in *Sabin's Reprints*, No. IV (New York, 1865).

As events later proved, protection was only one thing that the frontier Dissenters wanted. They saw that if they were going to improve their lot, they would have to gain more equitable representation in the Assembly.[10] The Quakers, on the other hand, realized that, given the great numerical superiority of the Presbyterians, truly representative government would mean the loss of political control to a group whom the Friends feared and hated.[11] Although the wealthy and status-conscious members of the proprietary party, both Anglicans and city Dissenters, had little more regard for the uncouth settlers than did the Quakers, they put aside their prejudices for a time and courted those whom they despised with demands for fair representation and protection for the back areas.

Franklin was reluctant to believe that his "Pupil" wrote *A Brief State*,[12] but the very next year, shortly after Smith offered to be Penn's propagandist,[13] he unleashed the vicious attack on the Quakers, *A Brief View of the Conduct of Pennsylvania*. Smith here carries out the logic inherent in his earlier work, calling the Friends "Infatuated Enthusiasts"[14] whose politics are religiously motivated.[15] The real reason they refuse to defend the five terrified back counties, he implies, is that the Quaker Assembly would rather see the settlers die than prosper, for they constitute a large majority in the colony and great numbers of them are *"Presbyterians from the North of Ireland. . . ."*[16] The provost diminishes the German population for the sake of appeal in this second pamphlet. Earlier he had called especially upon the Germans to rebel against the Assembly, but now he was summoning the Dissenters to unity and battle. He finally tries to enlist the support of the King and parliament on the side of the proprietor by repeating his charge that Quaker policy actually promotes the French cause in America.[17]

The Quakers and Franklin, however, enjoyed some revenge. Isaac Norris, second in command of the reorganized Quaker party,

[10]Brooke Hindle, "The March of the Paxton Boys," *William and Mary Quarterly*, Third Series, III (1946), 483-84.

[11]*The Paxton Papers*, ed. John R. Dunbar (The Hague: Martinus Nijhoff, 1957), pp. 85, 104, 205, 210, 339, 375-76.

[12]*Papers*, VI, 169, 216.

[13]*Ibid.*, VI, 213.

[14][William Smith], *A Brief View of the Conduct of Pennsylvania, for the Year 1755* (London: R. Griffiths, 1756), p. 23.

[15]*Ibid.*, p. 19.

[16]*Ibid.*, p. 53.

[17]*Ibid.*, pp. 6, 12-13.

wrote to its leader, Franklin, in England as agent for the province in the taxation dispute with Thomas Penn, that "Our old Inviterate Scribbler has at length wrote himself into a Jail."[18] Smith was imprisoned by the Assembly on January 6, 1758, for supporting a libel on that body and for seeing to its translation and publication in the *Philadelphische Zeitung.* There can be no doubt that the provost's role in the libel was the occasion rather than the sole reason for his confinement. Franklin himself had the opportunity of defending the Assembly's actions when Smith's request for a hearing in England was granted.

Yet more than revenge was involved in the matter. After all, the situation of the Assembly was delicate, and to imprison a man who had connections with the Archbishop of Canterbury and Thomas Penn was a very dangerous move—especially since Smith's case constituted the first time that any Assembly had ever tried a citizen for libel. Considering that the Quakers, who were skillful politicians, took the chance and that the normally cautious and shrewd Franklin supported the action, they must have considered the risk worth taking. And it was. Norris and Franklin saw Smith's attacks on the Assembly and his support of the frontier and the proprietary party in their proper context, and this context was by no means a merely political one. In his effort to gain backing for the Penn family Smith, as Norris said, "had been made a Tool of narrow Presbyterian Politicks. . . ."[19] Although the provost, like most Anglicans, feared, disliked and even opposed Presbyterianism,[20] he and the other Churchmen of the proprietary faction found themselves in a strong political alliance with them. Their demands for fair representation and protection for the back counties, in effect, were an insistence on greater power for the Dissenters who, the Quakers believed, were their most dangerous enemies on both religious and political grounds.[21] The allies of the proprietary party were able politicians who could work against each other along denominational lines while presenting a

[18]*Papers,* VII, 385.

[19]*Ibid.,* VII, 385-86.

[20]See, for example, Richard Peters' letter to Thomas Penn, June 20, 1752, POC, V. HSP; Peters to Penn, November 6, 1753, POC, VI. HSP; and Smith to Peters, [1765], Peters Papers, HSP.

[21]Even the city Presbyterians were afraid of their frontier brethren, one of the most fearful, for a time, being William Allen, one of their stauncher supporters and Penn's political strategist in America. See: *The Burd Papers. Extracts from Chief Justice William Allen's Letter Book,* I, ed. Lewis Burd Walker (Pottsville, Pennsylvania: Standard Publishing Co., 1897) , 25. Also, see: *Papers,* VIII, 81; Brooke Hindle, *William and Mary Quarterly,* Third Series, III, 478, 483-84; *Paxton Papers,* pp. 36, 85, 180 and 155-64.

united front against Franklin and the Assembly. The Anglicans took comfort in the fact that Thomas Penn was one of them and would not allow the Dissenters to become too powerful, while the Presbyterians, relying on their numerical advantage, were confident that the defeat of the Assembly would put them in the seat of political and church power.

Religion was also involved in the politicking over the College of Philadelphia. Although Smith and the Trustees of this institution who actually forced Franklin out of the school by rendering him ineffective were mostly members of Christ Church, they were expressing a policy that had very considerable religious and political significance for the Dissenters as well. And readers of the *Autobiography* will recall that Franklin had lost all regard for Congregationalists and Presbyterians by the time he was sixteen.[22]

Richard Peters confessed the underhanded nature of Franklin's removal from any position of influence in the school,[23] and the founder, of course, knew exactly what was happening and was understandably bitter. Writing from London to Ebenezer Kinnersley, master of the Academy or English school, Franklin said that the "Trustees had reap'd the full Advantage of my Head, Hands, Heart and Purse in getting through the first Difficulties" and then "laide me aside."[24] He exaggerated the openness of his purse, his contributions to the school being less than the average, but after he resigned as President of the Trustees he neither gave nor raised money for it at all. He was especially hurt that his ouster was the result of politics: "before I left Philadelphia, everything to be done in the Academy was privately preconcerted in a Cabal without my Knowledge or Patricipation and carried into Execution. The Schemes of Public Parties made it seem requisite to lessen my Influence wherever it could be lessened."[25] The letter, written more than three years after his resignation, during which time he had been abroad and involved in complex provincial matters, clearly indicates both the depth of Franklin's resentment and the fact that he blamed his political enemies among the Trustees for this personal tragedy.

In addition to being stripped of influence in the school, Franklin had the misfortune of seeing the Academy suffer from neglect. Most

[22]*The Autobiography of Benjamin Franklin*, ed. Leonard W. Labaree *et al.* (New Haven: Yale University Press, 1964), pp. 145-48, 167-68. Franklin did not make distinctions between Congregationalists and Presbyterians.

[23]Peters to Penn, February 14, 1757, Penn Letter Book. HSP.

[24]*Papers*, VIII, 415-16.

[25]*Ibid.*

of the Trustees and Smith were indifferent toward this branch of the institution and devoted their energies to improving the College, the classical school which could grant degrees and graduate ministers. In fact, the provost and his allies, as Franklin knew, were striving to make the College a virtual seminary for Church of England ministers.[26] This and especially Smith's politicking for the proprietary party brought the school into the religious battle between Anglicans and Presbyterians. Smith denied the fact, and even his recent apologist has insisted that he was above such deceit,[27] but Peters, who was an Anglican minister, President of the Trustees after Franklin, and Penn's secretary knew differently, as did Smith himself. Peters wrote to the Archbishop of Canterbury, who feared the Dissenters might become too powerful in the school, that it was the unstated intention and practice of the provost and the Trustees to hire Presbyterians as faculty *only* when there was a desperate need to fill positions and no Churchmen could be found for them.[28] Peters had earlier written to Smith, who was in England raising money for the College, about the same matter: "I blush to tell you that we have not one Church Tutor in all our Academy. There is not a Churchman upon the Continent as I can hear of that is fit to make a Tutor: and it is from downright necessity that we are obliged to take such as offer."[29] The provost, however, was confident that no part of the school would ever fall into Presbyterian hands. Trying to allay Anglican fears, he said that under his leadership, "the Church by soft and easy Means," would continue to gain influence in all branches of the institution. He reminded his correspondent, Rev. Philip Bearcroft, Secretary of the SPG, that with himself and nearly all the Trustees Anglican, there was little chance that the Dissenters would become influential. Moreover, twice each day the students were required to read the set prayers of the Church of England and were instructed solely from its catechism.[30] Smith knew better than the Secretary or other nervous Anglicans.

[26]Edward P. Cheyney, *History of the University of Pennsylvania, 1740-1940* (Philadelphia: University of Pennsylvania Press, 1940), p. 32.

[27]Albert F. Gegenheimer, *William Smith, Educator and Churchman, 1727-1803* (Philadelphia: University of Pennsylvania Press, 1943), *passim*.

[28]*Historical Collections Relating to the American Colonial Church*, ed. William S. Perry (5 vols.; Hartford, Connecticut: Printed for the Subscribers, 1870-78), II, 391.

[29]Peters to Smith, May 28, 1763, Dreer Collection, American Clergy. HSP. The letter has been published in the *Pennsylvania Magazine of History and Biography*, X (1886), 350-53.

[30]Horace W. Smith, *Life and Correspondence of the Rev. William Smith, D.D.* (2 vols.; Philadelphia: Ferguson Bros. & Co., 1880), I, 143.

Francis Alison, Presbyterian minister and scholar, could have borne witness to the provost's success. Alison resigned as head of a small seminary at New London, Pennsylvania, to become vice-provost of the College. He had hoped to turn out many more Old Side Dissenting ministers than he could have at the smaller school, thus enabling his faction to compete with the New Side Presbyterian graduates of the College of New Jersey. There seemed to be no other way for the Old Side to survive as a force in the Presbyterian Church. Smith and his allies, however, so thoroughly frustrated his plans that Alison was, after a time, "ready to resign my place in the College and retire to the country meerly thro chagrine." His feeling was undoubtedly shared by many in the Synod of Philadelphia. In 1752 this body, having been unable to offer an effective challenge to the College of New Jersey, appealed to Alison to use his new position in Philadelphia "not only to promote the good of the public, but also of the church"[31] by pushing through Old Side clergymen. By 1766, however, the chagrined Alison wrote to Ezra Stiles that the "Episcopal Trustees" controlled the College and were actually getting Presbyterian youth to take Anglican orders! This was being accomplished by acquainting the students with the "high life" they might expect as Anglican clergymen as well as by exploiting the lingering hostility between the nominally reunited Presbyterian parties.[32] Smith and the Trustees did indeed try to make the school an Anglican breeding ground (if not seminary), and during the Revolution suffered for their close connection with England and the Established Church by being forced out of the school.

For years prior to this event the air was filled with charges either that the institution was Presbyterian or, far more commonly, that it was Anglican. Some Church of England ministers, like Hugh Neill of Oxford, Pennsylvania, saw a Presbyterian behind every desk,[33] and no doubt Alison at times exaggerated the plight of his group. Yet the fear on both sides, even within the proprietary party, was so great that the Archbishop of Canterbury, Rev. Samuel Chandler, influential Presbyterian minister of Old Jewry, and Governor Richard Penn became involved. They finally agreed to demand that

---

[31] *Records of the Presbyterian Church in the United States*, ed. William H. Roberts (Enlarged ed. Philadelphia: Presbyterian Board of Publication and Sabbath-School Work, 1904) , p. 206.

[32] *Extracts from the Itineraries and Other Miscellanies of Ezra Stiles, 1755-1794, with a Selection from his Correspondence*, ed. Franklin B. Dexter (New Haven: Yale University Press, 1916) , p. 428.

[33] *Historical Collections*, ed. Perry, II, 389.

the Trustees guarantee the equal treatment of the "various denomi-nations."[34]

By the time of the letter, 1764, however, secular and church politics, which again were normally related, had already become an important part of the College of Philadelphia as they were in the other schools in the Middle Colonies. In spite of their political alliance, the proprietary Anglicans and the Presbyterians carried on a religious struggle for dominance that seriously affected the affairs of the school which Franklin had founded and which he had hoped would be free of sectarianism. Peters expressed the sentiments of the proprietary Anglican Trustees toward the Presbyterians in a letter to Thomas Penn. The Trustees, he wrote, did not want Alison on the faculty because he was a "Dissenter," and it was only his "uncommon Talents" that overcame the bigotry, if not the resentment, of his employers.[35] And Peters himself, for religious as well as social reasons, referred to the frontier Presbyterians, for whom he had sympathy when it was politically expedient, as "the very Scum of the Earth. . . ."[36] Smith, who was the chief promoter of fair representation and adequate defense for Dissenters, plotted with Peters to secure a quick and secret ordination for an Anglican minister of doubtful ability, a graduate of the College of Philadelphia, who would be sent to an area as yet unserviced by the Church of England. As Smith noted, the minister would actually be used as a bulwark against the Dissen-ters in "Gloster" and Egg Harbor, in which places Smith said that the people were degenerating so terribly that "the Presbyterians will soon get them all."[37]

On their part, the Presbyterians made life miserable and fearful for their Anglican friends. Rev. Thomas Barton complained bitterly of constant persecution by the Dissenters who insulted "both the Church & I" and prevented him from carrying on the Anglican ser-vice. Barton referred specifically to the New Side or evangelical and awakened Presbyterians, whom he called "Bigots and Enthusiasts."[38] The Dissenters also expressed their profound fear of the Church of

[34]*Benjamin Franklin and the University of Pennsylvania*, ed. Frances N. Thorpe (Washington: Government Printing Office, 1893), pp. 79-80. Also see: Thomas H. Montgomery, *A History of the University of Pennsylvania from Its Foundation to A.D. 1770* (Philadelphia: G. W. Jacobs & Co., 1900), p. 424.

[35]Peters to Penn, June 20, 1752, POC, V. HSP.

[36]Peters to Penn, November 6, 1753, POC, VI. HSP.

[37]Smith to Peters, [1765]. Peters Papers. HSP.

[38]*Pennsylvania Archives*, ed. Samuel Hazard (12 vols.; Philadelphia: Joseph Severins & Co., 1852-56), III, 450-51.

England by their unanimous opposition to an American bishopric. Peters, angered by their unrelenting hostility toward the idea, wrote to the Archbishop of Canterbury that the Presbyterians were "fond to a madness" of popular government "and would dislike Bishops on any footing."[39] This was written just one year before the election of 1764 in which the Presbyterians "to a Man" turned out to vote for the proprietary interest and defeat Franklin. The political coalition itself was nearly destroyed, however, when the Presbyterians discovered that Smith had tried to sabotage the Rev. Charles Beatty's efforts to raise money in England. The fund for which he was collecting was ostensibly for the relief of widows and orphans of Presbyterian ministers, but Smith told wealthy Anglicans, who might have otherwise given something, that the money was actually being used to propagate the Presbyterian faith. Word of Smith's actions got back to America and although he was able to mend some fences, he lost the friendship of William Allen and other important Dissenters.[40] The provost justified his efforts against Beatty privately by other Anglicans by in turn accusing the Presbyterian of trying to thwart the fund-raising campaign for the College of Philadelphia.[41]

In spite of their differences, both Anglicans and Old Side Presbyterians agreed that the Philadelphia community needed a degree-granting institution to compete with the College of New Jersey. Peters explained to Penn that unless a new charter was granted to permit the establishment of a college and not merely an Academy, the Philadelphia school would be "like to suffer much by the Neighbourhood of the Jersey College to which abundance of People send their sons for no other reason other than because they can there take Degrees."[42] Many of these young men, of course, became New Side ministers, and Peters reminded Penn that he had previously expressed his "apprehensions and Fears" that the Presbyterian institution would become a very important force in America and render the Academy ineffective as a bulwark against it.[43] Peters had formerly opposed the foundation of a college and Penn also had doubts as to the wisdom of such a venture; however, Smith changed their minds[44] and was soon

[39] *Historical Collections*, ed. Perry, II, 394.

[40] Peters to Smith, May 28, 1763, Dreer Collection. HSP.

[41] William Gordon to Charles Beatty, December 24, 1764. William Smith Papers, Penn-Peters Correspondence, II, 102. HSP.

[42] Peters to Penn, December 23, 1754, POC, VI. HSP.

[43] *Ibid.*

[44] *Ibid.*

able to thank the proprietor for the new charter, telling him that it had come just in time.[45]

The Old Side agreed, for shortly after the new charter was granted it presented a proposal asking permission to "ingraft a seminary" upon the institution. The plan called for having a minimum of six students read divinity with Alison while following a course of study in the College.[46] Eventually these students would become ministers who would be able to compete for souls with the Jersey graduates. The Old Side felt that Smith, their political ally, would encourage the plan. After all, he was known to be contemptuous of the New Side and had earlier discredited the evangelical preacher, Gilbert Tennent, while he was in England raising money for the Jersey school.[47] So intensive were Smith's efforts that, to the delight of the Old Side and the Anglicans alike, he turned the Rev. Samuel Chandler against the school for a time.[48] The provost was willing to let Alison have his seminary in the College, hoping to gain influence among his political compatriots and also to weaken the position of the New Side.[49] But as Alison and his fellow ministers were to discover, the Trustees and Smith, in spite of alliances, had little use for any Presbyterians. These allies used each other to further their private as well as common ends. However, when it looked to some that the Dissenters, because of their numerical superiority on the faculty and because Smith had indeed become the tool of the party which they dominated, were about to take over the College of Philadelphia, Smith and his fellow Anglicans stopped them, as they had promised the Archbishop of Canterbury they would.

Convinced that they would never get far in what they were sure was now an Anglican school, the Old Side clergy by 1766 were desperate for some sort of compromise with their New Side brethren. Their efforts to achieve one involved Presbyterians throughout the Middle Colonies, for they all feared their common religious enemies, Smith, the great majority of Trustees and their school. Old Side sympathizers therefore proposed a coalition between themselves and the New Side ministers and faculty of the College of New Jersey. They felt that either Alison or John Ewing, professor of natural philosophy in the Philadelphia school and an important Old Side leader, should

[45]Smith to Penn, April 10, 1755, POC, VI. HSP.

[46]Cheyney, *Pennsylvania*, p. 40.

[47]Smith, *Smith*, I, 103, 104.

[48]*Ibid.*, I, 103-6.

[49]*Ibid.*, I, 104-5.

be made president of the New Jersey institution.[50] This plan was unacceptable to the New Side and failed.

It did have much to recommend it to many Dissenters, however, who looked upon the College of Philadelphia as an Anglican school. Samuel Purviance, an Old Side politician who knew all matters and sentiments Presbyterian, expressed the feelings of many of his fellows in a letter to Ezra Stiles, President of Yale College and a Congregationalist minister, written just before the plan was rejected. Purviance expresses both the fear and malevolence of his party when, full of anticipation, he explained to Stiles that the departure of Alison and Ewing "will certainly ruin Phila. College. . . ."[51] Though one of Smith's chief political allies against the Assembly and Franklin, Purviance hoped that the plan would not only give the Old Side control over the Jersey school but also defeat the Churchmen and their dangerous college. The provost, he knew, like most Anglicans, took pleasure in the division within the nominally reunited Presbyterian Church, confident that the long struggle would weaken both factions enough to permit the Church of England to establish an American bishopric. Along with many other informed persons, Purviance was certain that Smith had been angling for the position himself. The best way to prevent a bishopric, to retaliate against Smith and to weaken the Anglican interest, Purviance felt, was to unite all Dissenters and "ruin" the College of Philadelphia.[52]

Once the plan had been rejected, the politician lapsed into despair. He was certain that the Church of England was an even greater threat to Presbyterians than the Quakers because it controlled a school with which it could turn out ministers. The Old Side would in particular suffer, he feared, for their young men would most probably have to be educated in Philadelphia, where each day they would be "perverted by the Intrigue of that designing subtile Mortal Dr. Smith. . . ."[53] Although the Dissenters continued striving to make headway in the Philadelphia college, the Trustees and the provost were too much for them, and by 1769 Alison, who was still at his post, was desperate. "Our Jersey College," he wrote of the school that had rejected him, "is now talking as if she was soon to be the bulwark against Episcopacy: I should rejoice to see her Pistols, like honest Teagues, grown up into great guns."[54] Alison's imagery was, unfor-

[50]*Stiles*, ed. Dexter, p. 429.
[51]*Ibid.*, p. 558.
[52]*Ibid.*, pp. 554-58.
[53]*Ibid.*, p. 559.
[54]*Ibid.*, p. 435.

tunately, appropriate, for the College of Philadelphia had become the battlefield on which an only partly submerged religious war was being waged. Franklin was kept informed of these and all important affairs in Philadelphia, and his efforts to sabotage the fund-raising drive in behalf of the school by arguing that it had been made a haven of bigotry and faction, referred not only to the political situation in the province, but far more significantly to the religious one.

Franklin despised religious battles and schemes above all others, for they seemed to him senseless. Yet his experiences with Calvinist Establishments in particular, both Congregationalist and Presbyterian, were very negative and he had often become involved in bitter disputes with them. In 1722, as Silence Dogood, the moralistic widow of a pious New England country minister, Franklin, at the age of sixteen, attacked the Boston area clergy, accusing them of being a parcel of lazy and ignorant good-for-nothings. They have, he charged, chosen the ministry because they look upon it as an easy way to make a living, and they are nothing more than conceited, fanatic and immoral tyrants.[55] Although he wrote the *Dogood Papers* pseudonymously, he may have been suspected of being their author. At least his general association with his brother James' *New England Courant*, which was born to do battle against the ministers and their allies in the government, and his frequent and unwise arguments in behalf of deism gained for him not only the applause of the unregenerate but the wrath of those who were still Puritans. On the whole he made more influential enemies than friends in a Boston that was not quite ready for emancipation, and he understandably became convinced that he would do better launching his career in New York or Philadelphia than in the city of his birth.[56]

He seems not to have forgotten his chief reasons for leaving Boston, for when he had become a rising young tradesman in Philadelphia, he used his own newspaper, the *Pennsylvania Gazette*, to lampoon Calvinists.[57] And in 1734 he used both the *Gazette* and his pen to defend Samuel Hemphill, a Presbyterian minister who was excommunicated by the Synod of Philadelphia for preaching something akin to rationalism or Christian deism rather than Calvinism. Such preaching was very acceptable to Franklin and others of his beliefs, but the Synod was less happy about it. Angrier than the religiously tolerant sage in the *Autobiography* ever becomes, the

[55]*Papers*, I, 8-13, 14-18, 21-26, 27-30, 30-32, 41-45.
[56]*Autobiography*, ed. Labaree *et al.*, p. 71.
[57]*Papers*, I, 119, 182-83, 187; II, 28-35, 37-126, 227; *Pennsylvania Gazette* for January 3, 1738, March 30, 1738, November 30, 1738, and December 6, 1738.

young printer thoroughly flayed the Synod in a series of sharp and even brutal pieces that attacked not only the Synod but its faith as well.[58] Five years later, as an interested spectator in the Great Awakening, Franklin learned how vicious the godly could become when they met head on. For a time he was impressed by the improvement in morals that seemed the result of the spectacular and effective preaching of George Whitefield, but Franklin grew disgusted with the great evangelist when he became increasingly Calvinistic in his doctrine.[59] By 1762, the year that Smith accused him of plotting against the College of Philadelphia, the philosopher felt little but disgust for Dissenters, a group of whom he was soon to condemn as a mob of bigoted and inhuman savages.[60] It is far more important, then, to see Franklin's efforts against the College in light of his long-held attitudes toward Calvinist Establishments rather than in a context of personal animosity or of political infighting. His Presbyterian contemporaries certainly saw matters in the context I am suggesting and spread the word that Franklin was not only a political opponent but underneath all, a dangerous enemy to their Church as well.[61]

Franklin did of course have a high regard for individual Presbyterians, but when the denomination, or any considerable faction of it acted in force and seemed to him to pose a threat, he responded negatively. Disgusted by the petty but dangerous religious and political rivalry in the school he founded and fearing that it might become a seminary, especially a Dissenting seminary, Franklin worked against the institution. As Smith noted to Peters, Franklin told potential contributors that the College of Philadelphia could have plenty of money from the Assembly, if Smith would only ask for it. It seems obvious that this was Franklin's attempt to gain control of the school and to make it completely secular, if not apolitical. If this effort were to fail, Franklin apparently came to believe, it would be better for the school to close its doors than for it to continue in its present course.

As I have previously indicated, Franklin's contributions to the College were small, even below the average. The school, however, was in dire financial straits and conducted a lottery each year between 1757 and 1764. These efforts brought in £ 9000,[62] hardly

[58]*Papers*, II, 27-33, 37-126.

[59]*Ibid.*, III, 88, 383; XI, 231-32.

[60]*Ibid.*, XI, 66.

[61]Allen to Penn, September 25, 1764, POC, IX. HSP; *Burd Papers*, I, ed. Walker, 56-58; *Stiles*, ed. Dexter, pp. 558-59.

[62]Cheyney, *Pennsylvania*, p. 61.

enough to guarantee the survival of the institution. Matters became so crucial that in 1761 Smith was sent to England and Scotland to raise money. He succeeded admirably, eventually getting about £ 12,000 in Pennsylvania currency. In 1762, however, all branches of the school were in very serious financial trouble.[63]

Throughout this continuing crisis, when many people of small means gave what little they could to the struggling school, the affluent Franklin gave nothing at all. Moreover, it had been the fervent hope and even expectation of the Trustees and other concerned parties that Franklin, while still in Philadelphia, would have persuaded the Assembly to grant money to the school, just as he had for the Pennsylvania Hospital in 1752. Though he had far more influence in the Assembly in 1756, the founder made no attempt to do so because of the religious and political hostilities between the Assembly and the Presbyterian controlled proprietary party.[64] His bitterness is also in part indicated by the fact that in making up his will before leaving for England, he left his "Electrical Apparatus" to Yale College.[65] It is true that Yale enjoyed a scientific tradition and doubtless made good use of the piece of electrical apparatus Franklin had already given them; however, the College of Philadelphia with Smith and especially with Kinnersley was by no means backward in this area of science, as Franklin well knew. Furthermore, President Clap of Yale had earlier ignored or rejected Franklin's urgent request that the school raise money for a "compleat Apparatus for Natural Philosophy" even after he generously offered to donate "the Electrical Part"[66] himself. Franklin made no such offer to the College of Philadelphia, and he did not mention it, the charity school that was also part of the institution, or even the Academy in his will.

Then, too, he went along with, and even encouraged, the Assembly's efforts to outlaw lotteries, which in Pennsylvania were very frequently run for the benefit of the College and its affiliated schools. A battle raged in the press between those who were certain that the lotteries were "ensnaring and delusive Practices"[67] that were robbing the people of their money and corrupting the morals of the province,[68] and those who defended them. There were to be sure people

[63]Joseph Y. Brinton, "Introduction" to *The Collection Books of Provost Smith* (Philadelphia: University of Pennsylvania Press, 1964), p. 7.

[64]Cheyney, *Pennsylvania*, p. 171.

[65]*Papers*, VII, 201.

[66]*Ibid.*, VII, 201n.

[67]*The Pennsylvania Journal and Weekly Advertiser*, November 30, 1758.

[68]*Ibid.*

who wished well to the school and opposed the lotteries on religious and moral grounds. But as one acute writer charged, there were many more who opposed them because they wanted to ruin the institution, particularly the College, which they felt was sectarian and political.⁶⁹ In any event, in 1759 the Assembly, having received a number of petitions against lotteries, gladly suppressed them. The King, however, repealed the law and the school raised money through lotteries until 1764.⁷⁰

Franklin, of course, was no enemy to lotteries on moral grounds, for he had made good use of them before and had begun the first one ever conducted in Philadelphia. However, an overlooked but important letter written by William Franklin, who served as his father's secretary, confidant and fellow schemer in England, makes it clear that Franklin not only knew about the Assembly's actions but had a hand in directing them. The letter, which was probably intended for Joseph Galloway, the elder Franklin's political ally and William's friend, further makes it apparent that the attacks on the lotteries were indeed designed "to prevent the ill Effects to the Province that [were] likely to proceed from the present Management of the College."⁷¹ The Assembly and others of the popular party had kept Franklin abreast of the various aspects of their political struggle and so he knew all about the "Scheme on foot" to hit at the proprietary party through the school. William slyly reported in the letter that "Parson [Jacob] Duché [Jr.]," a graduate of the College of Philadelphia and one of Smith's allies, came up to William and, in effect, blamed his father for being in back of the trouble over the lotteries. Duché also charged the elder Franklin with responsibility for the "many abominable Lies" concerning the efforts of the Trustees to make the institution a political and religious instrument.⁷² The minister would not have accused Franklin had he not been certain of his facts, for his father and Franklin were old friends and such close political compatriots that a disgusted Richard Peters referred to the elder Duché as one of the "meer Franklinists" among the Anglicans.⁷³ That the son was correct in his charges is confirmed not

⁶⁹*Ibid.*, February 1, 1759, February 8, 1759, February 22, 1759, and March 1, 1759.

⁷⁰Cheyney, *Pennsylvania*, p. 61.

⁷¹Letter of William Franklin, December 28, 1759. The original is at Yale, but there were two copies made of it. I have used the one in The American Philosophical Society.

⁷²*Ibid.*

⁷³Peters to Penn, June 1, 1756, POC, VI. HSP.

only by William's letter but by the elder Franklin's later actions toward the College of Philadelphia.

When Smith left for England to raise money for the school, he received explicit orders from the Trustees to gain the influential Franklin's aid in soliciting funds and in meeting the many wealthy people he knew.[74] The Trustees assumed that the two enemies would be able to put aside personal bitterness to help the struggling institution that the one had founded and the other was leading. Things did not, however, work out this way. Franklin at first claimed that he regretfully would be unable to aid Smith because he was preparing to return to Philadelphia. But he seems, having known about the plans to raise money in England and Scotland, to have found the time to discredit the school. Smith indeed complained of opposition from Franklin's friends among the fellows at St. John's and Balliol Colleges, where he had comparatively little success in collecting money.[75]

The provost's complaints seem justified. His very useful *Collection Books* which few scholars seem to have used, show that although he raised more than £ 12 on the average from each of the other Oxford and Cambridge colleges in 1762 and 1763, he collected nothing either from St. John's or Balliol.[76] Franklin had friends at both colleges and they knew of Smith's efforts to prevent him from receiving a doctorate. In fact, the provost had written to the president of St. John's in an attempt to blacken Franklin's character. The whole affair was well known at Oxford, and so it is understandable that those sympathetic to Franklin would believe what he had to say about Smith and the school and have nothing to do with either. It should be pointed out that when Smith reported his side of the affair to Peters on March 22, 1762, he merely noted that Franklin had "readily offered his assistance" but doubted that he could be of any help because he expected to leave England "in about six weeks. . . ."[77] Although he does not mention his own schemes, neither does he criticize his adversary. Indeed, there is a complete absence of rancor in the letter, which indicates, I believe, that the provost took Franklin at his word and was completely unprepared for what he subsequently discovered.

Nearly five months later Smith wrote once more to Peters, and this letter also shows that he had no idea that Franklin was an enemy

[74]Smith, *Smith*, I, 284.

[75]*Ibid.*, I, 335.

[76]*Collection Books*, pp. 19-20, 25-26.

[77]Gegenheimer, *Smith*, p. 150.

to the school. The two men parted on neither "the best Terms, nor the worst," and with the elder one on his way back to Philadelphia, Smith encouraged Peters to suspend his judgment of Franklin until he saw "what Part he takes in our Academy. If disposed to befriend it, you will not refuse his Aid; tho I think you should have more than one or two Marks of his Regard to it; before you admit him to take any Lead among you."[78] These instructions show that although Smith did not fully trust Franklin, he certainly had no definite idea yet that the founder felt any hostility toward the school or that he would use it as an arena for fighting other battles. Smith even thought it possible that Franklin would once again become a leader in the institution, which could have used his support.

Three weeks changed the complexion of everything. The provost's next two letters to Peters, which have often been cited but never analyzed, are worth careful consideration. The first is undated but is marked by Peters "rec'd 2n 8ber 1762," and in it Smith claims that "one Mr. Hanna, a very benevolent and wealthy gentleman of Barbadoes," told him that "he had enquired about the College of some Gentlemen from Phila. & was informed it was 'an Instrument of Dissension.' . . . ." Smith offered to disprove the charge but Hanna refused to become involved in the matter, "and gave me £ 25 intimating that he did not give it freely." The provost soon discovered "that Mr. Hanna had his information from an intimate Friend of his Mr. T. Allen, who had it from young Franklin, who is continually after Miss Downs, Allen's Sister in Law. . . . ." Determined to test his conclusion that the Franklins were trying to injure the school, Smith continues, he asked one Mr. Sergant for money. This gentleman, "who had large Dealings" in Philadelphia, "told me he would consult his Friend Dr Franklin to know what was proper to be done. . . . ." Franklin's advice was shocking. He asked Allen not to give money, for he thought the campaign a mere nuisance and that Smith "ought to apply" to the Assembly for funds. Sergant therefore refused to give money but did "give two Gold medals annually £ 5 Value, to some of the best Scholars, and had given his Directions about the Matter to Dr Franklin."[79]

Smith here seems to be reporting the matter accurately. As his *Collection Books* show, Mr. Hanna is George Hanna who, on April 22, 1762, did give £ 25.[80] Moreover, his friend, Mr. T. Allen was the

[78]*Ibid.*, p. 151.
[79]*Ibid.*, pp. 152-53.
[80]*Collection Books*, p. 14.

brother-in-law of Elizabeth Downes, whom William Franklin was courting and soon after married.[81] The "Mr. Sergant" whom Smith refers to is John Sargent of Sargent Aufere & Co., one of the firms that had been appointed recipient of Pennsylvania's share of the parliamentary grant for the 1759 campaign against the Indians.[82] Sargent did give medals instead of money and in August of 1762 sent the "Trifles" to Franklin. As he carefully notes, they cost him "5 Guineas each." The value of his donation was actually greater than the average one Smith collected in 1762-63, but though the provost accepted the gift he privately scorned it. What the College desperately needed was money, not medals.

Franklin knew that all branches of the school were very short of funds. He realized, however, that the lion's share of whatever Smith collected would be used for the College; and his hostility was directed primarily at this branch of the institution, for it had become the prize over which Anglicans and Presbyterians were battling, and it was in the College that Smith taught and, some believed, engaged in politics as well.[83] Convinced that the Academy was lost anyway because of neglect, Franklin was willing to sacrifice what remained of it in order to make certain that the College would not prosper. He could not reject Sargent's gift, for the man believed that he was expressing appreciation for handling the colony's financial business. What Franklin could and did do was to make certain that his gift would not be cash. Years before, when Franklin first recognized what was happening to the Academy and to the College, he tried to do exactly the same thing. He had been given £ 20 for the College and told to put the money to the best use. He did nothing for a time, but when he was about to embark for England he turned the money over to his friend William Coleman, treasurer of the school, explaining that he was asked by the benefactor to determine its use. Franklin insisted that the money be "put to interest, and that three Prizes [be] purchas'd with the yearly Produce, to be distributed yearly for the three best Pieces of Writing" done by the students.[84] It is no coincidence that Sargent's medals were to be awarded for excellence in writing. Furthermore, one of them was to be awarded to the Academy student that wrote the best English

[81]*Papers*, X, 108n.

[82]*Ibid.*, X, 3n.

[83]*Ibid.*, VII, 12n.

[84]*Ibid.*, VII, 134-35, 135n.

essay " 'on the reciprocal Advantages arising from a perpetual Union between Great Britain and her American Colonies.' . . ."[85]

A final word should be devoted to the subject of the English piece. Although Sargent had much to gain from "a perpetual Union" and though the topic was a familiar one on both sides of the Atlantic, it was an obsession with Franklin. His idealization of the glorious and monolithic British Empire was reaching its peak in these years just before his attempt to make Pennsylvania a Crown colony. Furthermore, his years in an England that had honored him and given him good and cultivated friends caused him to fall in love with the land and its people. He wished for nothing more, he said, than to leave America and settle there permanently.[86] The subject of the discourse, the fact that Sargent donated medals rather than money and Franklin's feelings toward the school leave little doubt, I believe, that he tried to prevent Smith's success in raising funds.

Just as pertinent is the role the provost attributed to William Franklin in thwarting the campaign. The father, perhaps because he felt guilt concerning his son's illegitimacy, developed a very close relationship with the young man and made certain that he would grow up a proper British gentleman. Because the young Franklin was unable to become a Harvard gentleman, he determined, having always been an unloyal Bostonian, that William would get even better than Harvard could offer, and the son was accordingly educated at the Middle Temple. Franklin carved out for William a career not unlike his own after his retirement from business. He had made William his successor as clerk of the Assembly and also as postmaster of Philadelphia. His legal training in England, Franklin knew, would help the young man's political career. Like his father, William, in 1762, was awarded a Crown position, as royal governor of New Jersey. Franklin instilled in his son his own veneration for the Empire and for nearly all things English. Part of William's training in becoming an influential English gentleman was handled by the father himself, for he had the young man accompany him to England in 1757 not only to study but to gain political experience. The son therefore served as his father's secretary and confidant. He further acted, under direction, as a competent propagandist for his father's causes. He knew the schemes of his father and he evidently gave his full assent to all of them. In fact, until the tragic years before the Revolution when the elder Franklin was to discover that he had

[85]*Ibid.*, X, 143.
[86]*Ibid.*, X, 169.

made his less pragmatic son too English, there is no evidence to indicate that the two men ever had a political disagreement. William's views were still his father's during the 1760's and even later. That the young man was an enemy to Smith and the proprietary party is clear. That he was involved in schemes to injure the College of Philadelphia is shown by his letter to Galloway. And if, as Hutson argues, Smith spread the word about William's birth, then both Franklins had additional reason to strike back at the provost in any way they could. There seems little doubt, then, that Smith was again reporting matters accurately when he accused the son along with the father of trying to damage the school.

Smith's second letter to Peters, dated "7ber 14th 1762," is of the same kind and also apparently true. It should be kept in mind, moreover, that the provost could gain no advantage from lying to Peters, who had five months earlier resigned as Penn's secretary and succeeded the late Rev. Robert Jenney as rector of Christ Church. This church was still suffering the effects of political and religious divisions, and so the position was bound to occupy most of Peter's time, leaving him little opportunity to confront Franklin in any manner. Smith's chief reason for writing to the rector, then, was to protect the College.

An unnamed "eminent Dissenter called on me," Smith wrote, "and let me know that Dr. Franklin took uncommon Pains to misrepresent our Academy before he went away to sundry of their People; saying that it was a narrow bigotted Institution, got into the Hands of Proprietary Party as an Engine of Government" and that "Dissenters had no Chance in it. . . ." According to the provost, Franklin said that were it not for these faults the Assembly would support the school and that Smith and the Trustees had no need "to beg," seeing that they had only to right matters to get sufficient funds. But, the letter continues, Franklin made himself disgusting to the Dissenter and once Smith proved to his satisfaction that the charges were false, the man donated "40 Guineas to the Design."[87]

Franklin, of course, was well aware of the lingering and only partly submerged hostility between Anglicans and Presbyterians on both sides of the Atlantic. Moreover, he believed what few people in England could posibly have felt—that the College was an instrument of proprietary politics. Smith's trial, after all, had ostensibly nothing to do with the struggle for political dominance in Pennsylvania but was rather a question of libel and of the Assembly's right

[87]Gegenheimer, *Smith*, pp. 151-52. Also see: Smith, *Smith*, I, 335, 336.

to punish one for such a crime. Further, on the surface the school was a catholic institution. Though Smith and the Trustees were Anglicans, nearly all the faculty were Presbyterian, and Kinnersley, one of its most distinguished members, was a Baptist. Only someone intimately familiar with the institution could know of the religious infighting that created a situation whereby "Dissenters had no Chance in it. . . ." Alison and others of the Old Side faction of the Presbyterian Church felt this to be the case but tried for many years to conceal the fact from their New Side brethren. It is also true that Franklin had actually made just such charges of which Smith accused him. For example, to his friend Peter Collinson, in 1756, after he lost influence in the school, Franklin wrote that the College had been declining seriously because of Smith's intrigues. The provost, he claimed, had become disliked by every one except the "Proprietary Faction"[88] which alone would benefit from his schemes. Then, in the previously quoted letter to Kinnersley, the disgusted Franklin, three years after he resigned as President, accused his political enemies of having betrayed him and the school for the sake of proprietary politics.[89] Finally, the charges Smith makes are altogether consistent with those made by the younger Duché to William Franklin and which the latter was in turn pleased to report to Galloway, his friend and his father's political ally.

There seems to be little doubt as to the truth of Smith's charges. No one knew better than Franklin that the stated intention of the original Trustees was to keep the school free of sectarian and political disputes. No one knew better than its disenchanted and angry founder that the institution desperately needed the support of people of different denominations who would give money to a truly catholic institution. No one knew better how to get back through the school, at the Old Side-Anglican coalition that seemed to the Assembly and Franklin to threaten Pennsylvania's cherished liberties and to supplant liberal Quaker rule by that of about half the Anglicans in the province and a horde of Presbyterians. Because he dreaded the consequences of a proprietary victory, and because he believed that the College had been made an instrument of this group's politics, Franklin used his intimate knowledge and his position to injure the institution of which he had once been the very "Soul."

[88]*Papers*, VII, 12.
[89]*Ibid.*, VIII, 415-16.

Brief of an Historical Investigation

Melvin H. Buxbaum, "Benjamin Franklin and William Smith: Their School and Their Dispute," Historical Magazine of the Protestant Episcopal Church, Vol. 39, (December, 1970), pp. 361-382.

I. The topic:

This research is concerned with the roles and relationships of Benjamin Franklin and William Smith at the Academy of Philadelphia in the 1760's. It makes a contribution to the history of American Education in colonial times.

Other recent research on the roles and relationships of Franklin and Smith has been published by Ralph Ketcham, James H. Hutson, and Bruce K. Lively. The Academy of Philadelphia was a combined "Latin" and "English" secondary school. It ultimately became the University of Pennsylvania.

Benjamin Franklin was the first President of the Board of Directors of the Academy, and William Smith was its first Provost. Franklin sponsored Smith for the position of Provost.

II. Analysis of the topic:

Independent Variable:

The variable investigated is the roles and relationships of Franklin and Smith at the Academy. They contended for control of the institution.

Descriptive Variables:

The roles and relationships of the two men ranged over several dimensions: 1. Personal relationships, 2. Political affiliations, 3. Religious affiliations, 4. Financial support of the Academy, and

5. Curriculum of the academy.

   <u>Mediating Variables</u>:

   Mediating variables in historical research are factors which are extrinsic to the independent variable but influence it. They are not controlled, but are the environment in which the independent variable existed. For this investigation, the mediating variables are conditions peculiar to the middle of the 18th century in which the dispute between Franklin and Smith occurred: colonial form of government, religious conflicts, frontier expansion, a mercantile agrarian economy, and limited educational opportunity in classical curriculum.

III. <u>Purposes of the research</u>

   The general purpose of the researcher is to re-establish the past record over this range of issues listed as descriptive variables.

   The specific purposes of the researcher are:

   1. to establish events for each descriptive variable.

   2. to sequence the events on each descriptive variable and across variables.

   3. to establish cause and effect relationships where feasible.

IV. <u>Hypotheses of the Investigation</u>:

   General hypothesis:

   The dispute was caused by factors from more than one descriptive variable.

   Specific hypotheses:

   1. Some specific events in one variable were caused by some specific causes within the same variable.

   2. Some specific events in one variable were caused by some specific causes across other variables.

V. Sources of the Investigation:

   The research utilized "classical" sources which had already
been adequately evaluated externally and internally: Papers of Benjamin
Franklin, Pennsylvania Magazine of History and Biography, etc.

VI. Criterion Data:

   Statements, persons, places, events, actions in each of the
descriptive variables.

VII. Reporting Design of the Investigation:

   Buxbaum cites briefly the recent publications of the topic.
He then states his hypothesis as to the causes of the dispute. The
article subsequently elaborates the evidence in support of his
thesis on each of the descriptive variables are treated as: 1. personal animosities, 2. political affiliations 3. religious affiliations,
with 4. curriculum disagreements sandwiched between the religious
involvements, and 5. financial support of the academy.

VIII. Interpretation of Sources:

   The process by which Buxbaum established the past record
is to make a statement about the topic and then quote sources in
support of the statement. References to the sources are numerous
and pertinent to the concept set forth. The interpretations are close
to the facts, and throughout the article the author presents ample
evidence in support of his reasoning.

IX. Findings of the Investigation:

   The author provides ample evidence to support his hypothesis
that causes of the dispute between Franklin and Smith existed in all
five of the descriptive variables. The hypothesis is well supported.

   1. Personal animosities:

      Franklin labeled Smith as a trouble maker. Smith rebelled,

publicized the illegitimacy of young Franklin.

2. Political affiliations:

   Franklin joined forces with Quakers and frontier settlers:
   Smith promoted interests of the Penn Family and Crown.

3. Religious conflict:

   Franklin disassociated himself from all institutional
   religious, Smith courted the Archbishop of Canterbury in
   hopes of a bishopric; he fought Franklin's irreligion and
   also promoted Anglican control of the Academy to the detriment
   of "Old Side" Presbyterions who were a majority on the
   faculty.

4. Curriculum Conflict:

   Franklin fought for equal treatment of the "English School"
   with the "Latin School"in the Academy; Smith favored the
   Latin School and suppressed the English School.

5. Financial Support:

   Franklin campaigned for public support of a non-sectarian
   Academy by the Pennsylvania Assembly; Smith engaged in fund
   raising for an Anglican Academy among affluent and influential
   church members in the colony and in England.

Summary:

Smith and associates connived to ease Franklin out of the Board
of Directors and all influence in the academy; Franklin had them all
fired during the Revolution because of their pro-British activities.

V. REPORTED PREDICTIVE INVESTIGATION

Associated with teaching:

Analysis of the Topic, Purposing,

Hypothesizing, Data Selection, Data

Collection, Tools for Collecting Data,

Critical Interpretation of Data,

Statistical Interpretation of Data,

Types of Research, and Written Report.

Accuracy of prediction is difficult to achieve, mainly because it is hard to find predictor variables (independent) which correlate highly with the predicted variable (dependent). Predictive investigations utilize the correlation and regression statistical processes.

PREDICTING GRADES FOR ALL SCHOOLS
IN A LARGE UNIVERSITY

JOHN R. HILLS and JOSEPH A. KLOCK

Regents of the University System of Georgia

INTRODUCTION

It has become commonplace to predict college grades on the basis of admission-test scores and high-school performance (Hills, Franz, and Emory, 1959; Hills, Emory, and Franz, 1960; Hills, Emory, and Masters, 1961; Hills, Emory, and Masters, 1962; Hills, Klock, and Lewis, 1963; Hills, Masters, and Emory, 1961; Swanson, Merwin, and Berdie, 1961). Many colleges do the appropriate multiple-regression analyses for themselves. Major national testing programs now provide, gratis, prediction formulas and tables for colleges that use their tests and submit criterion data.

As a first step in prediction, many admissions officers lump all students together and compute one regression equation. Later, with little more than a belief that it may make a difference, an admissions officer is likely to develop separate prediction equations for men and for women. These equations usually turn out to be sufficiently different in appearance so that the admissions officer decides to use them instead of one over-all equation. The next step is to compute different prediction equations for each sex in each of the schools, major fields, or programs in an institution. This will result in quite a large number of different prediction equations being used. Not only is this a bit of a nuisance, but since the freshman year is in many institutions so similar for all students and since students change major fields so often, one wonders whether these refined procedures are justified.

TESTING THE NEED FOR MORE THAN ONE PREDICTION EQUATION

To find out whether different prediction equations should be used with different groups of students, the regression tests for several samples formulated by Gulliksen and Wilks (1950) constitute a particularly suitable covariance procedure. In essence, Gulliksen and Wilks ask whether the same regression system applies to different groups. They provide tests of four hypotheses. The first is an over-all test of whether any of the subsequent tests are likely to be significant. The subsequent tests are of three hypotheses, each dependent upon nonsignificance of the

JOHN R. HILLS AND JOSEPH A. KLOCK

preceding one as an assumption. First, the differences among standard errors of estimate are tested. Second, if these differences are not found to be significant, the slopes of the population regression lines are tested for significant differences. If the standard errors of estimate and the slopes can be assumed to be equal, the third test is made—whether the regression intercepts are equal. If none of these tests shows significant differences, the same regression system applies to all the groups; and only one regression equation is needed.

APPLICATION OF THE TECHNIQUE

Freshmen at a large Southern public coeducational institution with many constituent schools were the subjects. A student must pick one of the schools to enter as a freshman, but the programs in all of the schools for the first year are very similar. There is a lot of changing about from one school to another after a student is enrolled. The university does not have an engineering program—that function being carried on by an institute of technology, located in a different community. Male freshmen usually enter one of the following schools at the university: Arts and Sciences, Business Administration, Journalism, Agriculture, Education, or Forestry. Female freshmen usually enter Arts and Sciences, Business Administration, Journalism, Education, or Home Economics.

The following data were collected on each student in the entering classes from 1957 through 1960: name, sex, high-school average grade (HSA), first-year average grade at the university (FAG), and the Verbal (V) and Mathematics (M) scores on the College Entrance Examination Board's *Scholastic Aptitude Test*. All students who entered as beginning freshmen in the fall quarter of the years 1957 through 1960 and who completed at least three quarters were included in the study. The relevant data are shown in Tables 1 and 2.

TABLE 1

Description of Males Entering in 1957–1960

Year	Sample Size	Mean FAG*	Mean SAT V	Mean SAT M	Mean HSA†
1957	395	71.278	398.79	439.18	24.694
1958	482	72.896	403.81	446.95	25.556
1959	559	71.961	402.85	449.21	25.293
1960	668	72.725	423.89	459.53	26.001

* FAG is first-year average grade where $A = 93$, $B = 83$, $C = 73$, $D = 63$, and $F = 43$.
† HSA is high-school average grade where $A = 40$, $B = 30$, $C = 20$, $D = 10$, and $F = 0$.

PREDICTING GRADES

TABLE 2

Description of Females Entering in 1957–1960

Year	Sample Size	Mean FAG*	Mean SAT V	Mean SAT M	Mean HSA†
1957	356	77.278	416.92	402.84	29.461
1958	476	76.275	420.98	414.71	29.540
1959	502	76.426	420.06	408.20	29.462
1960	600	76.435	439.08	426.79	30.750

* FAG is first-year average grade where $A = 93$, $B = 83$, $C = 73$, $D = 63$, and $F = 43$.

† HSA is high-school average grade where $A = 40$, $B = 30$, $C = 20$, $D = 10$, and $F = 0$.

COMBINING CLASSES

The first application of the Gulliksen-Wilks technique* was to determine whether data from all four years within each sex could be treated with a single regression equation. For males none of the tests yielded results significant at the .05 level, but for females significant differences between the intercepts were found. In fact, the constant term for the 1960 class of females was about .3 of a letter grade less than that for the 1957 entering class. This indicates that with the same level of aptitude, as measured by V, M, and HSA, a girl would be predicted to make a letter-grade average as a freshman in 1960 about .3 lower than in 1957.

COMBINING SCHOOLS WITHIN A YEAR

For the 1960 entering class, the Gulliksen-Wilks technique was applied to separate groups of students of each sex entering the different schools. Data about these groups appear in Tables 3 and 4.

Neither the analysis for males nor the analysis for females yielded any results significant at the .05 level. Thus, the same regression system can properly be applied to students of the same sex entering the different schools at the university in 1960. Nevertheless, some of the differences between means on the predictor variables were statistically significant. For instance, the means for all four measures were significantly higher (at the .05 level) among males enrolled in Arts and Sciences than among males enrolled in Business Administration. However, covariance analysis indicates that the males in Business Administration received grades about in line with their aptitudes—as did the males enrolled in Arts and Sciences.

---

* Dr. James Walker of the School of Mathematics at Georgia Institute of Technology programed the Gulliksen-Wilks analysis for the computer and provided some helpful additions to their conceptions. The work was done at the Rich Electronic Computer Center at the Institute.

JOHN R. HILLS AND JOSEPH A. KLOCK

TABLE 3

Means and Standard Deviations of Males Entering Various Colleges
in the University in 1960

		FAG	SAT V	SAT M	HSA
Arts and Sciences	Mean	73.8	445.8	482.2	27.1
(N = 320)	SD	9.3	92.7	81.0	7.2
Business	Mean	71.6	400.6	435.8	24.3
(N = 210)	SD	8.2	83.8	85.6	6.4
Journalism	Mean	74.3	456.2	455.0	25.6
(N = 27)	SD	8.0	75.2	80.2	5.9
Agriculture	Mean	71.1	398.3	450.7	27.2
(N = 51)	SD	8.9	91.3	72.4	6.1
Education	Mean	70.9	382.9	415.8	23.1
(N = 29)	SD	6.9	89.9	79.1	6.7
Forestry	Mean	72.3	407.7	445.5	27.2
(N = 31)	SD	9.6	96.2	86.2	6.4

TABLE 4

Means and Standard Deviations of Females Entering Various Colleges
in the University in 1960

		FAG	SAT V	SAT M	HSA
Arts and Sciences	Mean	77.5	459.6	442.4	31.1
(N = 297)	SD	8.8	88.1	81.7	6.5
Business	Mean	74.4	386.6	392.5	29.6
(N = 48)	SD	7.6	67.8	74.9	6.2
Journalism	Mean	77.5	451.0	420.4	29.3
(N = 37)	SD	9.1	83.1	78.0	6.0
Education	Mean	75.4	418.2	415.8	30.6
(N = 142)	SD	8.1	85.2	79.1	5.9
Home Economics	Mean	75.0	420.4	408.6	30.7
(N = 69)	SD	8.6	81.3	74.0	6.7

COMBINING SEXES WITHIN A YEAR

Since the same prediction system can be used for men in all schools
and another same system for women in all schools, perhaps a single
system can be used for men and women combined. This was the next
problem for analysis. The 1960 data were used. The result was failure to
reject the hypotheses that the standard errors of estimate were equal and
that the regression coefficients were equal. However, the hypothesis that
the intercepts were equal was rejected at the .05 level of significance. These
results indicate that accuracy of prediction for the two sexes is not de-
tectably different, that the predictors combine in the same manner for
both sexes, but that higher grades will be predicted for one sex than for
the other.

PREDICTING GRADES

The favored sex is female; the margin is not great—about .1 of a letter grade. The prediction equation without the constant term was:

$$\text{Predicted FAG} = .028V + .016M + .559(\text{HSA}).$$

The constant term to be added for males was 36.299; that to be added for females was 37.379. In this case, HSA was measured on a scale in which A = 45, B = 35, C = 25, D = 15, and F = 5 points. The multiple correlation between letter grades and the three predictor variables in the entire group was .66, and the standard error of estimate was .67 grade point. For all practical purposes, it would be wise to split the difference between the intercepts for males and females and use 36.839 as the constant term for everyone.

Discussion

If other institutions investigating this matter obtain results similar to those reported here, it may well be that for predicting first-year grades there is little to be gained by refining the groups on whom the predictions are based. In fact, it may be more important to keep the prediction equations current than to provide separate ones for different schools, curricula, or sexes. Two considerations should be pointed out, however. First, if there had been engineering students at the university used in the present study, the first-year engineering curriculum might have been sufficiently different from the curricula of other students to make the use of a different prediction equation desirable for engineering applicants. Second, this university is beginning to practice some selectivity in admissions. This fact is reflected in the data of Tables 1 and 2. The most noticeable change occurred between 1959 and 1960. This may be the cause of the significant change among female students admitted over those years. An institution that is admitting students on the basis of academic potential will probably find that grading standards will change (Aiken, 1963; Webb, 1959) and that lower first-year grades will be predicted as time goes on for students at the same level of academic aptitude.

References

Aiken, Lewis R., Jr. "The Grading Behavior of a College Faculty." *Educational and Psychological Measurement* 23: 319–22; Summer 1963.

Gulliksen, Harold, and Wilks, Samuel S. "Regression Tests for Several Samples." *Psychometrika* 15: 91–114; March 1950.

Hills, John R.; Emory, Linda B.; and Franz, Gretchen. *Freshman Norms for the University System of Georgia, 1958–59*. Atlanta: Regents of the University System of Georgia, 1960. 91 pp.

Hills, John R.; Emory, Linda B.; and Masters, Pauline B. *Freshman Norms for the University System of Georgia, 1959–60*. Atlanta: Regents of the University System of Georgia, 1961. 65 pp.

JOHN R. HILLS AND JOSEPH A. KLOCK

HILLS, JOHN R.; EMORY, LINDA B.; and MASTERS, PAULINE B. *Freshman Norms for the University System of Georgia, 1960–61*. Atlanta: Regents of the University System of Georgia, 1962. 65 pp.

HILLS, JOHN R.; FRANZ, GRETCHEN; and EMORY, LINDA B. *Counselor's Guide to Georgia Colleges*. Atlanta: Regents of the University System of Georgia, 1959. 32 pp.

HILLS, JOHN R.; KLOCK, JOSEPH A.; and LEWIS, SANDRA C. *Freshman Norms for the University System of Georgia, 1961–62*. Atlanta: Regents of the University System of Georgia, 1963. 65 pp.

HILLS, JOHN R.; MASTERS, PAULINE B.; and EMORY, LINDA B. *Supplement: Counselor's Guide to Georgia Colleges*. Atlanta: Regents of the University System of Georgia, 1961. 35 pp.

SWANSON, EDWIN O.; MERWIN, JACK C.; and BERDIE, RALPH F. "Expectancy Tables for Freshmen Entering Minnesota Colleges." *Minnesota Test-Norms and Expectancy Tables*. St. Paul: State of Minnesota, Department of Education, 1961. pp. 87–123.

WEBB, SAM C. "Measured Changes in College Grading Standards." *College Board Review*, Fall 1959 (No. 39). pp. 27–30.

300

BRIEF OF A PREDICTIVE INVESTIGATION

John R. Hills and Joseph A. Klock, "Predicting Grades for All
Schools in a Large University," American Educational Research Journal,
Vol. 2 (May, 1965), pp. 145-150.

I. Topic of the Investigation:

This investigation is concerned with predicting first-year average

grade in college. Specifically, the question is whether different

prediction formulas are needed for male and female students, and for

students entering different schools of the university, rather than one

single over-all equation to predict grades for any and all students of

the university.

The investigation makes a contribution to improving college

admissions and instruction.

Previous related research had been done by Hills, Franz, and Emory,

1959 and 1960; Hills, Emory, and Masters, 1961 and 1962; Hills, Klock,

and Lewis, 1963; and Swanson, Merwin, and Berdie, 1961.

First-year average grade was operationally defined as: A=93,

B=83, C=73, D=63, and F=43.

High School average grade was operationally defined as: A=40,

B=30, C=20, D=10, and F=0.

II. Analysis of the Topic:

1. Independent Variables:

The independent variables were the measurements used to predict

first-year college grade. The three predictors were: a. Verbal Score

on college entrance Examination Board's Scholastic Aptitude Test,

b. Mathematics score on the same test, and c. high-school average
grade. Multiple regression, involving all three predictors in a
single formula was used rather than linear regression, using one predictor in each of three prediction formulas.

2. Dependent Variable:

The dependent variable (predicted) was first-year average
grade in college. The dependent variable included first-year average
grade of males and/or females, who entered schools of Arts and Sciences,
Business Administration, Journalism, Agriculture, Education, Forestry,
and Home Economics.

3. Mediating Variables:

The mediating variables are extrinsic to the independent variable
but influence it. They are not controlled, but are different
environments for testing the hypothesis. For this topic, the mediating
variables are: a large institution, a state university - but not
including the school of Engineering, location in a Southeastern state,
and the post-sputnik time period 1957-1960.

III. Purposes of the Investigation:

The general purpose is to answer the question: Can the same
prediction formula be used for all students in all schools (except
Engineering) to predict first-year average grades.

The specific purposes involved in the general purpose are:

1. Can the same prediction formula be used for female students
and male students.

2. Can the same formula be used for male and/or female students
entering: Arts and Sciences, Business Administration, Journalism,
Agriculture, Education, Forestry, and Home Economics?

3. Can the same formula be used for male and/or female students entering all majors within the schools in the university?

IV. Hypotheses of the Investigation:

The general hypothesis is: The same prediction formula can be used for all students in all schools (except Engineering) to predict first-year letter grades.

The specific hypotheses involved in the general hypothesis are:

1. The same formula can be used for male and female student grades.

2. The same formula can be used for predicting grades of students entering all schools of the university except engineering.

3. The same formula can be used in predicting grades of students entering all majors in all aforesaid schools of the university.

The justifications for these hypotheses for predicting first-year average grades are that courses of all freshmen are similar, and that many students change majors during the freshman year.

V. Criterion Data in the Investigation:

The criterion data on the dependent variable (predicted) are first-year average grades of male students and female students in the various schools. Criterion data on the independent variables (predictors), are verbal and mathematics scores on the Scholastic Aptitude Test, and high school average grades for the same students. The multiple correlation between first-year college grades and the combined three predictor variables for the entire group was .66, and the standard error of the estimate was .67 of a grade point.

VI. Sample of the Investigation:

There were 2104 male students in the investigation, and 1934 female

students. The male students entered colleges as follows: Arts and
Sciences, 320; Business, 210; Journalism, 27; Agriculture, 51;
Education, 29; and Forestry, 31. The female students enrolled in
college as follows: Arts and Sciences, 297; Business, 48; Journalism,
37; Education 142; and Home Economics, 69. The sample is not representative of any universe beyond itself.

VII. Instruments for Collecting Data in the Investigation

The only test used for obtaining scores was the College Entrance
Examination Board Scholastic Aptitude Test. The high-school average
and first-year average grade were collected from student record
files, and operationally defined, as reported under "I Topic," in this
brief.

VIII. Statistical Interpretation of Data

A statistical rationale by Gulliksen and Wilks was utilized.

The first statistical treatment was an over-all test of differences
among the predicted first-year grades of students in the various schools.

Three further statistical treatments were computed, all regression
analysis:

1. test of significanceof differences among standard errors of
estimates of the groups.

2. test of significance of differences among regression coeffi-
ciencts (slopes) of the groups.

3. test of significance of differences among the constant terms
(intercepts)of the groups.

Along with these analyses, the regression formulas for predicting
first-year average grades for each group were computed. These formulas
were of the type reported under "IX. Findings", below.

IX. Findings of the Investigation:

1. the prediction formula for males was:

Predicted FAG = .028 V + .016M + .559 HSA + 36.299

FAG = First-year average grade.
V = Verbal, SAT score   M= Mathematics, SAT score
HSA = High-School average grade.

2. The prediction formula for females was:
Predicted FAG = .028 V + .016 M + .599 HSA + 37.379

3. The hypothesis that no statistical differences existed among
standard errors of estimates could not be rejected. Neither could
the hypothesis of no statistical differences among regression
coefficients be rejected. But there were significant differences
among constant terms (intercepts) between men and women, at the .05
level. Because of this finding the difference between intercepts for
males and females should be split to be 36.839.

4. Therefore, a single prediction formula can be used for male
and/or females of all schools to predict first-year average grades:

FAG = .028 V + .016 M + .559 HSA + 36.839

X. Discussion

It is more important for an institution to keep a single over-all
prediction formula for students updated from year to year rather
than to provide separate ones for different schools, curricula, and sexes
without updating them.

If Engineering students had been included in the investigation,
they might have shown need for a separate formula.

If students are admitted on academic potential, the findings of
this investigation might be different over the years if the faculty
change their grading behaviors.

Institutions should conduct their own local research on predicting
first-year average grades of students.

———————————————————————————

XXV. A RESEARCHER-MADE QUESTIONNAIRE. (Reading Instruction)

Associated with teaching tools for

Collecting Data.

Tools for collecting educational research
data are the key to validity and reliability of
the measurements and observations. Data collecting devices regulate the empirical tone of the
research. It is important that the research
tools be oriented toward the purposes of the research, hence the researcher is often obligated
to devise research tools of his own.

Beverly M. Dernbach
1039 Rolling Drive
Lisle, Illinois   60532

Dear Teacher:

It is with a great deal of excitement on my part that I am at
last presenting my questionnaire about the Individualized Reading
Program to you. I believe that we have a mutual bond in our interest in this plan. I am sure your opinion for or against Individualized Reading is already formed and that is ideal for my work.

I am doing this study under the direction of Dr. Alfred L.
Papillon, School of Education, DePaul University, as partial ful-
fillment of the requirements for my Master of Arts degree in
Education. It is my combined position as a student, teacher, and
parent that has encouraged my interest in this controversial
subject.

This questionnaire has been set up to use a minimum amount of
your time (fifteen minutes) and yet accomplish my purpose of discovering:

> What is the basic format in the Individualized Reading
>   Program?
> How do you, the teacher, evaluate it?
> What are common problems that we can discover in order
>   to better prepare future teachers?
> Is this a myth or a must in our system?

Please answer this questionnaire at your earliest convenience.
Check as many answers as fit you particular situation. If some
questions are not applicable to your class, omit those items. If
you are no longer using the Individualized Reading Program, please
answer the questions in relation to the last term in which you used
this system.

I have already indicated to your principal that I will send
a short summary of the results to your school, if it is desired.

Thank you for your help. The success of my many months of
work depends on YOU. Every teacher has a different relationship
with his/her class. I need to know about YOU and your class
anonymously, of course.

Sincerely,

_____

Beverly M. Dernbach

Enclosure: Stamped, addressed envelope

QUESTIONNAIRE ABOUT THE INDIVIDUALIZED READING PROGRAM

Part One   Initiating the Program

1. How was the Individualized Reading Program brought to your attention?
    ___Superintendent   ___An educational conference
    ___Principal   ___Parents
    ___Other teachers   ___Your own idea
    ___Educational magazines   ___The children

2. Why was the Individualized Reading Program tried?
    ___Lack of interest in the basal reader
    ___Difference in reading abilities in the classroom
    ___Need for more personalized approach
    ___Lack of motivation when using the group-ability plan
    ___Variety of interest among the children
    ___Variety of backgrounds of the children
    ___Desire to try a new approach in reading
    ___Suggestion of a supervisor

3. Were you in favor of trying the Individualized Reading Program?
    ___yes   ___no

4. Are you in favor of the program now?
    ___yes   ___no

5. Whom did you notify when you began the Individualized Reading Program?
    ___The district superintendent   ___The public librarian
    ___Your supervisor   ___Other teachers in your school
    ___Your principal   ___The children
    ___The parents   ___None of these
    ___The school librarian

6. How many years have you taught?_____

7. How many years have you used the Individualized Reading Program?

    _____

8. With what grades have you used the Individualized Reading Program?

    _____

9. What is your class membership?_____

10. What was the largest class with which you used this program?

    _____

11. What was the smallest class with which you used this program?

    _____

12. How was the program initiated in your room?
___Started with the top group
___Started with the middle group
___Started with the bottom group
___Started with the whole class

13. How long is your reading period (per day)?_____

14. What activities are usually included in a daily reading period?
___Selecting books   ___Group meetings
___Individual conferences   ___Sharing time
___Individual activities   ___Activity for class as a whole
___Silent reading

15. What levels of ability are present in your class?
___Above average ability   ___Below average ability
___Average ability

16. Have you excluded any child from this program?
___yes   ___no

17. What was the reason for excluding the child?
___Immaturity   ___Inability to work independently
___Lack of native ability   ___Troublesome nature of child
___Rebellion to plan   ___Lack of interest in plan
___Failure to cooperate

18. Do you keep an individual record on each child?
___yes   ___no
a) Is this a running record noting problems and achievements over
   the course of the year?
   ___yes   ___no
b) Do you make a notation during or following the individual
   conference with a child?
   ___yes   ___no
c) How often is something written about each child?
   ___Daily   ___Twice a month
   ___Twice a week   ___Once a month
   ___Once a week   ___Following the conferences

19. Does each child keep some type of record of his reading?
___yes   ___no
a) What type of record is used?
   ___A standard form adopted by the class
   ___Individual child selects his own form
   ___A variety of recording methods used by each child
b) Do you make a periodical check on the child's individual record
   to see that it is in order?
   ___yes   ___no
c) Do the children keep a list of new words that they have encountered?
   ___yes   ___no

20. Are there any visible charts, graphs, or tallies in the room which
show the number of books read by each child?
___yes   ___no

21. Are there any charts or graphs showing the variety of material read by the individuals?
___yes   ___no

22. Are there any charts or graphs showing the reading level of the books read by each child?
___yes   ___no

Part Two Selecting Material

1. Do you use a basal reader?
   ___Not at all
   ___Finish it before starting Individualized Reading
   ___As a supplementary book
   ___Children may select these books if they want to read them
   ___Alternate it with Individualized Reading on different days
   ___Alternate it with Individualized Reading on same day

2. Do you use the Science Research Associates (SRA) material?
   ___yes   ___no

3. Approximately how many books per child are in your room?_____

4. How are the reading materials selected?
   ___Textbooks   ___School library
   ___Supplementary books   ___Public library
   ___Trade books*   ___Book sales
   ___Newspapers   ___Auctions
   ___Magazines   ___Children bring books from home
   ___Reference books

5. How often do you change books in the classroom?
   ___Every week   ___Twice a year
   ___Twice a month   ___Once a year
   ___Once a month   ___A few books at a time
   ___2-3 months

6. What is the reading level of the children in the room?
   Grade_____to Grade_____.

7. What reading levels are represented by the books in the room?
   Grade_____to Grade_____.

8. How are the books arranged for selection?
   ___No arrangement   ___Size of book
   ___Subject matter   ___Fiction-nonfiction
   ___Level of difficulty

*Trade books - books designed for the general bookstore and library rather than for text use.

9. How does a child select his book?
   ___The teacher aids in finding something suitable
   ___The child finds it entirely on his own
   ___Other children help by means of book reports, skits, etc.

10. What usually motivates a child to choose a particular book?
    ___The teacher   ___Size of book
    ___The child   ___Difficulty of book
    ___Other children   ___Type of book
    ___Other books by this author   ___Pictures in the book

11. Must the children read a book once they have selected it?
    ___yes   ___Usually
    ___no   ___Except in certain cases where
                                   the decision was unwise

12. What is the approximate number of books read by the children
    during the course of one school year?
    _____The average amount read
    _____The most any child read
    _____The least any child read

13. What if a child keeps selecting the same type of book?
    ___Insist on a change   ___Leave him alone
    ___Encourage a change   ___This has never happened

14. How do you stop a child from constantly reading books beneath
    his reading level?
    ___Insist a change   ___Leave him alone
    ___Encourage a change   ___This has never happened

15. Is there a public library convenient to your school?
    ___yes   ___no

16. How many children have a library card?
    ___25%   ___75%
    ___50%   ___100%

Part Three Development of Skills

1. How do you normally develop reading skills?
   ___The entire class
   ___Certain permanently established groups
   ___Temporary groups who need the same skill
   ___The individual when he needs a skill

2. Do you follow a sequential development as in the Basal Reading
   Plan?
   ___yes   ___no   ___With some children

3. Do you check on certain skills with each child during the course
   of the year?
   ___yes   ___no

4. Do you teach only those skills that you notice the child is lacking?
___yes   ___no

5. How is seatwork distributed?
___To some children
___To the whole class
___The individual creates his own

6. Do you use reading workbooks?
___For the whole room   ___For the faster children
___For certain groups   ___For the average children
___For particular individuals   ___For those needing vocabulary help
___For the slower children   ___For those needing help with a
                                      certain skill

7. How do you use the workbooks?
___Follow the order in the book
___Use certain pages when the need arises

8. How do you take care of remedial reading
___In the individual conference   ___Don't even consider this concept
___In small groups   since the child is working at
                                      his own pace

9. Is the oral reading in your room?
___yes   ___no

10. Who is the audience?
___One or two other children   ___You in the individual conference
___A group of children   ___The whole class

11. Who helps with unknown words?
___The teacher   ___Dictionaries
___Another child   ___Content and context clues
___Make a word list   ___Skip over

Part Four   Guiding Learning

1. How many individual conferences do you average (per day)?_____

2. How often do you see each child individually for a reading conference?
_____

3. How is the need for a reading conference established?
___The child indicates   ___The teacher selects the child
___Rotation in a definite order

4. Do you see some children more often than others?
___yes   ___no

5. Which children do you see more often?
___The slower ones   ___The brighter ones
___The average ones   ___Varies according to current needs
                                      of the child

6. In the individual conference what do you try to determine?
   ___How the child feels about reading in general
   ___How he is enjoying his particular book
   ___What difficulties he is having with the book
   ___What skills he needs to be taught
   ___If he could profit from some group work
   ___How good his oral reading is
   ___What related activities he is doing
   ___Establish a personal relationship between yourself and
      the child

7. Do you have grouping of any kind?
   ___yes   ___no
   a) Is the grouping temporary?
      ___yes   ___no
   b) What is the specific purpose for the group?
      ___A particular skill   ___Enjoyment of a particular story
      ___Remedy of a difficulty   ___Work on a group project
      ___Similar reading material

8. Do you have a sharing time during your reading period when different children are allowed to present their reading experiences
   to the class in a variety of ways?
   ___yes   ___no

9. How often do you have a sharing time?
   ___Daily   ___Every other week
   ___Twice a week   ___Once a month
   ___Once a week

10. List the methods used most often by your class to report on their
    reading._____
    _____

Part Five Personal Opinions and Observations

1. What seems to be the reaction of your group toward the Individualized
   Reading Program?
   ___Much in favor   ___Not particulary in favor
   ___Moderatily in favor   ___Definitely against
   ___Slightly in favor

2. What is the reaction of the parents?
   ___Much in favor   ___Not particularly in favor
   ___Moderately in favor   ___Definitely against
   ___Slightly in favor   ___Not particularly interested

3. What is the reaction of the other teachers in your school?
   ___Much in favor   ___Not particulary in favor
   ___Moderately in favor   ___Definitely against
   ___Slightly in favor   ___Not particularly interested

4. What is the reaction of your principal?
   ___Much in favor   ___Not particularly in favor
   ___Moderately in favor   ___Definitely against
   ___Slightly in favor   ___Not particularly interested

5. How does Individualized Reading affect the child? (Indicate
                                                     yes or no)
   Progresses at own rate   ___ ___
   Slow reader not stigmatized   ___ ___
   Shows much enthusiasm   ___ ___
   Sustained interest in reading   ___ ___
   Competes with himself   ___ ___
   Reads more books   ___ ___
   Reads a variety of books   ___ ___
   Increase in reading ability   ___ ___

6. Does the child seem to enjoy the personal conference?
   ___yes   ___Little enthusiam noticed
   ___no   ___Most of the time

7. Do you enjoy the individual conference?
   ___yes   ___Most of the time
   ___no   ___Some of the time

8. Do you believe that the personal conference is usually beneficial?
   ___yes   ___no

9. Do you believe that a child should have a conference only when he
   seeks you out?
   ___yes   ___no

10. What teachers should use this method?
    ___All teachers   ___Only experienced teachers
    ___All those interested in trying it

11. Do you think this method can be used effectively in any
    elementary grade?

    ___yes   ___no

12. Is there any grade where you think this system would be par-
    ticularly effective?_____

13. In what size class would you consider this plan to be most
    effective?_____

14. If your membership were as follows would you want to use the
    Individual Reading Program (IRP), the Basal Reading Plan(BRP)
    or not teach this size group(N)?
    ___1-20   ___26-30   ___36-40   ___46-50
    ___21-25   ___31-35   ___41-45   ___More than 50

15. How does the discipline compare with discipline under the Basal
    Reading Plan?
    ___Easier than with Basal Reading
    ___About the same
    ___Harder to maintain

16. What is your opinion of the record keeping?
    ___Tedious   ___Time consuming
    ___Essential   ___Rewarding
    ___Non-essential

17. Does this system call for more preparation on your part?
    ___yes   ___no

18. Do you find it more rewarding to teach?
    ___yes   ___no

19. Does this system seem to increase the children's reading outside of school?
    ___yes   ___no

20. Do you believe that the children develop into better readers through the use of this plan?
    ___yes   ___no

21. In relation to these reading skills how would you say your children have progressed? (Consider the children's abilities.)
    E - Excellent; G - Good; F - Fair; U - Unsatisfactory

    ___The children are able to see and hear words clearly and recognize their meanings.
    ___The children are able to understand sentences, paragraphs, pages and stories.
    ___The children are creative readers.
    ___The children are able to find the information they need and seek.
    ___The children are able to read aloud effectively.

XXVI. A RESEARCHER-MADE LIKERT SCALE

Associated with teaching tools for
Collecting Data.

Even more than tests, which measure cognitive characteristics, scales, which measure
affective traits must suit specific purposes
and hypotheses. The items in the sample scale
reproduced here were all arrived at by having
students write short essays on the topic "What
does reading mean to me?" All of the items
were culled from these essays and are hence
presumably relevant to students.

SCALE FOR MEASURING STUDENT ATTITUDE TOWARD READING

by Ronald Frye

Directions: All of the following statements express
either a favorable or an unfavorable attitude toward
reading. Read each statement carefully and then check
the extent to which you approve or disapprove of it in
the columns opposite the statement.

The improtant thing to remember when you check each
statement is to indicate whether you personally approve
or disapprove of it.

Statement	SA	A	N	D	SD
1. Reading has nothing to offer me.					
2. I believe reading can help my future.					
3. All reading is boring and it doesn't mean anything anyway.					
4. Reading is more necessary to me than any other subject.					
5. One should read only when he has nothing else to do.					
6. Reading can improve my vocabulary.					

Statement	SA	A	N	D	SD
7. Reading often helps to understand people around us.					
8. Reading is basically an enjoyable experience.					
9. Reading only helps me to pass tests. Beyond that it is a waste of time.					
10. Reading helps improve the mind.					
11. Students read because teachers think it is important, not because they like to read.					
12. Ability to read can help one to find a job.					
13. Reading is an activity for girls rather than for boys.					
14. Reading is an activity for spare time and relaxation.					
15. There is no value in reading.					
16. I can share someone else's experiences through reading.					
17. Whenever I read I enjoy it.					
18. The last thing to do in your spare time is read.					
19. Reading can help me to be more effective when I talk to other people.					
20. If I never read, I feel as though I am missing out on something.					

Statement	SA	A	N	D	SD
21. My favorite subject is reading even though it is not my most necessary subject.					
22. I read only because the career that I an interested in calls for a lot of reading.					
23. To spend one hour reading a book or magazine is too long.					
24. Since I cannot remember everything I read it hardly makes sense to read more.					
25. Reading can help me to improve my speech.					
26. Unless a book is very interesting throughout it does not make sense to continue reading it.					
27. Reading has never been of help to me. Therefore, I do not think it will help my future.					
28. There are a lot of people who are better off because they do not know how to read.					
29. The more I read the better I like it.					
30. Reading only helps those people who are already good readers.					

Statement	SA	A	N	D	SD
31. Reading is difficult, so it is better to find something else to do.					
32. The more a person reads the more creative he can be.					
33. A person should read just for the sake of reading. It doesn't matter whether or not he enjoys it.					
34. Reading can help me to discover new ideas.					
35. A person should read only to find out something he needs to know now.					
36. Reading just takes up too much valuable time.					
37. Most reading deals with nothing but words: there are no real life situations in books.					
38. Reading can help me to solve problems that I may meet in life.					
39. I think that reading skill will help me to earn more money.					
40. A lot of self-improvement can come from reading.					
41. A good thing about reading is that you only have it in school.					

Statement	SA	A	N	D	SD
42. One way to understand anything is to read about it.					
43. Reading is not going to help me or anyone else in dealing with others.					
44. I can learn more by looking at television than I can by reading.					
45. A person who reads a great deal will probably have something interesting to say.					
46. I will be able to understand myself better through reading.					
47. Sometimes after reading one book on a subject a student can be inspired to read another book in order to find out more about the subject.					
48. No person is completely educated usless he is a good reader.					
49. Being a good reader gives a person confidence in himself.					
50. Practicing citizenship fully requires the ability to read.					

LIBRARY OF STATISTICAL PROGRAMS TAPES

1.	SIGMA	Sum of a Series
2.	MEAN	Average of a Series
3.	STDEV	Standard Deviation: Ungrouped Scores
4.	GRMEDN	Median of Grouped Scores
5.	GRMSTD	Mean and Standard Deviation: Grouped Scores
6.	TSTU	t-test: Independent Means
7.	TCOR	t-test: Correlated Means
8.	RANK	Papillon Score Ranking Program
9.	RPEAR	Pearson Correlation Coefficient
10.	RSPEAR	Spearman Correlation Coefficient
11.	SIMCHI	Chi-Square for Equiprobability
12.	CHISQR	Chi-Square for Independence
13.	ANOVA	One-Way Analysis of Variance
14.	FPAIRS	Post Mortem Pairs of ANOVA Means
15.	ANOVA2	Two-Way Analysis of Variance
16.	KRUWAL	KRUSKAL-WALLIS ANOVA with Ranks
17.	ANCOVA	Analysis of Covariance
18.	REGFOR	Regression formula
19.	FRIEDM	Friedman two-way ANOVA with Ranks
20.	INTFR	Two-Way Analysis of Variance without Replications: Intraclass Correlations
21.	DEP	Discrepancy Evaluation Program
22.	SDEV	Standard Deviation with Original Measurements

Appendix

Table A.   Table of Squares and Square Roots of Numbers

Table B.   Percent of Total Area under the Normal Curve
              between Mean Ordinate and Ordinate at any
              Given Sigma-Distance from the Mean

Table C.   Table of Random Sampling Numbers

Table D.   Values of the Correlation Coefficient for
              Different Levels of Significance

Table E.   Values of the Rank-Order Correlation Coefficient
              (rho) at the 5% and 1% Levels of Significance

Table F.   Levels of Significance of the "t"-Test

Table G.   Values of the F-Ratio at the 5% and 1%, Levels
              of Significance

Table H.   Levels of Significance of Chi-Square

Table A.

Table of Squares and Square Roots of Numbers

Taken from ELEMENTARY STATISTICAL PROCEDURES by Clinton
I. Chase. 1967, 1976. McGraw-Hill Book Co.
Reproduced with the permission of McGraw-Hill Book Company
Suggestions for Expanding the Table

The student may increase the flexibility of this table (1) by using the Square column as the Number column and the Number column as the Square-root column and (2) by manipulating the decimal point in the terms in the Number and in the Square-root columns.

If I multiply 4 × 4 and get 16, then the number I began with, 4, is the square root of 16.   Similarly, if I wish the square root of a number beyond 1,000, I may find it, at least to the significant figures necessary for work in this book, by looking in the column labeled Square.   Then moving to the left I find the square root of this number in the column labeled Number. For example, suppose I want the square root of 1,300.   I move down the Square column until I find a number as near as possible to 1,300.   It is 1,296.   To the left of 1,296 is 36, which is almost exactly the square root of 1,300.   (The exact square root of 1,300 is 36.056.   The more precise student may wish to make interpolations to arrive at the exact values; however, in the great majority of problems in this book interpolations will not alter the significant figures involved.)

The square root of 1,300 may also be found by manipulating the decimal point in the number and in its square root.   The value of 1,300 is equal to 13 × 100, and so its square root must be equal to $\sqrt{13} \times \sqrt{100}$, or $\sqrt{13} \times 10$.

212

Our table contains the square root of 13; it is 3.6056. And if we multiply this value by 10, we have 36.056, which is the square root of 1,300.

Here is another example. What is the square root of 47,100? This number is equal to 471 × 100, and its square root is $\sqrt{471} \times \sqrt{100}$, or 21.7025 × 10, or 217.025.

What is the square root of 4.21? This number is equal to 421 × $\frac{1}{100}$, and its square root is $\sqrt{421} \times 1/\sqrt{100}$, or 20.5183 × $\frac{1}{10}$, or 2.05 retaining only two decimal places.

Some practice with the above suggestions should make it unnecessary for the student to have to compute square roots by the long method typically taught in high school mathematics classes. However, in all cases the student should inspect his figures to see if his square root when multiplied by itself would reasonably be equal to the number for which the root was taken.

Number	Square	Square root	Number	Square	Square root
1	1	1.0000	41	16 81	6.4031
2	4	1.4142	42	17 64	6.4807
3	9	1.7321	43	18 49	6.5574
4	16	2.0000	44	19 36	6.6332
5	25	2.2361	45	20 25	6.7082
6	36	2.4495	46	21 16	6.7823
7	49	2.6458	47	22 09	6.8557
8	64	2.8284	48	23 04	6.9282
9	81	3.0000	49	24 01	7.0000
10	1 00	3.1623	50	25 00	7.0711
11	1 21	3.3166	51	26 01	7.1414
12	1 44	3.4641	52	27 04	7.2111
13	1 69	3.6056	53	28 09	7.2801
14	1 96	3.7417	54	29 16	7.3485
15	2 25	3.8730	55	30 25	7.4162
16	2 56	4.0000	56	31 36	7.4833
17	2 89	4.1231	57	32 49	7.5498
18	3 24	4.2426	58	33 64	7.6158
19	3 61	4.3589	59	34 81	7.6811
20	4 00	4.4721	60	36 00	7.7460
21	4 41	4.5826	61	37 21	7.8102
22	4 84	4.6904	62	38 44	7.8740
23	5 29	4.7958	63	39 69	7.9373
24	5 76	4.8990	64	40 96	8.0000
25	6 25	5.0000	65	42 25	8.0623
26	6 76	5.0990	66	43 56	8.1240
27	7 29	5.1962	67	44 89	8.1854
28	7 84	5.2915	68	46 24	8.2462
29	8 41	5.3852	69	47 61	8.3066
30	9 00	5.4772	70	49 00	8.3666
31	9 61	5.5678	71	50 41	8.4261
32	10 24	5.6569	72	51 84	8.4853
33	10 89	5.7446	73	53 29	8.5440
34	11 56	5.8310	74	54 76	8.6023
35	12 25	5.9161	75	56 25	8.6603
36	12 96	6.0000	76	57 76	8.7178
37	13 69	6.0828	77	59 29	8.7750
38	14 44	6.1644	78	60 84	8.8318
39	15 21	6.2450	79	62 41	8.8882
40	16 00	6.3246	80	64 00	8.9443

* By permission from h. Sorenson, "Statistics for Students of Psychology and Education," copyright 1936, McGraw-Hill Book Company, New York.

Number	Square	Square root	Number	Square	Square root
81	65 61	9.0000	121	1 46 41	11.0000
82	67 24	9.0554	122	1 48 84	11.0454
83	68 89	9.1104	123	1 51 29	11.0905
84	70 56	9.1652	124	1 53 76	11.1355
85	72 25	9.2195	125	1 56 25	11.1803
86	73 96	9.2736	126	1 58 76	11.2250
87	75 69	9.3274	127	1 61 29	11.2694
88	77 44	9.3808	128	1 63 84	11.3137
89	79 21	9.4340	129	1 66 41	11.3578
90	81 00	9.4868	130	1 69 00	11.4018
91	82 81	9.5394	131	1 71 61	11.4455
92	84 64	9.5917	132	1 74 24	11.4891
93	86 49	9.6437	133	1 76 89	11.5326
94	88 36	9.6954	134	1 79 56	11.5758
95	90 25	9.7468	135	1 82 25	11.6190
96	92 16	9.7980	136	1 84 96	11.6619
97	94 09	9.8489	137	1 87 69	11.7047
98	96 04	9.8995	138	1 90 44	11.7473
99	98 01	9.9499	139	1 93 21	11.7898
100	1 00 00	10.0000	140	1 96 00	11.8322
101	1 02 01	10.0499	141	1 98 81	11.8743
102	1 04 04	10.0995	142	2 01 64	11.9164
103	1 06 09	10.1489	143	2 04 49	11.9583
104	1 08 16	10.1980	144	2 07 36	12.0000
105	1 10 25	10.2470	145	2 10 25	12.0416
106	1 12 36	10.2956	146	2 13 16	12.0830
107	1 14 49	10.3441	147	2 16 09	12.1244
108	1 16 64	10.3923	148	2 19 04	12.1655
109	1 18 81	10.4403	149	2 22 01	12.2066
110	1 21 00	10.4881	150	2 25 00	12.2474
111	1 23 21	10.5357	151	2 28 01	12.2882
112	1 25 44	10.5830	152	2 31 04	12.3288
113	1 27 69	10.6301	153	2 34 09	12.3693
114	1 29 96	10.6771	154	2 37 16	12.4097
115	1 32 25	10.7238	155	2 40 25	12.4499
116	1 34 56	10.7703	156	2 43 36	12.4900
117	1 36 89	10.8167	157	2 46 49	12.5300
118	1 39 24	10.8628	158	2 49 64	12.5698
119	1 41 61	10.9087	159	2 52 81	12.6095
120	1 44 00	10.9545	160	2 56 00	12.6491

Number	Square	Square root	Number	Square	Square root
161	2 59 21	12.6886	201	4 04 01	14.1774
162	2 62 44	12.7279	202	4 08 04	14.2127
163	2 65 69	12.7671	203	4 12 09	14.2478
164	2 68 96	12.8062	204	4 16 16	14.2829
165	2 72 25	12.8452	205	4 20 25	14.3178
166	2 75 56	12.8841	206	4 24 36	14.3527
167	2 78 89	12.9228	207	4 28 49	14.3875
168	2 82 24	12.9615	208	4 32 64	14.4222
169	2 85 61	13.0000	209	4 36 81	14.4568
170	2 89 00	13.0384	210	4 41 00	14.4914
171	2 92 41	13.0767	211	4 45 21	14.5258
172	2 95 84	13.1149	212	4 49 44	14.5602
173	2 99 29	13.1529	213	4 53 69	14.5945
174	3 02 76	13.1909	214	4 57 96	14.6287
175	3 06 25	13.2288	215	4 62 25	14.6629
176	3 09 76	13.2665	216	4 66 56	14.6969
177	3 13 29	13.3041	217	4 70 89	14.7309
178	3 16 84	13.3417	218	4 75 24	14.7648
179	3 20 41	13.3791	219	4 79 61	14.7986
180	3 24 00	13.4164	220	4 84 00	14.8324
181	3 27 61	13.4536	221	4 88 41	14.8661
182	3 31 24	13.4907	222	4 92 84	14.8997
183	3 34 89	13.5277	223	4 97 29	14.9332
184	3 38 56	13.5647	224	5 01 76	14.9666
185	3 42 25	13.6015	225	5 06 25	15.0000
186	3 45 96	13.6382	226	5 10 76	15.0333
187	3 49 69	13.6748	227	5 15 29	15.0665
188	3 53 44	13.7113	228	5 19 84	15.0997
189	3 57 21	13.7477	229	5 24 41	15.1327
190	3 61 00	13.7840	230	5 29 00	15.1658
191	3 64 81	13.8203	231	5 33 61	15.1987
192	3 68 64	13.8564	232	5 38 24	15.2315
193	3 72 49	13.8924	233	5 42 89	15.2643
194	3 76 36	13.9284	234	5 47 56	15.2971
195	3 80 25	13.9642	235	5 52 25	15.3297
196	3 84 16	14.0000	236	5 56 96	15.3623
197	3 88 09	14.0357	237	5 61 69	15.3948
198	3 92 04	14.0712	238	5 66 44	15.4272
199	3 96 01	14.1067	239	5 71 21	15.4596
200	4 00 00	14.1421	240	5 76 00	15.4919

* By permission from H. Sorenson, "Statistics for Students of Psychology and Education," copyright 1936, McGraw-Hill Book Company, New York.

Number	Square	Square root	Number	Square	Square root
241	5 80 81	15.5242	281	7 89 61	16.7631
242	5 85 64	15.5563	282	7 95 24	16.7929
243	5 90 49	15.5885	283	8 00 89	16.8226
244	5 95 36	15.6205	284	8 06 56	16.8523
245	6 00 25	15.6525	285	8 12 25	16.8819
246	6 05 16	15.6844	286	8 17 96	16.9115
247	6 10 09	15.7162	287	8 23 69	16.9411
248	6 15 04	15.7480	288	8 29 44	16.9706
249	6 20 01	15.7797	289	8 35 21	17.0000
250	6 25 00	15.8114	290	8 41 00	17.0294
251	6 30 01	15.8430	291	8 46 81	17.0587
252	6 35 04	15.8745	292	8 52 64	17.0880
253	6 40 09	15.9060	293	8 58 49	17.1172
254	6 45 16	15.9374	294	8 64 36	17.1464
255	6 50 25	15.9687	295	8 70 25	17.1756
256	6 55 36	16.0000	296	8 76 16	17.2047
257	6 60 49	16.0312	297	8 82 09	17.2337
258	6 65 64	16.0624	298	8 88 04	17.2627
259	6 70 81	16.0935	299	8 94 01	17.2916
260	6 76 00	16.1245	300	9 00 00	17.3205
261	6 81 21	16.1555	301	9 06 01	17.3494
262	6 86 44	16.1864	302	9 12 04	17.3781
263	6 91 69	16.2173	303	9 18 09	17.4069
264	6 96 96	16.2481	304	9 24 16	17.4356
265	7 02 25	16.2788	305	9 30 25	17.4642
266	7 07 56	16.3095	306	9 36 36	17.4929
267	7 12 89	16.3401	307	9 42 49	17.5214
268	7 18 24	16.3707	308	9 48 64	17.5499
269	7 23 61	16.4012	309	9 54 81	17.5784
270	7 29 00	16.4317	310	9 61 00	17.6068
271	7 34 41	16.4621	311	9 67 21	17.6352
272	7 39 84	16.4924	312	9 73 44	17.6635
273	7 45 29	16.5227	313	9 79 69	17.6918
274	7 50 76	16.5529	314	9 85 96	17.7200
275	7 56 25	16.5831	315	9 92 25	17.7482
276	7 61 76	16.6132	316	9 98 56	17.7764
277	7 67 29	16.6433	317	10 04 89	17.8045
278	7 72 84	16.6733	318	10 11 24	17.8326
279	7 78 41	16.7033	319	10 17 61	17.8606
280	7 84 00	16.7332	320	10 24 00	17.8885

* By permission from H. Sorenson, "Statistics for Students of Psychology and Education," copyright 1936, McGraw-Hill Book Company, New York.

Number	Square	Square root	Number	Square	Square root
321	10 30 41	17.9165	361	13 03 21	19.0000
322	10 36 84	17.9444	362	13 10 44	19.0263
323	10 43 29	17.9722	363	13 17 69	19.0526
324	10 49 76	18.0000	364	13 24 96	19.0788
325	10 56 25	18.0278	365	13 32 25	19.1050
326	10 62 76	18.0555	366	13 39 56	19.1311
327	10 69 29	18.0831	367	13 46 89	19.1572
328	10 75 84	18.1108	368	13 54 24	19.1833
329	10 82 41	18.1384	369	13 61 61	19.2094
330	10 89 00	18.1659	370	13 69 00	19.2354
331	10 95 61	18.1934	371	13 76 41	19.2614
332	11 02 24	18.2209	372	13 83 84	19.2873
333	11 08 89	18.2483	373	13 91 29	19.3132
334	11 15 56	18.2757	374	13 98 76	19.3391
335	11 22 25	18.3030	375	14 06 25	19.3649
336	11 28 96	18.3303	376	14 13 76	19.3907
337	11 35 69	18.3576	377	14 21 29	19.4165
338	11 42 44	18.3848	378	14 28 84	19.4422
339	11 49 21	18.4120	379	14 36 41	19.4679
340	11 56 00	18.4391	380	14 44 00	19.4936
341	11 62 81	18.4662	381	14 51 61	19.5192
342	11 69 64	18.4932	382	14 59 24	19.5448
343	11 76 49	18.5203	383	14 66 89	19.5704
344	11 83 36	18.5472	384	14 74 56	19.5959
345	11 90 25	18.5742	385	14 82 25	19.6214
346	11 97 16	18.6011	386	14 89 96	19.6469
347	12 04 09	18.6279	387	14 97 69	19.6723
348	12 11 04	18.6548	388	15 05 44	19.6977
349	12 18 01	18.6815	389	15 13 21	19.7231
350	12 25 00	18.7083	390	15 21 00	19.7484
351	12 32 01	18.7350	391	15 28 81	19.7737
352	12 39 04	18.7617	392	15 36 64	19.7990
353	12 46 09	18.7883	393	15 44 49	19.8242
354	12 53 16	18.8149	394	15 52 36	19.8494
355	12 60 25	18.8414	395	15 60 25	19.8746
356	12 67 36	18.8680	396	15 68 16	19.8997
357	12 74 49	18.8944	397	15 76 09	19.9249
358	12 81 64	18.9209	398	15 84 04	19.9499
359	12 88 81	18.9473	399	15 92 01	19.9750
360	12 96 00	18.9737	400	16 00 00	20.0000

* By permission from H. Sorenson, "Statistics for Students of Psychology and Education," copyright 1936, McGraw-Hill Book Company, New York.

Number	Square	Square root	Number	Square	Square root
401	16 08 01	20.0250	441	19 44 81	21.0000
402	16 16 04	20.0499	442	19 53 64	21.0238
403	16 24 09	20.0749	443	19 62 49	21.0476
404	16 32 16	20.0998	444	19 71 36	21.0713
405	16 40 25	20.1246	445	19 80 25	21.0950
406	16 48 36	20.1494	446	19 89 16	21.1187
407	16 56 49	20.1742	447	19 98 09	21.1424
408	16 64 64	20.1990	448	20 07 04	21.1660
409	16 72 81	20.2237	449	20 16 01	21.1896
410	16 81 00	20.2485	450	20 25 00	21.2132
411	16 89 21	20.2731	451	20 34 01	21.2368
412	16 97 44	20.2978	452	20 43 04	21.2603
413	17 05 69	20.3224	453	20 52 09	21.2838
414	17 13 96	20.3470	454	20 61 16	21.3073
415	17 22 25	20.3715	455	20 70 25	21.3307
416	17 30 56	20.3961	456	20 79 36	21.3542
417	17 38 89	20.4206	457	20 88 49	21.3776
418	17 47 24	20.4450	458	20 97 64	21.4009
419	17 55 61	20.4695	459	21 06 81	21.4243
420	17 64 00	20.4939	460	21 16 00	21.4476
421	17 72 41	20.5183	461	21 25 21	21.4709
422	17 80 84	20.5426	462	21 34 44	21.4942
423	17 89 29	20.5670	463	21 43 69	21.5174
424	17 97 76	20.5913	464	21 52 96	21.5407
425	18 06 25	20.6155	465	21 62 25	21.5639
426	18 14 76	20.6398	466	21 71 56	21.5870
427	18 23 29	20.6640	467	21 80 89	21.6102
428	18 31 84	20.6882	468	21 90 24	21.6333
429	18 40 41	20.7123	469	21 99 61	21.6564
430	18 49 00	20.7364	470	22 09 00	21.6795
431	18 57 61	20.7605	471	22 18 41	21.7025
432	18 66 24	20.7846	472	22 27 84	21.7256
433	18 74 89	20.8087	473	22 37 29	21.7486
434	18 83 56	20.8327	474	22 46 76	21.7715
435	18 92 25	20.8567	475	22 56 25	21.7945
436	19 00 96	20.8806	476	22 65 76	21.8174
437	19 09 69	20.9045	477	22 75 29	21.8403
438	19 18 44	20.9284	478	22 84 84	21.8632
439	19 27 21	20.9523	479	22 94 41	21.8861
440	19 36 00	20.9762	480	23 04 00	21.9089

* By permission from H. Sorenson, "Statistics for Students of Psychology and Education," copyright 1936, McGraw-Hill Book Company, New York.

Number	Square	Square root	Number	Square	Square root
481	23 13 61	21.9317	521	27 14 41	22.8254
482	23 23 24	21.9545	522	27 24 84	22.8473
483	23 32 89	21.9773	523	27 35 29	22.8692
484	23 42 56	22.0000	524	27 45 76	22.8910
485	23 52 25	22.0227	525	27 56 25	22.9129
486	23 61 96	22.0454	526	27 66 76	22.9347
487	23 71 69	22.0681	527	27 77 29	22.9565
488	23 81 44	22.0907	528	27 87 84	22.9783
489	23 91 21	22.1133	529	27 98 41	23.0000
490	24 01 00	22.1359	530	28 09 00	23.0217
491	24 10 81	22.1585	531	28 19 61	23.0434
492	24 20 64	22.1811	532	28 30 24	23.0651
493	24 30 49	22.2036	533	28 40 89	23.0868
494	24 40 36	22.2261	534	28 51 56	23.1084
495	24 50 25	22.2486	535	28 62 25	23.1301
496	24 60 16	22.2711	536	28 72 96	23.1517
497	24 70 09	22.2935	537	28 83 69	23.1733
498	24 80 04	22.3159	538	28 94 44	23.1948
499	24 90 01	22.3383	539	29 05 21	23.2164
500	25 00 00	22.3607	540	29 16 00	23.2379
501	25 10 01	22.3830	541	29 26 81	23.2594
502	25 20 04	22.4054	542	29 37 64	23.2809
503	25 30 09	22.4277	543	29 48 49	23.3024
504	25 40 16	22.4499	544	29 59 36	23.3238
505	25 50 25	22.4722	545	29 70 25	23.3452
506	25 60 36	22.4944	546	29 81 16	23.3666
507	25 70 49	22.5167	547	29 92 09	23.3880
508	25 80 64	22.5389	548	30 03 04	23.4094
509	25 90 81	22.5610	549	30 14 01	23.4307
510	26 01 00	22.5832	550	30 25 00	23.4521
511	26 11 21	22.6053	551	30 36 01	23.4734
512	26 21 44	22.6274	552	30 47 04	23.4947
513	26 31 69	22.6495	553	30 58 09	23.5160
514	26 41 96	22.6716	554	30 69 16	23.5372
515	26 52 25	22.6936	555	30 80 25	23.5584
516	26 62 56	22.7156	556	30 91 36	23.5797
517	26 72 89	22.7376	557	31 02 49	23.6008
518	26 83 24	22.7596	558	31 13 64	23.6220
519	26 93 61	22.7816	559	31 24 81	23.6432
520	27 04 00	22.8035	560	31 36 00	23.6643

Number	Square	Square root	Number	Square	Square root
561	31 47 21	23.6854	601	36 12 01	24.5153
562	31 58 44	23.7065	602	36 24 04	24.5357
563	31 69 69	23.7276	603	36 36 09	24.5561
564	31 80 96	23.7487	604	36 48 16	24.5764
565	31 92 25	23.7697	605	36 60 25	24.5967
566	32 03 56	23.7908	606	36 72 36	24.6171
567	32 14 89	23.8118	607	36 84 49	24.6374
568	32 26 24	23.8328	608	36 96 64	24.6577
569	32 37 61	23.8537	609	37 08 81	24.6779
570	32 49 00	23.8747	610	37 21 00	24.6982
571	32 60 41	23.8956	611	37 33 21	24.7184
572	32 71 84	23.9165	612	37 45 44	24.7385
573	32 83 29	23.9374	613	37 57 69	24.7588
574	32 94 76	23.9583	614	37 69 96	24.7790
575	33 06 25	23.9792	615	37 82 25	24.7992
576	33 17 76	24.0000	616	37 94 56	24.8193
577	33 29 29	24.0208	617	38 06 89	24.8395
578	33 40 84	24.0416	618	38 19 24	24.8596
579	33 52 41	24.0624	619	38 31 61	24.8797
580	33 64 00	24.0832	620	38 44 00	24.8998
581	33 75 61	24.1039	621	38 56 41	24.9199
582	33 87 24	24.1247	622	38 68 84	24.9399
583	33 98 89	24.1454	623	38 81 29	24.9600
584	34 10 56	24.1661	624	38 93 76	24.9800
585	34 22 25	24.1868	625	39 06 25	25.0000
586	34 33 96	24.2074	626	39 18 76	25.0200
587	34 45 69	24.2281	627	39 31 29	25.0400
588	34 57 44	24.2487	628	39 43 84	25.0599
589	34 69 21	24.2693	629	39 56 41	25.0799
590	34 81 00	24.2899	630	39 69 00	25.0998
591	34 92 81	24.3105	631	39 81 61	25.1197
592	35 04 64	24.3311	632	39 94 24	25.1396
593	35 16 49	24.3516	633	40 06 89	25.1595
594	35 28 36	24.3721	634	40 19 56	25.1794
595	35 40 25	24.3926	635	40 32 25	25.1992
596	35 52 16	24.4131	636	40 44 96	25.2190
597	35 64 09	24.4336	637	40 57 69	25.2389
598	35 76 04	24.4540	638	40 70 44	25.2587
599	35 88 01	24.4745	639	40 83 21	25.2784
600	36 00 00	24.4949	640	40 96 00	25.2982

* By permission from H. Sorenson, "Statistics for Students of Psychology and Education," copyright 1936, McGraw-Hill Book Company, New York.

Number	Square	Square root	Number	Square	Square root
641	41 08 81	25.3180	681	46 37 61	26.0960
642	41 21 64	25.3377	682	46 51 24	26.1151
643	41 34 49	25.3574	683	46 64 89	26.1343
644	41 47 36	25.3772	684	46 78 56	26.1534
645	41 60 25	25.3969	685	46 92 25	26.1725
646	41 73 16	25.4165	686	47 05 96	26.1916
647	41 86 09	25.4362	687	47 19 69	26.2107
648	41 99 04	25.4558	688	47 33 44	26.2298
649	42 12 01	25.4755	689	47 47 21	26.2488
650	42 25 00	25.4951	690	47 61 00	26.2679
651	42 38 01	25.5147	691	47 74 81	26.2869
652	42 51 04	25.5343	692	47 88 64	26.3059
653	42 64 09	25.5539	693	48 02 49	26.3249
654	42 77 16	25.5734	694	48 16 36	26.3439
655	42 90 25	25.5930	695	48 30 25	26.3629
656	43 03 36	25.6125	696	48 44 16	26.3818
657	43 16 49	25.6320	697	48 58 09	26.4008
658	43 29 64	25.6515	698	48 72 04	26.4197
659	43 42 81	25.6710	699	48 86 01	26.4386
660	43 56 00	25.6905	700	49 00 00	26.4575
661	43 69 21	25.7099	701	49 14 01	26.4764
662	43 82 44	25.7294	702	49 28 04	26.4953
663	43 95 69	25.7488	703	49 42 09	26.5141
664	44 08 96	25.7682	704	49 56 16	26.5330
665	44 22 25	25.7876	705	49 70 25	26.5518
666	44 35 56	25.8070	706	49 84 36	26.5707
667	44 48 89	25.8263	707	49 98 49	26.5895
668	44 62 24	25.8457	708	50 12 64	26.6083
669	44 75 61	25.8650	709	50 26 81	26.6271
670	44 89 00	25.8844	710	50 41 00	26.6458
671	45 02 41	25.9037	711	50 55 21	26.6646
672	45 15 84	25.9230	712	50 69 44	26.6833
673	45 29 29	25.9422	713	50 83 69	26.7021
674	45 42 76	25.9615	714	50 97 96	26.7208
675	45 56 25	25.9808	715	51 12 25	26.7395
676	45 69 76	26.0000	716	51 26 56	26.7582
677	45 83 29	26.0192	717	51 40 89	26.7769
678	45 96 84	26.0384	718	51 55 24	26.7955
679	46 10 41	26.0576	719	51 69 61	26.8142
680	46 24 00	26.0768	720	51 84 00	26.8328

* By permission from H. Sorenson, "Statistics for Students of Psychology and Education," copyright 1936, McGraw-Hill Book Company, New York.

Number	Square	Square root	Number	Square	Square root
721	51 98 41	26.8514	761	57 91 21	27.5862
722	52 12 84	26.8701	762	58 06 44	27.6043
723	52 27 29	26.8887	763	58 21 69	27.6225
724	52 41 76	26.9072	764	58 36 96	27.6405
725	52 56 25	26.9258	765	58 52 25	27.6586
726	52 70 76	26.9444	766	58 67 56	27.6767
727	52 85 29	26.9629	767	58 82 89	27.6948
728	52 99 84	26.9815	768	58 98 24	27.7128
729	53 14 41	27.0000	769	59 13 61	27.7308
730	53 29 00	27.0185	770	59 29 00	27.7489
731	53 43 61	27.0370	771	59 44 41	27.7669
732	53 58 24	27.0555	772	59 59 84	27.7849
733	53 72 89	27.0740	773	59 75 29	27.8029
734	53 87 56	27.0924	774	59 90 76	27.8209
735	54 02 25	27.1109	775	60 06 25	27.8388
736	54 16 96	27.1293	776	60 21 76	27.8568
737	54 31 69	27.1477	777	60 37 29	27.8747
738	54 46 44	27.1662	778	60 52 84	27.8927
739	54 61 27	27.1846	779	60 68 41	27.9106
740	54 76 00	27.2029	780	60 84 00	27.9285
741	54 90 81	27.2213	781	60 99 61	27.9464
742	55 05 64	27.2397	782	61 15 24	27.9643
743	55 20 49	27.2580	783	61 30 89	27.9821
744	55 35 36	27.2764	784	61 46 56	28.0000
745	55 50 25	27.2947	785	61 62 25	28.0179
746	55 65 16	27.3130	786	61 77 96	28.0357
747	55 80 09	27.3313	787	61 93 69	28.0535
748	55 95 04	27.3496	788	62 09 44	28.0713
749	56 10 01	27.3679	789	62 25 21	28.0891
750	56 25 00	27.3861	790	62 41 00	28.1069
751	56 40 01	27.4044	791	62 56 81	28.1247
752	56 55 04	27.4226	792	62 72 64	28.1425
753	56 70 09	27.4408	793	62 88 49	28.1603
754	56 85 16	27.4591	794	63 04 36	28.1780
755	57 00 25	27.4773	795	63 20 25	28.1957
756	57 15 36	27.4955	796	63 36 16	28.2135
757	57 30 49	27.5136	797	63 52 09	28.2312
758	57 45 64	27.5318	798	63 68 04	28.2489
759	57 60 81	27.5500	799	63 84 01	28.2666
760	57 76 00	27.5681	800	64 00 00	28.2843

* By permission from H. Sorenson, "Statistics for Students of Psychology and Education," copyright 1936, McGraw-Hill Book Company, New York.

Number	Square	Square root	Number	Square	Square root
801	64 16 01	28.3019	841	70 72 81	29.0000
802	64 32 04	28.3196	842	70 89 64	29.0172
803	64 48 09	28.3373	843	71 06 49	29.0345
804	64 64 16	28.3549	844	71 23 36	29.0517
805	64 80 25	28.3725	845	71 40 25	29.0689
806	64 96 36	28.3901	846	71 57 16	29.0861
807	65 12 49	28.4077	847	71 74 09	29.1033
808	65 28 64	28.4253	848	71 91 04	29.1204
809	65 44 81	28.4429	849	72 08 01	29.1376
810	65 61 00	28.4605	850	72 25 00	29.1548
811	65 77 21	28.4781	851	72 42 01	29.1719
812	65 93 44	28.4956	852	72 59 04	29.1890
813	66 09 69	28.5132	853	72 76 09	29.2062
814	66 25 96	28.5307	854	72 93 16	29.2233
815	66 42 25	28.5482	855	73 10 25	29.2404
816	66 58 56	28.5657	856	73 27 36	29.2575
817	66 74 89	28.5832	857	73 44 49	29.2746
818	66 91 24	28.6007	858	73 61 64	29.2916
819	67 07 61	28.6082	859	73 78 81	29.3087
820	67 24 00	28.6356	860	73 96 00	29.3258
821	67 40 41	28.6531	861	74 13 21	29.3428
822	67 56 84	28.6705	862	74 30 44	29.3598
823	67 73 29	28.6880	863	74 47 69	29.3769
824	67 89 76	28.7054	864	74 64 96	29.3939
825	68 06 25	28.7228	865	74 82 25	29.4109
826	68 22 76	28.7402	866	74 99 56	29.4279
827	68 39 29	28.7576	867	75 16 89	29.4449
828	68 55 84	28.7750	868	75 34 24	29.4618
829	68 72 41	28.7924	869	75 51 61	29.4788
830	68 89 00	28.8097	870	75 69 00	29.4958
831	69 05 61	28.8271	871	75 86 41	29.5127
832	69 22 24	28.8444	872	76 03 84	29.5296
833	69 38 89	28.8617	873	76 21 29	29.5466
834	69 55 56	28.8791	874	76 38 76	29.5635
835	69 72 25	28.8964	875	76 56 25	29.5804
836	69 88 96	28.9137	876	76 73 76	29.5973
837	70 05 69	28.9310	877	76 91 29	29.6142
838	70 22 44	28.9482	878	77 08 84	29.6311
839	70 39 21	28.9655	879	77 26 41	29.6479
840	70 56 00	28.9828	880	77 44 00	29.6648

* By permission from H. Sorenson, "Statistics for Students of Psychology and Education," copyright 1936, McGraw-Hill Book Company, New York.

Number	Square	Square root	Number	Square	Square root
881	77 61 61	29.6816	921	84 82 41	30.3480
882	77 79 24	29.6985	922	85 00 84	30.3645
883	77 96 89	29.7153	923	85 19 29	30.3809
884	78 14 56	29.7321	924	85 37 76	30.3974
885	78 32 25	29.7489	925	85 56 25	30.4138
886	78 49 96	29.7658	926	85 74 76	30.4302
887	78 67 69	29.7825	927	85 93 29	30.4467
888	78 85 44	29.7993	928	86 11 84	30.4631
889	79 03 21	29.8161	929	86 30 41	30.4795
890	79 21 00	29.8329	930	86 49 00	30.4959
891	79 38 81	29.8496	931	86 67 61	30.5123
892	79 56 64	29.8664	932	86 86 24	30.5287
893	79 74 49	29.8831	933	87 04 89	30.5450
894	79 92 36	29.8998	934	87 23 56	30.5614
895	80 10 25	29.9166	935	87 42 25	30.5778
896	80 28 16	29.9333	936	87 60 96	30.5941
897	80 46 09	29.9500	937	87 79 69	30.6105
898	80 64 04	29.9666	938	87 98 44	30.6268
899	80 82 01	29.9833	939	88 17 21	30.6431
900	81 00 00	30.0000	940	88 36 00	30.6594
901	81 18 01	30.0167	941	88 54 81	30.6757
902	81 36 04	30.0333	942	88 73 64	30.6920
903	81 54 09	30.0500	943	88 92 49	30.7083
904	81 72 16	30.0666	944	89 11 36	30.7246
905	81 90 25	30.0832	945	89 30 25	30.7409
906	82 08 36	30.0998	946	89 49 16	30.7571
907	82 26 49	30.1164	947	89 68 09	30.7734
908	82 44 64	30.1330	948	89 87 04	30.7896
909	82 62 81	30.1496	949	90 06 01	30.8058
910	82 81 00	30.1662	950	90 25 00	30.8221
911	82 99 21	30.1828	951	90 44 01	30.8383
912	83 17 44	30.1993	952	90 63 04	30.8545
913	83 35 69	30.2159	953	90 82 09	30.8707
914	83 53 96	30.2324	954	91 01 16	30.8869
915	83 72 25	30.2490	955	91 20 25	30.9031
916	83 90 56	30.2655	956	91 39 36	30.9192
917	84 08 89	30.2820	957	91 58 49	30.9354
918	84 27 24	30.2985	958	91 77 64	30.9516
919	84 45 61	30.3150	959	91 96 81	30.9677
920	84 64 00	30.3315	960	92 16 00	30.9839

* By permission from H. Sorenson, "Statistics for Students of Psychology and Education," copyright 1936, McGraw-Hill Book Company, New York.

Number	Square	Square root	Number	Square	Square root
961	92 35 21	31.0000	981	96 23 61	31.3209
962	92 54 44	31.0161	982	96 43 24	31.3369
963	92 73 69	31.0322	983	96 62 89	31.3528
964	92 92 96	31.0483	984	96 82 56	31.3688
965	93 12 25	31.0644	985	97 02 25	31.3847
966	93 31 56	31.0805	986	97 21 96	31.4006
967	93 50 89	31.0966	987	97 41 69	31.4166
968	93 70 24	31.1127	988	97 61 44	31.4325
969	93 89 61	31.1288	989	97 81 21	31.4484
970	94 09 00	31.1448	990	98 01 00	31.4643
971	94 28 41	31.1609	991	98 20 81	31.4802
972	94 47 84	31.1769	992	98 40 64	31.4960
973	94 67 29	31.1929	993	98 60 49	31.5119
974	94 86 76	31.2090	994	98 80 36	31.5278
975	95 06 25	31.2250	995	99 00 25	31.5436
976	95 25 76	31.2410	996	99 20 16	31.5595
977	95 45 29	31.2570	997	99 40 09	31.5753
978	95 64 84	31.2730	998	99 60 04	31.5911
979	95 84 41	31.2890	999	99 80 01	31.6070
980	96 04 00	31.3050	1,000	100 00 00	31.6228

* By permission from H. Sorenson, "Statistics for Students of Psychology and Education," copyright 1936, McGraw-Hill Book Company, New York.

Table B.

Per Cent of Total Area under the Normal Curve between Mean Ordinate and Ordinate at Any Given Sigma-Distance from the Mean

$\frac{x}{\sigma}$	.00	.01	.02	.03	.04	.05	.06	.07	.08	.09
0.0	00.00	00.40	00.80	01.20	01.60	01.99	02.39	02.79	03.19	03.59
0.1	03.98	04.38	04.78	05.17	05.57	05.96	06.36	06.75	07.14	07.53
0.2	07.93	08.32	08.71	09.10	09.48	09.87	10.26	10.64	11.03	11.41
0.3	11.79	12.17	12.55	12.93	13.31	13.68	14.06	14.43	14.80	15.17
0.4	15.54	15.91	16.28	16.64	17.00	17.36	17.72	18.08	18.44	18.79
0.5	19.15	19.50	19.85	20.19	20.54	20.88	21.23	21.57	21.90	22.24
0.6	22.57	22.91	23.24	23.57	23.89	24.22	24.54	24.86	25.17	25.49
0.7	25.80	26.11	26.42	26.73	27.04	27.34	27.64	27.94	28.23	28.52
0.8	28.81	29.10	29.39	29.67	29.95	30.23	30.51	30.78	31.06	31.33
0.9	31.59	31.86	32.12	32.38	32.64	32.90	33.15	33.40	33.65	33.89
1.0	34.13	34.38	34.61	34.85	35.08	35.31	35.54	35.77	35.99	36.21
1.1	36.43	36.65	36.86	37.08	37.29	37.49	37.70	37.90	38.10	38.30
1.2	38.49	38.69	38.88	39.07	39.25	39.44	39.62	39.80	39.97	40.15
1.3	40.32	40.49	40.66	40.82	40.99	41.15	41.31	41.47	41.62	41.77
1.4	41.92	42.07	42.22	42.36	42.51	42.65	42.79	42.92	43.06	43.19
1.5	43.32	43.45	43.57	43.70	43.83	43.94	44.06	44.18	44.29	44.41
1.6	44.52	44.63	44.74	44.84	44.95	45.05	45.15	45.25	45.35	45.45
1.7	45.54	45.64	45.73	45.82	45.91	45.99	46.08	46.16	46.25	46.33
1.8	46.41	46.49	46.56	46.64	46.71	46.78	46.86	46.93	46.99	47.06
1.9	47.13	47.19	47.26	47.32	47.38	47.44	47.50	47.56	47.61	47.67
2.0	47.72	47.78	47.83	47.88	47.93	47.98	48.03	48.08	48.12	48.17
2.1	48.21	48.26	48.30	48.34	48.38	48.42	48.46	48.50	48.54	48.57
2.2	48.61	48.64	48.68	48.71	48.75	48.78	48.81	48.84	48.87	48.90
2.3	48.93	48.96	48.98	49.01	49.04	49.06	49.09	49.11	49.13	49.16
2.4	49.18	49.20	49.22	49.25	49.27	49.29	49.31	49.32	49.34	49.36
2.5	49.38	49.40	49.41	49.43	49.45	49.46	49.48	49.49	49.51	49.52
2.6	49.53	49.55	49.56	49.57	49.59	49.60	49.61	49.62	49.63	49.64
2.7	49.65	49.66	49.67	49.68	49.69	49.70	49.71	49.72	49.73	49.74
2.8	49.74	49.75	49.76	49.77	49.77	49.78	49.79	49.79	49.80	49.81
2.9	49.81	49.82	49.82	49.83	49.84	49.84	49.85	49.85	49.86	49.86
3.0	49.87									
3.5	49.98									
4.0	49.997									
5.0	49.99997									

* The original data for Table B came from *Tables for statisticians and biometricians*, edited by Karl Pearson, published by Cambridge University Press, and are used here by permission of the publisher. The adaptation of these data is taken from Lindquist, E. L., *A first course in statistics* (revised edition), with permission of the publisher, Houghton Mifflin Company.

Table C.
Table of Random Sampling Numbers

340

ROW	1	2	3	4	5	6	7	8	9	10	11	12	13	14	15	16	17	18	19	20	21	22	23	24	25	26	27	28	29	30	31	32	ROW
1	2	7	8	9	4	0	7	2	3	2	5	4	2	6	7	1	6	8	5	9	1	3	5	4	0	3	6	6	7	6	5	1	1
2	2	2	6	0	4	1	7	7	3	8	7	3	6	7	9	4	2	1	3	8	9	0	3	4	9	0	2	6	3	0	9	8	2
3	9	1	6	6	3	9	4	9	1	0	5	1	5	2	2	7	5	2	5	3	4	1	3	9	5	8	1	3	8	2	9	2	3
4	7	0	5	5	9	2	7	5	7	8	0	8	8	5	0	6	0	5	9	0	5	7	4	5	2	0	6	1	6	4	2	0	4
5	4	7	3	6	6	3	9	8	2	1	7	9	7	6	4	2	4	9	6	0	3	6	3	5	3	9	9	1	8	5	1	3	5
6	8	2	0	2	8	7	7	6	0	2	2	3	1	1	1	6	4	8	5	2	2	3	4	2	2	6	5	2	2	4	9	6	6
7	0	8	7	5	3	3	6	4	2	6	8	3	1	6	5	0	0	5	5	7	8	1	0	1	2	9	1	4	3	4	7	6	7
8	9	4	1	9	0	8	4	6	6	8	6	3	3	2	2	3	7	4	7	5	1	5	7	6	3	7	9	4	5	5	3	5	8
9	5	0	0	6	7	4	0	0	0	1	9	5	9	9	1	8	1	4	7	4	9	8	7	2	4	3	0	8	6	4	2	7	9
10	1	9	5	4	1	5	2	6	2	9	4	1	1	5	8	4	4	4	6	1	8	7	8	6	4	8	7	4	4	0	5	8	10
11	5	6	4	4	1	8	7	2	8	3	6	1	5	9	8	6	2	2	9	1	9	0	4	8	1	0	1	3	5	3	4	4	11
12	7	9	2	5	1	9	7	9	3	1	8	6	8	7	7	6	6	5	0	3	8	1	1	2	4	7	8	9	1	7	5	2	12
13	3	3	3	5	9	5	1	4	0	8	2	5	6	3	5	4	4	6	5	7	2	6	7	8	9	9	9	8	0	9	1	5	13
14	1	9	0	4	0	0	9	9	5	7	4	1	5	9	4	7	6	4	8	2	6	4	4	1	8	8	1	5	4	3	8	0	14
15	5	4	4	7	2	0	3	7	9	1	0	9	6	2	9	7	4	7	6	1	1	6	1	2	2	9	5	8	4	4	8	6	15
16	2	9	8	2	5	5	9	3	2	0	4	9	0	6	4	4	2	1	5	7	3	6	5	5	4	5	7	9	6	6	4	0	16
17	9	7	6	2	6	7	7	3	3	3	1	7	5	0	9	6	1	1	3	9	2	1	1	0	0	1	3	7	7	3	7	3	17
18	5	8	2	4	3	3	0	8	5	3	5	7	5	8	3	5	9	3	4	5	4	6	3	9	2	7	1	1	4	9	1	3	18
19	4	3	4	9	5	0	3	6	2	9	7	4	6	2	5	6	9	8	3	6	1	4	0	3	5	9	7	1	8	0	6	9	19
20	1	1	9	8	4	8	0	6	7	0	9	7	9	6	9	9	4	0	6	0	0	5	9	6	5	1	4	2	0	4	1	9	20
21	6	9	1	8	3	3	7	5	9	6	6	7	7	6	0	4	5	3	4	5	7	3	0	6	1	0	3	0	0	3	5	0	21
22	7	0	0	3	8	1	3	4	7	9	5	2	6	9	9	7	3	2	5	0	2	3	5	3	9	7	4	8	9	4	1	5	22
23	3	7	2	0	8	1	5	6	9	0	1	7	8	9	6	6	6	0	7	8	1	9	6	7	4	8	9	6	3	6	5	1	23
24	2	7	0	0	0	6	5	0	6	5	6	0	3	2	9	3	1	7	2	2	8	4	9	0	4	3	2	4	5	5	1	2	24
25	3	0	7	0	7	8	4	9	4	2	8	2	4	7	4	9	6	0	4	3	8	1	7	7	0	9	8	4	6	3	1	2	25
26	6	2	9	3	3	1	7	7	5	2	2	3	4	6	4	2	2	4	7	5	4	4	4	1	7	1	6	7	1	2	6	8	26
27	5	4	9	2	1	4	8	5	7	0	9	6	4	7	2	1	8	9	7	6	1	3	3	4	6	6	5	9	0	7	0	3	27
28	0	3	7	0	1	7	3	8	0	3	6	2	3	1	0	9	5	5	2	5	9	2	0	2	8	7	7	2	0	2	7	2	28
29	9	3	6	6	2	2	0	9	7	2	3	9	2	8	7	3	1	0	7	0	8	9	3	8	8	5	3	1	3	1	0	9	29
30	2	9	5	6	9	9	5	6	9	8	2	8	0	0	4	4	8	8	5	7	2	1	3	4	9	5	2	6	8	3	6	6	30
31	8	5	7	2	9	2	6	5	9	3	9	7	1	8	3	5	6	6	1	2	1	5	5	5	6	1	7	1	5	7	5	9	31
32	8	4	5	7	7	9	9	5	1	4	5	5	0	9	5	3	1	3	9	3	7	8	1	4	0	5	4	1	5	4	4	0	32
33	8	7	9	8	1	8	4	1	4	3	7	7	0	0	9	1	9	4	6	1	3	8	6	5	9	2	2	8	1	6	9	0	33
34	7	3	2	5	1	8	6	3	2	8	5	8	6	9	3	4	5	2	6	1	9	0	6	9	0	5	4	6	8	0	3	2	34
35	8	9	9	0	1	8	8	8	9	5	7	5	0	4	1	1	6	0	3	1	3	0	3	5	8	9	2	7	8	8	7	1	35
36	0	2	9	7	8	8	1	7	6	1	6	7	6	4	2	5	0	5	8	3	2	4	7	7	2	2	6	2	6	8	6	0	36
37	0	5	2	3	2	3	8	1	8	8	1	6	2	3	0	7	3	0	1	2	6	2	6	8	3	7	4	4	3	8	9	9	37
38	2	2	6	8	1	6	9	6	2	6	7	9	1	7	8	0	2	4	8	0	4	7	3	3	8	4	4	8	4	3	3	8	38
39	0	7	8	4	9	5	8	8	0	7	2	1	8	1	7	5	3	0	7	4	1	0	3	2	0	1	2	8	6	5	9	4	39
40	4	8	0	7	0	5	9	9	4	9	6	9	8	2	0	6	4	0	7	8	1	1	4	2	1	6	7	0	7	3	1	2	40
41	9	2	0	1	6	7	2	8	3	9	8	8	3	4	7	8	4	0	5	1	6	8	7	8	3	5	4	5	0	4	0	6	41
42	0	8	8	3	4	0	9	2	2	8	1	5	0	4	8	2	6	2	9	2	1	9	8	5	3	1	0	7	8	5	3	9	42
43	2	0	6	9	7	5	2	8	2	5	5	4	0	7	7	1	7	6	8	6	8	5	1	3	7	8	2	7	1	9	3	6	43
44	3	1	8	6	8	3	5	6	3	2	7	4	1	8	9	4	5	6	8	0	6	4	6	4	1	0	9	1	9	8	1	4	44
45	0	0	8	6	1	7	5	0	8	5	6	5	0	8	2	7	1	1	6	3	4	6	0	0	9	4	7	9	2	4	8	7	45
46	3	3	2	9	4	2	5	3	3	8	2	4	2	6	2	5	2	9	0	1	3	7	6	5	9	1	4	6	0	1	0	0	46
47	8	4	7	4	0	4	5	1	2	1	0	4	2	5	7	7	9	4	6	5	8	3	3	8	1	0	3	7	7	7	8	6	47
48	0	2	4	3	0	2	0	7	2	8	8	0	8	4	1	6	0	2	3	5	9	7	5	1	3	6	3	2	8	7	5	8	48
49	4	6	5	6	3	0	4	5	2	0	1	5	2	7	9	5	3	0	2	2	1	6	1	1	0	0	9	1	6	1	7	7	49
50	3	4	8	3	2	5	8	7	5	9	7	1	6	3	9	9	0	9	4	2	5	8	9	5	3	3	3	6	4	5	2	0	50

Table D.

Values of the Correlation Coefficient for Different Levels of
Significance

df	P = .10	.05	.02	.01
1	.988	.997	.9995	.9999
2	.900	.950	.980	.990
3	.805	.878	.934	.959
4	.729	.811	.882	.917
5	.669	.754	.833	.874
6	.622	.707	.789	.834
7	.582	.666	.750	.798
8	.549	.632	.716	.765
9	.521	.602	.685	.735
10	.497	.576	.658	.708
11	.476	.553	.634	.684
12	.458	.532	.612	.661
13	.441	.514	.592	.641
14	.426	.497	.574	.623
15	.412	.482	.558	.606
16	.400	.468	.542	.590
17	.389	.456	.528	.575
18	.378	.444	.516	.561
19	.369	.433	.503	.549
20	.360	.423	.492	.537
21	.352	.413	.482	.526
22	.344	.404	.472	.515
23	.337	.396	.462	.505
24	.330	.388	.453	.496
25	.323	.381	.445	.487
26	.317	.374	.437	.479
27	.311	.367	.430	.471
28	.306	.361	.423	.463
29	.301	.355	.416	.456
30	.296	.349	.409	.449
35	.275	.325	.381	.418
40	.257	.304	.358	.393
45	.243	.288	.338	.372
50	.231	.273	.322	.354
60	.211	.250	.295	.325
70	.195	.232	.274	.302
80	.183	.217	.256	.283
90	.173	.205	.242	.267
100	.164	.195	.230	.254

SOURCE: Table D is reprinted from Table V.A. of Fisher & Yates, *Statistical Methods for Research Workers*, published by Oliver and Boyd Ltd., Edinburgh, and by permission of the author and publishers.

NOTE: ' The probabilities given are for a two-tailed test of significance, that is with the sign of r ignored. For a one-tailed test of significance, the tabled probabilities should be halved.

Reproduced with permission of Hafner Press, as found in EDUCATIONAL STATISTICS; USE AND INTERPRETATION by W. James Popham. 1967. Harper and Row, Publishers.

Table E
Values of the Rank–Order Correlation
Coefficient (rho) at the 5% and 1% Levels of Significance

Additional Values of r at the 5 and 1 Per Cent Levels of Significance

df	.05	.01	df	.05	.01	df	.05	.01
32	.339	.436	48	.279	.361	150	.159	.208
34	.329	.424	55	.261	.338	175	.148	.193
36	.320	.413	65	.241	.313	200	.138	.181
38	.312	.403	75	.224	.292	300	.113	.148
42	.297	.384	85	.211	.275	400	.098	.128
44	.291	.376	95	.200	.260	500	.088	.115
46	.284	.368	125	.174	.228	1,000	.062	.081

TABLE E. Table of Critical Values of
r_s, the Spearman Rank Correlation
Coefficient

N	Significance level (one-tailed test)	
	.05	.01
4	1.000	
5	.900	1.000
6	.829	.943
7	.714	.893
8	.643	.833
9	.600	.783
10	.564	.746
12	.506	.712
14	.456	.645
16	.425	.601
18	.399	.564
20	.377	.534
22	359	.508
24	.343	.485
26	.329	.465
28	.317	.448
30	.306	.432

SOURCE: E. G. Olds, "Distributions of
Sums of Squares of Rank Differences for
Small Numbers of Individuals," *Ann. Math.
Statist.* **9,** 133–148 (1938).

Table F.
Levels of Significance of the "t"–Test

df	Level of significance for one-tailed test					
	.10	.05	.025	.01	.005	.0005
	Level of significance for two-tailed test					
	.20	.10	.05	.02	.01	.001
1	3.078	6.314	12.706	31.821	63.657	636.619
2	1.886	2.920	4.303	6.965	9.925	31.598
3	1.638	2.353	3.182	4.541	5.841	12.941
4	1.533	2.132	2.776	3.747	4.604	8.610
5	1.476	2.015	2.571	3.365	4.032	6.859
6	1.440	1.943	2.447	3.143	3.707	5.959
7	1.415	1.895	2.365	2.998	3.499	5.405
8	1.397	1.860	2.306	2.896	3.355	5.041
9	1.383	1.833	2.262	2.821	3.250	4.781
10	1.372	1.812	2.228	2.764	3.169	4.587
11	1.363	1.796	2.201	2.718	3.106	4.437
12	1.356	1.782	2.179	2.681	3.055	4.318
13	1.350	1.771	2.160	2.650	3.012	4.221
14	1.345	1.761	2.145	2.624	2.977	4.140
15	1.341	1.753	2.131	2.602	2.947	4.073
16	1.337	1.746	2.120	2.583	2.921	4.015
17	1.333	1.740	2.110	2.567	2.898	3.965
18	1.330	1.734	2.101	2.552	2.878	3.922
19	1.328	1.729	2.093	2.539	2.861	3.883
20	1.325	1.725	2.086	2.528	2.845	3.850
21	1.323	1.721	2.080	2.518	2.831	3.819
22	1.321	1.717	2.074	2.508	2.819	3.792
23	1.319	1.714	2.069	2.500	2.807	3.767
24	1.318	1.711	2.064	2.492	2.797	3.745
25	1.316	1.708	2.060	2.485	2.787	3.725
26	1.315	1.706	2.056	2.479	2.779	3.707
27	1.314	1.703	2.052	2.473	2.771	3.690
28	1.313	1.701	2.048	2.467	2.763	3.674
29	1.311	1.699	2.045	2.462	2.756	3.659
30	1.310	1.697	2.042	2.457	2.750	3.646
40	1.303	1.684	2.021	2.423	2.704	3.551
60	1.296	1.671	2.000	2.390	2.660	3.460
120	1.289	1.658	1.980	2.358	2.617	3.373
∞	1.282	1.645	1.960	2.326	2.576	3.291

SOURCE: Table F is abridged from Table III of Fisher & Yates: *Statistical Tables for Biological, Agricultural, and Medical Research,* published by Oliver & Boyd Ltd., Edinburgh, and by permission of the authors and publishers.

Table F is taken from Table III of Fisher and Yates: STATISTICAL TABLES FOR BIOLOGICAL, AGRICULTURAL AND MEDICAL RESEARCH, published by Longman Group, Ltd., London. (previously published by Oliver and Boyd, Edinburgh), and by permission of the authors and publishers.

Reproduced as found in EDUCATIONAL STATISTICS: USE AND INTERPRETATION by W. James Popham. 1967. Harper and Row, Publishers.

Table G.
Values of the F-Ratio and the 5% and 1%
Levels of Significance

(df ASSOCIATED WITH THE DENOMINATOR)		1	2	3	4	5	6	7	8	9
1	5%	161	200	216	225	230	234	237	239	241
	1%	4052	5000	5403	5625	5764	5859	5928	5982	6022
2	5%	18.5	19.0	19.2	19.2	19.3	19.3	19.4	19.4	19.4
	1%	98.5	99.0	99.2	99.2	99.3	99.3	99.4	99.4	99.4
3	5%	10.1	9.55	9.28	9.12	9.01	8.94	8.89	8.85	8.81
	1%	34.1	30.8	29.5	28.7	28.2	27.9	27.7	27.5	27.3
4	5%	7.71	6.94	6.59	6.39	6.26	6.16	6.09	6.04	6.00
	1%	21.2	18.0	16.7	16.0	15.5	15.2	15.0	14.8	14.7
5	5%	6.61	5.79	5.41	5.19	5.05	4.95	4.88	4.82	4.77
	1%	16.3	13.3	12.1	11.4	11.0	10.7	10.5	10.3	10.2
6	5%	5.99	5.14	4.76	4.53	4.39	4.28	4.21	4.15	4.10
	1%	13.7	10.9	9.78	9.15	8.75	8.47	8.26	8.10	7.98
7	5%	5.59	4.74	4.35	4.12	3.97	3.87	3.79	3.73	3.68
	1%	12.2	9.55	8.45	7.85	7.46	7.19	6.99	6.84	6.72
8	5%	5.32	4.46	4.07	3.84	3.69	3.58	3.50	3.44	3.39
	1%	11.3	8.65	7.59	7.01	6.63	6.37	6.18	6.03	5.91
9	5%	5.12	4.26	3.86	3.63	3.48	3.37	3.29	3.23	3.18
	1%	10.6	8.02	6.99	6.42	6.06	5.80	5.61	5.47	5.35
10	5%	4.96	4.10	3.71	3.48	3.33	3.22	3.14	3.07	3.02
	1%	10.0	7.56	6.55	5.99	5.64	5.39	5.20	5.06	4.94
11	5%	4.84	3.98	3.59	3.36	3.20	3.09	3.01	2.95	2.90
	1%	9.65	7.21	6.22	5.67	5.32	5.07	4.89	4.74	4.63
12	5%	4.75	3.89	3.49	3.26	3.11	3.00	2.91	2.85	2.80
	1%	9.33	6.93	5.95	5.41	5.06	4.82	4.64	4.50	4.39
13	5%	4.67	3.81	3.41	3.18	3.03	2.92	2.83	2.77	2.71
	1%	9.07	6.70	5.74	5.21	4.86	4.62	4.44	4.30	4.19
14	5%	4.60	3.74	3.34	3.11	2.96	2.85	2.76	2.70	2.65
	1%	8.86	6.51	5.56	5.04	4.70	4.46	4.28	4.14	4.03
15	5%	4.54	3.68	3.29	3.06	2.90	2.79	2.71	2.64	2.59
	1%	8.68	6.36	5.42	4.89	4.56	4.32	4.14	4.00	3.89

(df ASSOCIATED WITH THE NUMERATOR)

* Merrington, M., and Thompson, C. M. Tables of percentage points of the inverted beta (F) distribution, *Biometrika*, 1943, 33, 73–88, by permission of the editor. Reproduced with the permission of the Biometrika Trustees and Houghton Mifflin Company, as found in ELEMENTARY STATISTICS, by Janet T. Spence, et. al. Second edition; 1968. Houghton Mifflin Company.

Values of F at the 5% and 1% Significance Levels, continued

(df ASSOCIATED WITH THE DENOMINATOR)		(df ASSOCIATED WITH THE NUMERATOR)								
16	5%	4.49	3.63	3.24	3.01	2.85	2.74	2.66	2.59	2.54
	1%	8.53	6.23	5.29	4.77	4.44	4.20	4.03	3.89	3.78
17	5%	4.45	3.59	3.20	2.96	2.81	2.70	2.61	2.55	2.49
	1%	8.40	6.11	5.18	4.67	4.34	4.10	3.93	3.79	3.68
18	5%	4.41	3.55	3.16	2.93	2.77	2.66	2.58	2.51	2.46
	1%	8.29	6.01	5.09	4.58	4.25	4.01	3.84	3.71	3.60
19	5%	4.38	3.52	3.13	2.90	2.74	2.63	2.54	2.48	2.42
	1%	8.18	5.93	5.01	4.50	4.17	3.94	3.77	3.63	3.52
20	5%	4.35	3.49	3.10	2.87	2.71	2.60	2.51	2.45	2.39
	1%	8.10	5.85	4.94	4.43	4.10	3.87	3.70	3.56	3.46
21	5%	4.32	3.47	3.07	2.84	2.68	2.57	2.49	2.42	2.37
	1%	8.02	5.78	4.87	4.37	4.04	3.81	3.64	3.51	3.40
22	5%	4.30	3.44	3.05	2.82	2.66	2.55	2.46	2.40	2.34
	1%	7.95	5.72	4.82	4.31	3.99	3.76	3.59	3.45	3.35
23	5%	4.28	3.42	3.03	2.80	2.64	2.53	2.44	2.37	2.32
	1%	7.88	5.66	4.76	4.26	3.94	3.71	3.54	3.41	3.30
24	5%	4.26	3.40	3.01	2.78	2.62	2.51	2.42	2.36	2.30
	1%	7.82	5.61	4.72	4.22	3.90	3.67	3.50	3.36	3.26
25	5%	4.24	3.39	2.99	2.76	2.60	2.49	2.40	2.34	2.28
	1%	7.77	5.57	4.68	4.18	3.86	3.63	3.46	3.32	3.22
26	5%	4.23	3.37	2.98	2.74	2.59	2.47	2.39	2.32	2.27
	1%	7.72	5.53	4.64	4.14	3.82	3.59	3.42	3.29	3.18
27	5%	4.21	3.35	2.96	2.73	2.57	2.46	2.37	2.31	2.25
	1%	7.68	5.49	4.60	4.11	3.78	3.56	3.39	3.26	3.15
28	5%	4.20	3.34	2.95	2.71	2.56	2.45	2.36	2.29	2.24
	1%	7.64	5.45	4.57	4.07	3.75	3.53	3.36	3.23	3.12
29	5%	4.18	3.33	2.93	2.70	2.55	2.43	2.35	2.28	2.22
	1%	7.60	5.42	4.54	4.04	3.73	3.50	3.33	3.20	3.09
30	5%	4.17	3.32	2.92	2.69	2.53	2.42	2.33	2.27	2.21
	1%	7.56	5.39	4.51	4.02	3.70	3.47	3.30	3.17	3.07
40	5%	4.08	3.23	2.84	2.61	2.45	2.34	2.25	2.18	2.12
	1%	7.31	5.18	4.31	3.83	3.51	3.29	3.12	2.99	2.89
60	5%	4.00	3.15	2.76	2.53	2.37	2.25	2.17	2.10	2.04
	1%	7.08	4.98	4.13	3.65	3.34	3.12	2.95	2.82	2.72
120	5%	3.92	3.07	2.68	2.45	2.29	2.18	2.09	2.02	1.96
	1%	6.85	4.79	3.95	3.48	3.17	2.96	2.79	2.66	2.56

Table H.
Levels of Significance of Chi-Square

df	.99	.98	.95	.90	.80	.70	.50	.30	.20	.10	.05	.02	.01	.001
1	.0³157	.0⁴628	.00393	.0158	.0642	.148	.455	1.074	1.642	2.706	3.841	5.412	6.635	10.827
2	.0201	.0404	.103	.211	.446	.713	1.386	2.408	3.219	4.605	5.991	7.824	9.210	13.815
3	.115	.185	.352	.584	1.005	1.424	2.366	3.665	4.642	6.251	7.815	9.837	11.341	16.268
4	.297	.429	.711	1.064	1.649	2.195	3.357	4.878	5.989	7.779	9.488	11.668	13.277	18.465
5	.554	.752	1.145	1.610	2.343	3.000	4.351	6.064	7.289	9.236	11.070	13.388	15.086	20.517
6	.872	1.134	1.635	2.204	3.070	3.828	5.348	7.231	8.558	10.645	12.592	15.033	16.812	22.457
7	1.239	1.564	2.167	2.833	3.822	4.671	6.346	8.383	9.803	12.017	14.067	16.622	18.475	24.322
8	1.646	2.032	2.733	3.490	4.594	5.527	7.344	9.524	11.030	13.362	15.507	18.168	20.090	26.125
9	2.088	2.532	3.325	4.168	5.380	6.393	8.343	10.656	12.242	14.684	16.919	19.679	21.666	27.877
10	2.558	3.059	3.940	4.865	6.179	7.267	9.342	11.781	13.442	15.987	18.307	21.161	23.209	29.588
11	3.053	3.609	4.575	5.578	6.989	8.148	10.341	12.899	14.631	17.275	19.675	22.618	24.725	31.264
12	3.571	4.178	5.226	6.304	7.807	9.034	11.340	14.011	15.812	18.549	21.026	24.054	26.217	32.909
13	4.107	4.765	5.892	7.042	8.634	9.926	12.340	15.119	16.985	19.812	22.362	25.472	27.688	34.528
14	4.660	5.368	6.571	7.790	9.467	10.821	13.339	16.222	18.151	21.064	23.685	26.873	29.141	36.123
15	5.229	5.985	7.261	8.547	10.307	11.721	14.339	17.322	19.311	22.307	24.996	28.259	30.578	37.697
16	5.812	6.614	7.962	9.312	11.152	12.624	15.338	18.418	20.465	23.542	26.296	29.633	32.000	39.252
17	6.408	7.255	8.672	10.085	12.002	13.531	16.338	19.511	21.615	24.769	27.587	30.995	33.409	40.790
18	7.015	7.906	9.390	10.865	12.857	14.440	17.338	20.601	22.760	25.989	28.869	32.346	34.805	42.312
19	7.633	8.567	10.117	11.651	13.716	15.352	18.338	21.689	23.900	27.204	30.144	33.687	36.191	43.820
20	8.260	9.237	10.851	12.443	14.578	16.266	19.337	22.775	25.038	28.412	31.410	35.020	37.566	45.315
21	8.897	9.915	11.591	13.240	15.445	17.182	20.337	23.858	26.171	29.615	32.671	36.343	38.932	46.797
22	9.542	10.600	12.338	14.041	16.314	18.101	21.337	24.939	27.301	30.813	33.924	37.659	40.289	48.268
23	10.196	11.293	13.091	14.848	17.187	19.021	22.337	26.018	28.429	32.007	35.172	38.968	41.638	49.728
24	10.856	11.992	13.848	15.659	18.062	19.943	23.337	27.096	29.553	33.196	36.415	40.270	42.980	51.179
25	11.524	12.697	14.611	16.473	18.940	20.867	24.337	28.172	30.675	34.382	37.652	41.566	44.314	52.620
26	12.198	13.409	15.379	17.292	19.820	21.792	25.336	29.246	31.795	35.563	38.885	42.856	45.642	54.052
27	12.879	14.125	16.151	18.114	20.703	22.719	26.336	30.319	32.912	36.741	40.113	44.140	46.963	55.476
28	13.565	14.847	16.928	18.939	21.588	23.647	27.336	31.391	34.027	37.916	41.337	45.419	48.278	56.893
29	14.256	15.574	17.708	19.768	22.475	24.577	28.336	32.461	35.139	39.087	42.557	46.693	49.588	58.302
30	14.953	16.306	18.493	20.599	23.364	25.508	29.336	33.530	36.250	40.256	43.773	47.962	50.892	59.703

For larger values of df, the expression $\sqrt{2\chi^2} - \sqrt{2df-1}$ may be used as a normal deviate with unit variance, remembering that the probability for χ^2 corresponds with that of a single tail of the normal curve.

source: Table I is reprinted from Table IV of Fisher & Yates: *Statistical Tables for Biological, Agricultural, and Medical Research*, published by Oliver & Boyd Ltd., Edinburgh, and by permission of the authors and publishers.

Table H is taken from Table IV of Fisher and Yates: STATISTICAL TABLES FOR BIOLOGICAL, AGRICULTURAL AND MEDICAL RESEARCH, published by Longman Group, Ltd., London. (previously published by Oliver and Boyd, Edinburgh), and by permission of the authors and publishers.

Reproduced as found in EDUCATIONAL STATISTICS: USE AND INTERPRETATION by W. James Popham. 1967. Harper and Row, Publishers.